ANNE LISTER, ANN WALKER, AND ME

Lynn Pharaoh

This book is dedicated to Julie, my soulmate.

And thanks to my sister, Caroline, for the lovely artwork on the book cover.

CONTENTS

Title Page
Dedication
Chapter 1: Gentleman Jack   1
Chapter 2: Miss Lister of Shibden Hall   9
Chapter 3: Oddity   12
Chapter 4: Miss Lister courts Miss Walker   30
Chapter 5: Separated   112
Chapter 6: Reunited   128
Chapter 7: Commitment   136
Chapter 8: A taste of married life   152
Chapter 9: Back to Heworth Grange   160
Chapter 10: The honeymoon   168
Chapter 11: Setting up home at Shibden   198
Chapter 12: Christmas 1834   217
About The Author   225

CHAPTER 1: GENTLEMAN JACK

This is the story of the lives of two amazing 19th century women, a wonderful television series which captured a crucial moment in lesbian cultural history, and the effect this had on me and other lesbians. The two women were Anne Lister and Ann Walker, both members of the English landed gentry, both with their own independent incomes, and both unmarried. They lived on their own extensive estates near the town of Halifax, in the county of Yorkshire, in northern England, and, although their homes were only two miles apart, for most of their lives they had only been slightly acquainted. However, in 1832 these two women met up and fell in love. Their story was dramatized in the brilliant BBC/HBO tv show titled 'Gentleman Jack', written by Sally Wainwright, and first aired in the UK on Sunday, May 19th, 2019. The title 'Gentleman Jack' was a nickname given to Anne Lister, for reasons which will become clear. The key to the telling of this love story was the fact that Anne Lister was a prolific diarist. As it turns out, she was probably one of the most prolific diarists that ever lived. Her diaries, which she referred to as her journal, are in the care of the West Yorkshire Archive Service (WYAS) and have been added to UNESCO's Memory of the World register.

I had known of Anne Lister and Ann Walker and had visited Shibden Hall, Anne Lister's home, many years previously, but for some reason, I had never fully engaged with their story. Well, I watched the first episode of the Gentleman Jack tv series and to say I was blown away was an understatement. The wonderful performances of Suranne Jones and Sophie Rundle, portraying Anne Lister and Ann Walker, brought these two inspirational and brave women back to life for me in a way that I could never have foreseen. Every episode of Gentleman Jack was an absolute joy. I watched them, over and over again. I mean, not one, but two amazing lesbians on the tv, well it's not what us lesbians are used to. Seeing them come alive on the tv screen totally fired up my interest. My sister told me about a Facebook group called 'Gentleman Jack Fans' which I joined and found thousands of other women who were as addicted to Gentleman Jack as I was. We call ourselves the Lister Sisters. Some of their posts are edits from the tv show, others have historical information, and some include passages they have transcribed from Anne Lister's diaries. I say 'transcribed' because Anne Lister's diaries are actually quite difficult to read. When Anne made an entry in her journal, she wrote partly in a secret code, referred to as her crypt hand and the rest in plain hand, in which most of the words were significantly abbreviated. The plain hand describes, in minute detail, how Anne lived her life, and in crypt hand, she describes, also in minute detail, her sexual activities with other women. I discovered from the Facebook group that Anne Lister's diaries had been made available to view online by the WYAS and that they were looking for volunteers to help with the transcribing of the diaries to make them readily accessible for people to read. I contacted them and they sent two diary pages, a copy of the key to the crypt hand and asked me to have a go at transcribing, send them back, and they would see if I had done a good enough job to be accepted as a volunteer. A couple of weeks later I was accepted and was sent my first batch of diary pages to transcribe. I have now transcribed many pages from different times in Anne's life. What a joy! When I am transcribing, I feel like I have been transported back to the nineteenth century and Anne Lister is actually talking to me. It is truly wonderful.

Desperate to go back to Shibden Hall, I booked a cottage in Hebden Bridge, about a 20 minute drive from Halifax, and on Tuesday, September 3rd, 2019, my wife and I took up residence there for a few days. On the first day, we drove to Shibden Hall. This time, as I walked around the Hall, I could picture Anne Lister striding through the housebody to the parlour, sitting writing her journal in the study, shagging Mariana in the bedroom ...... (more about Mariana later). It could have been my imagination, but I genuinely felt as if I could sense Anne Lister's presence. Shibden Hall is a stunning 15th century manor house set in 90 acres of parkland. Of course, over the centuries, the Hall has been changed and added to, but the most extensive renovations were undertaken by Anne Lister, it is very much her house, her home.

After a lovely lunch at Shibden cafe, by the lake, we followed in Anne Lister's footsteps down the steep cobbled path, which she always referred to as 'old bank', into Halifax, to the Halifax Minster. This is a beautiful 15th century church, with boxed pews dating from the 17th century, and many painted ceiling panels showing the coat-of-arms of famous Halifax families, including the Listers. Anne Lister was both baptised and buried at this church. The Lister family vault is believed to be at the west end of the Holdsworth chapel. It is not certain that Anne was interred in the family vault because her gravestone was uncovered, in March 2000, in the opposite corner of the church. As we walked into the church, an older man, one of the church attendants, approached us and asked if we were there to see Anne Lister's gravestone. I expect there had been many lesbian visitors to the Minster since the airing of Gentleman Jack, and clearly, he could now spot a lesbian couple a mile off. He directed us to her gravestone which, sadly, is badly damaged, but I have to say I did find the sight of it very moving.

The 2nd day of our trip took us back to Halifax and a visit to the Central Library to see a display containing two of Anne Lister's diaries and a small painting of her that I had read about on one of her diary pages I had transcribed for WYAS. Seeing actual, real, 'in the flesh' diary pages was incredible. I tried to do a spot of transcribing but unfortunately had forgotten my reading glasses. From the library we went to the Piece Hall, a stunning building built in 1779 and renovated relatively recently. The main reason for the visit was to get a bit of lunch but I had read that Anne Lister had visited the Piece Hall to view a balloonist taking off, so there was indeed a connection. Next, we were off to the Bankfield museum, a good walk from the Piece Hall but so worth the visit. The museum had an exhibition of the clothes worn by members of the cast in the Gentleman Jack tv show. Now, as a rule, I am not into clothes (a fact everyone who knows me would be happy to confirm) but this was different. The top hat worn by Suranne Jones, when acting in the role of Anne Lister, even had its own display case.

Day 3 took us to Lightcliffe in search of Ann Walker's grave at old St. Matthew's Church. Lightcliffe is a lovely village about 3 miles east of Halifax and about 2 miles from Shibden Hall. As we walked along the main road through Lightcliffe we passed the entrance gate to the carriage road that led to Crow Nest which was a mansion on the huge Walker estate which Ann Walker and her family had moved into when she was six years old. The other large properties on the Walker estate, included Cliff Hill, New House, and Lidgate House. Crow Nest and New House have since been demolished but the other two buildings still stand. We soon came to St. Matthew's Church but as we walked up the path to the entrance door, we heard a woman's voice call to us "are you looking for Ann Walker's grave?" The woman, who I think was one of the church attendants, told us that there were two St. Matthew's churches in Lightcliffe and that we were at the wrong one. The St. Matthew's Church that we wanted had been demolished in the 1960's (or 70's) leaving just its tower and its graveyard and is currently cared for by an organization called the Friends of Friendless Churches. We found its location further along the main road opposite the Sun Country Inn, an old Georgian coaching inn, that had been part of the Walker estate, and yes, as we entered the graveyard, we were approached by a man who asked if we were looking for the location where Ann Walker was buried. He kindly showed us to the marked position below which was the old church's vault where Ann Walker was laid to rest, so we were able to pay her our respects. A rainbow bracelet and a sympathy card had been left there so we knew we were not the first lesbians to visit. After this we went for lunch at the Lightcliffe Tea Rooms and I had one of the best fruit scones I have ever eaten. Then off home, delighted with our trip.

My transcribing for WYAS, and also, by now, having read quite extensively about Anne Lister and Ann Walker, showed me that the city of York played a part in both their lives, but particularly so for Anne Lister. I decided that a visit there for a few days, just before Christmas 2019, would be perfect. York is a beautiful city, and I will tell you about this trip in a later chapter. Having got so much enjoyment from reading the posts of my fellow Lister Sisters on Facebook, and also posting my own photos from my trips to York and Halifax, I decided to get an Instagram account and set up my own Anne Lister page. I discovered that many other people had had the same idea. Having even more Anne Lister stuff to read was great and it was now beginning to dawn on me that the Gentleman Jack tv show had touched the lives of lesbians from all over the world. In fact, the passion for Anne Lister and Ann Walker amongst lesbians had gone global and many were travelling great distances to visit Shibden Hall, which was fast becoming an international focal point for gay women. Don't get me wrong, I know that many straight women and some men are equally fascinated by the lives of Anne Lister and Ann Walker, but I cannot over emphasise how momentous all this was for the world's lesbian community. Events were even being planned to celebrate Anne Lister's birthday in Halifax on April 3rd, 2020. The organisation planning many of the events was called ALBW (Anne Lister's Birthday Weekend) run by an American woman named Pat Esgate. One of the events organised by Pat was to involve Sally Wainwright talking about the making of the Gentleman Jack tv show and was to be held at the Halifax Minster. I was thrilled when I managed to get tickets because they had apparently sold incredibly quickly. About the same time, WYAS invited the transcribers of Anne Lister's diaries to a meeting at their office in Halifax on the morning of the same day as the Minster event. Very excited, I realised it was time to get a hotel booked in Halifax.

A month or two passed and I was getting quicker at transcribing Anne's diaries and loving every minute of it. Anyway, watching the news on the tv it was becoming clear that an outbreak of some new virus in China was getting increasingly serious. Then, even as it started to spread to Europe, the UK government was telling us that it was nothing to worry about, the risk to the UK was low. God knows what they based that opinion on. The situation did, of course, get worse. Events involving large gatherings were being postponed and it was only a matter of time before the Anne Lister Birthday Weekend events would be postponed too. So, there I was in lockdown, still transcribing, still re-watching episodes of Gentleman Jack, kindly kept available to us by the BBC on iplayer, and still reading anything I could find about Anne Lister and Ann Walker. I felt, from my diary transcribing for WYAS, that I was getting to know Anne Lister, and had discovered that she was both kind and generous to her friends. For example, friends would write to her asking for advice or needing her support, which she always happily gave. Prior to inheriting the Shibden estate in 1826, Anne had relatively little money at her disposal, so, instead of buying new clothes, she repeatedly repaired her old clothes so she could save money to purchase gifts for her friends and buy books to help continue her education. By this time, I had read two books about Anne Lister's life. One of these books portrayed Anne in a positive way, the other was very negative. I found this contradiction puzzling, but as I continued transcribing, I found a possible explanation. As I have previously mentioned, the crypt hand sections in Anne's diaries contained details of her sex life. They also contained details of her menstruation, her bowel activity, and, from time to time, there was a good old rant. Basically, when a friend or acquaintance upset or annoyed her, she did not like to show that this was the case, she stayed calm, not wanting to say anything unkind or that she might later regret. But, to get the upset or annoyance out of herself, she would write about it, in crypt hand, in her journal. Her use of language, in this case, could be quite extreme because she was essentially venting her spleen. You may not be familiar with this old saying, but I think it sums up what she did perfectly. This method of coping with upset almost always worked for Anne Lister, she felt better for it and was able to move on. Most of the content in Anne's diaries is in plain hand and details the majority of her daily interactions with others. To get a real understanding of Anne Lister, I believe it is important to pay as much attention to the plain hand as the crypt hand, and study extracts from the diaries over an extended period of time, not just a few years. It is also best to see her occasional diary rant for what it was, and not take it too literally. So, too much focus on the crypt hand, taking her occasional rants at face value, and focussing on a limited time interval, could possibly lead to a false impression of Anne Lister's character. I have now realised, based on extensive reading of the diaries, that Anne Lister was, in fact, a brilliant woman with a kind heart.

By early 2020, my knowledge of Ann Walker was still minimal, based only on what I had read in books, there having been only fleeting references to her in the diaries I had transcribed for WYAS. I was interested in finding out more about Ann Walker, partly because she was potentially a very important part of lesbian history, but mostly because I was just plain nosey about her and Anne Lister's relationship. Anyway, one morning in April 2020, during lockdown, I was doing some transcribing and a thought suddenly occurred to me out of the blue: I should write my own book and within a second or two, the title just popped into my head: 'Anne Lister, Ann Walker, and me.' I was very surprised by the 'and me' but soon realised that it must have come from the massive impact the 'Gentleman Jack' tv show had had on me. In that moment I decided that everything I wrote about Anne and Ann's relationship had to come directly from my own transcribing of the diaries. Although this may seem a huge undertaking, it was, in fact, a labour of love, motivated by my own desire to tell their story.

CHAPTER 2: MISS LISTER OF SHIBDEN HALL

When Anne Lister was born, in 1791, to Jeremy and Rebecca Lister, the chances of her eventually inheriting the Shibden estate were incredibly slim and had, most probably, never even crossed the minds of any of members of the Lister family. Anne's father, Jeremy, had three older brothers that had survived to adulthood: John, James, and Joseph all of whom would have a prior claim to the estate over Jeremy. Jeremy's eldest brother John died aged 24 in 1769, so when their father died in 1788, the 2nd oldest son, James was the primary heir although the 3rd oldest, Joseph, inherited Northgate House in Halifax, also part of the Shibden estate. The income from the Shibden estate would also have provided an income for Jeremy's two unmarried younger sisters, Martha and Anne (more of Anne later). As the youngest son, and therefore with no prospect of ever inheriting anything of significance on his father's death, Jeremy had joined the army in 1770, reaching the rank of captain. In 1788, he married Rebecca Battle, who, fortunately for him, received an inheritance, enabling him, in 1793, to purchase the Skelfler estate in Market Weighton, about 60 miles from Halifax. Jeremy and Rebecca's first child, a boy named John, died in infancy. Anne was their 2nd child, followed by Samuel, Marian, another John, and Jeremy, who also died in infancy. Around 1805, Jeremy and Rebecca moved the family from Market Weighton to Halifax to live at Ellen Royd, on part of the Shibden estate. Two years later John died aged 15, most likely of influenza, and then in 1813, Samuel died, aged 20. This just left Anne and Marian.

Anne's Uncle James, who had inherited Shibden in 1788, did not marry, so had no descendents. Anne's Uncle Joseph, despite marrying twice, had no children, so no descendents, and

Jeremy, of course, had no surviving male children. So, Uncle James, wanting to ensure that Shibden remained in the hands of a Lister, decided that a distant male cousin, living in Wales, would be his heir. However, Anne, had other ideas. Throughout her childhood Anne had frequently visited Uncle James and Aunt Anne at Shibden and had grown particularly close to them. She was a highly intelligent child, who loved to read, and was fascinated by just about everything. She was unusually well educated for a girl in Georgian England having, herself, insisted on being tutored, particularly in mathematics, although for the most part, she was self taught. When Anne visited Shibden, she would help her Uncle James with the running of the Shibden estate, and when she moved into Shibden permanently in 1815, aged 24, Uncle James was happy to leave more and more estate matters in her capable hands. Uncle James, knowing just how exceptional a woman Anne was, and, after a conversation with her on May 28th, 1817, when she convinced him that she would never marry, and, promised that the Welsh Lister's would be her heirs, he made the decision that she would inherit Shibden. You may be wondering why it was not Jeremy, Anne's father, who inherited Shibden. Apparently, within the family, it was well known that Jeremy had very little business sense, so there was no way that James would leave Shibden to him, although he did leave Jeremy a life share in the income from the Shibden estate.

Jeremy Lister's Skelfler estate at Market Weighton was very much smaller than Shibden. It is my understanding that Jeremy moved his family from Market Weighton to Halifax in 1805 so he could rent out the estate to try to increase his income. Some years later he moved his family back to Market Weighton, and it was here, in November 1817, that Anne's mother, Rebecca, died. I have got the impression that there was never any possibility of Marian inheriting a share of the Shibden estate. But don't be too concerned, she did eventually inherit her father's Market Weighton estate.

Just a quick word about Aunt Anne. Anne Lister absolutely

adored her aunt, who she felt had been more of a mother to her than Rebecca had ever been. In 1834, writing about her, then very frail, aunt, Anne Lister: *'My poor aunt suffers a martyrdom and may still survive some months. It was her arms that first held me. Hers was like a mother's care and to her liberal kindness were owing half the comforts of my early life. I see her sinking slowly and painfully into the grave. I shall feel lonely when she is gone'*. (For future reference, quotes from Anne's diaries will appear like this, that is, in italics, between inverted commas.)

So, there we have it. In 1826, Anne's Uncle James died and she became mistress of Shibden Hall (although the income from the estate was to be shared between her, Jeremy and Aunt Anne).

CHAPTER 3: ODDITY

To understand how it came about that Anne Lister and Ann Walker fell in love and moved in together, it helps to know what prompted Anne Lister to seek out and court Ann Walker after their reacquaintance in July 1832.

From my transcribing of the diaries, I have come to the rather obvious conclusion that Anne Lister was an extremely intelligent, well-educated, and highly engaging person. However, the key to truly recognising the extraordinary woman that she was, is an appreciation of what she referred to as her '*oddity*', essentially her lesbian nature, the powerful driving force of her life. I'll let Anne put you in the picture regarding her oddity, then I'll tell you about some of the women she loved, and who loved her.

Anne Lister knew from a young age that she was different to most other girls. Interestingly, she was more fascinated than fazed by this realisation. On Wednesday, November 13th, 1816, the twenty-five-year-old Anne was in conversation with her friend, Anne Belcombe, who was staying with her at Shibden. Anne Lister described her feelings for women: '*the strength of natural feeling and instinct, for so I might call it, as I had always had, the same turn from infancy, that it had been made known to me, as it were, by intuition, that I had never varied, and no effort on my part had been able to counteract it, that the girls liked me, and always had liked me, that I had never been refused by anyone*'.

On November 25th, 1819, Anne Lister, aged 28, was writing about a conversation she had had with her friend, Elizabeth Brown: '*this led to the subject of my oddity, I owned I was, very. She would never meet another. Such peculiar feelings, peculiar circumstances, made me what I was.. ...She said I was very agreeable, everybody, even those who had only seen me five minutes, all owned this... She liked my oddity. I said I was aware of that and knew that all ladies did like it. It was my oddity that made me so agreeable'.*

On Monday, January 29th, 1821, Anne Lister, aged 30, was at Shibden and had been sorting through some old letters. Some were letters from friends and some from acquaintances. Anne burnt a few of the letters, then came across a letter from a male admirer, which she also burnt. Anne Lister: *'Mr. Montagu's farewell verses, that no trace of any man's admiration may remain, it is not meet for me. I love and only love the fairer sex and thus beloved by them in turn my heart revolts from any other love than theirs'.* This last sentence is quoted on the mug I bought from Shibden Hall, and from which I am drinking tea, as I type.

On the morning of July 12th, 1823, Anne Lister: *'Could not sleep last night. Dozing, hot and disturbed... ...a violent longing for a female companion came over, never remember feeling it so painfully before, held out a good while, but at last fancied it would really comfort me and relieve me and so I gave way'.* Although Anne did have some ethical concerns regarding masturbation, she very much believed in the physical benefits of the pleasure and relief it provided.

On Thursday, July 24th, 1823, Anne had been working hard on the Shibden estate helping and organising the men bringing in the hay. Anne Lister: *'all this ordering work and exercise seemed to excite my manly feelings. I saw a pretty young girl go up the lane and desire rather came over me'.*

Anne Lister met her first lover, Eliza Raine, in 1805, at the age of fourteen. Anne had been sent to boarding school in York on account of her parents being unable to cope with her at home. The school she was sent to was called the Manor School; the building still stands in York (Kings Manor, Exhibition Square). Well, not surprisingly, she saw this as a great opportunity to practice flirting with the other girls and, it appears she made quite an impact. A Mr. Mather, a medical man who attended the pupils at the school, subsequently described the effect that Anne had on the other pupils: *'all the girls passions were so excited, it was quite shocking'.* Anne was assigned an attic room as her bedroom and was required to share this with another pupil, Eliza Raine. Eliza's older sister Jane also attended the school but for some reason, not as a boarder. Eliza and Jane arrived in England from India in December 1802 having been parted from their Indian mother and sent to England after the death of their British father, to be in the care of their father's friends, a Mr. and Mrs. Duffin of Micklegate, York. Anne and Eliza were instantly attracted to each other, and the attic room they shared gave them the privacy to explore their developing sexual relationship. In the early summer of 1806, when they were both 15 years old, Anne left the Manor School. There have been several suggestions as to why Anne left the school, but I have not come across definite confirmation of any of these. It is possible that she was asked to leave because the staff had become aware of the intensity of her and Eliza's relationship or maybe because of the effect she was having on the other girls, or it may simply be that her family could not afford the fees. Now that the girls were apart, they wrote to each other almost daily. Their writing was so prolific that Anne started to keep a record of the letters she received from Eliza and those she sent to her. This record would lead to Anne keeping a diary which would later develop into the detailed journal of her life. The secret code of the crypt hand in Anne's journal was devised by Eliza and Anne so that they could communicate their private thoughts in their letters to each other without having to fear that someone else might discover the sexual nature of their relationship. In the school summer holiday of 1806, Eliza went to stay with Anne and her family at Ellen Royd in Halifax as she had done the previous summer. Although still only children, Eliza and Anne had promised themselves to each other, and the time Eliza spent with the Listers made her feel very much part of the family, becoming particularly close to Rebecca, Anne's mother.

Anne and Eliza continued to spend time together, visiting each other in Halifax or York. In April 1808, against Mr Duffin's wishes, Eliza's sister, Jane, married Henry Boulton, a cadet in the Madras Infantry and left for Calcutta. Knowing that she was unlikely to ever see her sister again, Eliza had become very depressed, so Anne invited her to spend the summer with her in Halifax. The two seventeen-year-olds had a happy time together. Towards the end of 1808 and into 1809, Anne, aged 17, was starting to flex her adolescent muscles, became rebellious and endeavoured to try to limit her parents attempts to control her. She was dressing in a more masculine manner and was keeping male company (nothing sexual of course) that her parents did not approve of. This was alluded to in season 1 episode 3, of the Gentleman Jack tv show, in a clip which has Anne playing cards with a group of soldiers based in Halifax. Although writing less frequently, Eliza and Anne kept in touch. They spent July and August 1809 together in Scarborough and Christmas of that year in York with the Duffins. Anne became close to the Duffins and remained friends with them all her life. In 1810, on one of her visits to York, Anne was introduced to the Norcliffe family, friends of the Duffins. The Norcliffes were very wealthy, and Anne was blown away by their luxurious lifestyle. Not surprising really, given that the Shibden estate was not particularly profitable, so Anne's own family had relatively little spare cash. The eldest daughter of the Norcliffes was Isabella. In Isabella, Anne had found an older, more worldly-wise woman. Anne broke up with Eliza and she and Isabella became lovers, Anne was nineteen and Isabella, twenty-five.

In her journal of 1825, Anne, then aged 34, recorded a conversation with her Aunt Anne in which they discussed Eliza Raine, who Anne described as *'the best I had ever known'*. Anne, clearly feeling guilty about her break-up with Eliza, explained to her aunt that she was only 15 years old when she made a commitment to Eliza. She also said to her aunt that Eliza: *'gave me up to Isabella because she thought it for my interest and happiness. She had behaved to me more like an angel than anything else and I was too thoughtless to return it as I ought'*. Anne obviously regretted how the relationship ended, but, in fairness to her, they were both children when they expressed their commitment to each other, and Anne's adventurous spirit was always going to drive her to spread her wings and experience the world that so fascinated and excited her.

Isabella Norcliffe, known as Tib, was very different to Eliza Raine. She was in some ways more like Anne herself. She liked to ride horses and enjoyed shooting and hunting on the Norcliffes' estate, Langton Hall, near Malton, about 20 miles north-east of York. In Anne's diaries, I have come across numerous entries where game that Tib had shot at Langton had been sent to Shibden. When Anne was at Langton, she loved to take part in these activities with Tib. However, there was another side to Tib that was less pleasing to Anne. She was a heavy drinker and had a particularly bad temper when under the influence of alcohol. Tib was in the fortunate position of being born into a very wealthy family which meant that she had an income for life and so would not be forced into marriage as so many other less well-off lesbians in the 19th century must have been. Anne enjoyed Tib's company, and they became life-long friends with Anne making frequent extended visits over the years to Langton, and Tib visiting Shibden. Anne also became very fond of Tib's mother who always showed kindness and understanding towards her.

Although six years older, it was Tib that was very much besotted with Anne. In my transcriptions of some of Anne's diaries, it is clear that Anne was sexually attracted to women who dressed and behaved in a more feminine manner, so I suppose it was unlikely that Anne and Tib's sexual relationship would be exclusive for any length of time. Having said this, they did have sex every time they visited each other, well, there was no tv to watch in those days. Besides Langton, the Norcliffes owned a property on Petergate in York where they had neighbours, the Belcombe family, who were also their good friends. Dr. and Mrs. Belcombe had six children, five daughters, Anne, Mariana, Harriet, Eliza and Louisa, and one son, Steph, who eventually became a doctor and took over his father's practice. At some point in 1812, the Belcombes had been invited by the Norcliffes to an event at Langton Hall, at a time when Anne Lister was also staying there with Tib. It was on this occasion that Anne first met Mariana Belcombe, and they fell instantly in love. Anne was 21 and Mariana was 22 years old. Sadly, some of Anne's diaries are missing so we have little detail of her early relationship with Isabella or the first few years of her relationship with Mariana. However, it is clear from subsequent diaries, whilst sex was a hugely important part of Anne and Mariana's relationship, with Anne writing in reference to Mariana: *'in bed she is excellent',* that each would be the other's grand passion for getting on for twenty years.

As early as 1814, a wealthy landowner, Charles Lawton was showing an interest in Mariana Belcombe. His wife, Ann, was still living at this point and it appears that Charles would make up to Mariana in front of her, what a wretch! In her journal, Anne records a conversation she had with Louisa Belcombe, one of Mariana's sisters, who described observing this behaviour when she, Mariana and their mother visited Charles and his wife at Lawton Hall in Cheshire. Charles' wife died in November 1814. Louisa told Anne that she always knew that Mariana would marry Charles and she recalled the moment when they heard of Ann Lawton's death: *'they were all sitting at dinner, Mariana burst out laughing and so did they all'.*

Obviously, Mariana and her family knew that they should soon expect a marriage proposal from Charles. Anne was not even aware that Charles Lawton had designs on Mariana, so when she eventually found out that they planned to marry she was shocked. Anne Lister: *'I knew nothing of it, then it came on me like a thunderbolt after my return from Market Weighton, in November eighteen hundred and fifteen'.* Anne had always believed that she and Mariana would eventually live together, so discovering that Mariana was to marry Charles Lawton broke her heart. Indeed, throughout her diaries, Anne repeatedly returns to her pain over Mariana's marriage, and it would be many years later before Mariana fully realised the massive hurt her marriage had caused Anne. In fairness to Mariana, she may have had little choice but to accept the offer of marriage from Charles Lawton. Her parents were not particularly wealthy and would have been keen to marry off as many of their daughters as possible, since there was no way for women of their class to earn their own income. Mariana had other suitors before Charles, but at twenty-six years of age, it was likely that she would have felt obliged to do what was in the best interests of her family.

On March 8th, 1816, Mariana married Charles Lawton, seventeen years her senior. At the time it was common practice for a relative and/or friend of the bride to join the married couple on the honeymoon and subsequently in the marital home, for a period of time, whilst the bride adjusted to married life. Amazingly, Anne and Mariana's older sister Anne, accompanied Mariana and Charles for five months after the wedding. Goodness knows why Anne Lister agreed to do this, as it must have been so painful for her. Most likely Mariana asked her, and she felt she could not refuse a request.

When the diary resumed, in August 1816, Anne Lister and Anne Belcombe were still accompanying Mariana and Charles on their extended honeymoon. The four of them were staying in Buxton, Derbyshire. Anne Lister was six years younger than Anne Belcombe and it appears she had been finding comfort in the older woman's arms. Monday, August 19th, 1816, Anne Lister: *'Anne let me look at her. A lock of queer's [pubic] hair'*. Wednesday, August 21st, Anne Lister: *'all but connected with Anne'*.

Anne Lister was back home at Shibden on Friday, August 23rd, 1816. On Thursday, November 7th, 1816, Anne Belcombe arrived at Shibden for a visit. On the Friday night, Anne Lister: *'we went great lengths, as we had often done before, such as feeling her all over, pushing my finger up her, but still did not get to the last extremity. I asked her several times to let me get nearer her and to have a proper kiss. She seemed as if she would by no means have disliked it, but as if she thought it right to refuse, which she did very languidly'.* I have discovered from my transcribing of Anne's diaries that the phrases *'last extremity', 'getting near', 'kiss'* and *'being connected'* did, for the most part, all mean the same thing, that is, achieving an orgasm with vulva-to-vulva contact during classic lesbian scissoring, a technique that Anne and Mariana had totally perfected, achieving two, sometimes three, simultaneous orgasms without even losing contact. Anyway, Anne had decided it was time to give Anne Belcombe the benefit of her knowledge. On Monday, November 11th, Anne Lister: *'had a very good kiss last night, Anne gave it with pleasure not thinking it necessary to pretend to refuse any longer'*. And, over the following days, Anne Lister: *'A good kiss last night. Anne certainly improves in the art. Owns she likes it better than she did at first and does not now deny it gives her pleasure'* and *'had a good kiss last night. Anne has always an abundance of moisture and never fails to give me full gratification'*.

On Saturday, November 23rd, 1816, Anne Lister received a letter from Mariana *'expressing her fears about my prudence with Anne, alas, is too late'*. Just bit! Anne wrote back to Mariana *'assuring her of my love and affection. That my only wish and study were to deserve and gain her confidence and that I neither had done, nor would do in future, anything imprudent to Anne. Never did I deceive Mariana before. Would to God I had not obliged myself to do it now'*. It does seem a little unfair that, having married Charles Lawton, Mariana was trying to prevent Anne from having sex with anyone but her. Well, with Anne's heightened libido, it was a futile attempt anyway. The following day, Anne Lister: *'Had a long but rather lazy kiss last night. Nantz [Anne Belcombe] and I had a rummage in the morning'*. Anne Belcombe returned to York on November 29th, 1816, I assume, well satisfied.

Anne Lister had planned to meet up with Mariana on Monday,

January 27th, 1817, when Mariana was meant to be travelling via Halifax to York, to visit her family. However, there had been an unfortunate occurrence. Charles Lawton, Mariana's husband, had, for some reason, opened Mariana's writing box and read one of her letters from Anne, in which Anne had implied that the hope of something happening to Charles at some point in the future was worth the wait. Not surprisingly Charles was not best pleased. Basically, the shit hit the fan, big time. There was even talk of divorce. Mariana asked Anne to write to Charles and smooth things over, which of course she did, albeit reluctantly. However, on Wednesday, January 29th, much to everyone's surprise, Mariana turned up at Shibden Hall, in a hack-chaise, alone. It transpired that Charles had decided that he would travel with Mariana, essentially to keep her away from Anne, and, that they would travel on the Wednesday instead of the Monday. However, some financial matter arose, and he could not travel with her. Anne wrote in her journal that Charles *'had let Mariana come without him, in spite of all that had just happened, crying and roaring like a child when she left him. Mariana was delighted to see us all and get to Shibden again, and we spent the evening most happily'.* It appears that Charles had expected Mariana to stay overnight at the inn in Halifax that they had already pre-booked, so that was what she did, but she took Anne with her, of course. The next morning, Anne: *'Mariana gave me two good kisses last night, one directly after the other, and had two very good ones herself. She told me that Charles had never yet given her any pleasure, indeed that such was her affection for me, she had quite a disgust for the thing with anybody else and did not believe it possible for any other ever to inspire her with the smallest sentiment of love'.* Mariana and Anne decided that it would be best if Anne did not see Charles for the foreseeable. Mariana continued on her journey to York, but not before entreating Anne to try to be faithful to her.

Mariana returned to Shibden a few weeks later on Friday, February 21st, 1817, having travelled from York. Apparently, Charles was expected in York in a week or so and Mariana had wanted to spend some time with Anne before he arrived. Mariana stayed at Shibden for a week, returning to York on Thursday, February 27th. The two women had great sex every night, except Wednesday, when Mariana had a bad back. When Mariana left, Anne wrote: *'how dreary and forlorn I am without my darling. No sooner was she come than she is gone. Her having been here seems like a dream, but it has done me good and I will think only of our happiness in future'.* Sadly, in reality, there was no prospect of the two women having any kind of future together, apart from the occasional fleeting meeting, when Mariana was able to engineer an opportunity to get away from her husband.

By Friday, July 11th, 1817, almost five months had passed without Anne getting to see Mariana, she wrote: *'As I was getting into bed, thinking how little confidence I had in Mariana, how little likely it was that we should ever get together. I was very low. I felt that my happiness depended upon having some female companion whom I could love and depend upon'.* The intensity of Anne and Mariana's relationship fluctuated over the twenty or so years that it continued. There were times when they did not see each other for many months, sometimes even longer. At one point, Anne had reports from Mariana's sisters that Mariana had settled well into life with her wealthy husband, and even had her own carriage, which wasn't really what Anne wanted to hear. However, although the Belcombe sisters were close, there was a rivalry between them for Anne Lister's attention, so this information regarding Mariana, may, or may not, have been true.

Anne Lister longed for female company, so, of course, there were to be other women in her life to make up for the long separations from Mariana. She frequently stayed at Langton Hall, the home of the Norcliffes, just outside York. On one such occasion, she had an extended winter stay from October 5th, 1820, till January 8th, 1821. During her stay she enjoyed the company of her dear friend Isabella (Tib) and her younger sister, Charlotte, their friend Mary Valance, Anne Belcombe and her married sister, Harriet Milne. Well, there was flirting with Harriet and kissing with Charlotte, but with Tib, Anne Belcombe and Mary things went much further. Just a few of many similar journal entries: December 13th, Anne Lister: *'good kiss of Tib last night'.* December 21st, Anne Lister: *'With Anne alone in her room, dawdling and lovemaking till three. Then went to Mary Valance, took her on my knee, held her with my right arm and grubbled with the second finger of the left. I kept it nearly still and she gave the action, so that I am sure she felt enough. We were a goodish while at it and had only just done when Charlotte came in'.* I get the impression that Anne endeavoured to keep her sexual activity with each one secret from the other two. Whether she succeeded, I do not know.

Anne Lister attached a great importance to maintaining a correspondence with her friends. Interestingly, virtually all the women with whom she had had a sexual relationship, wanted to keep in touch with her long after the physical side of their relationship was over. In the early nineteenth century it took a long time to travel anywhere so friends may not see each other for months or even years at a time, so maintaining contact was essentially done through the writing of letters. Anne endeavoured to write entertaining letters, and, being a particularly knowledgeable person, her friends were apt to write to her for advice which she kindly gave. In my transcribing for WYAS I came across a copy of a letter in Anne's journal, on June 2nd, 1824, from Mary Valance: *'I am an egotist, I dwell upon myself because I fancy the subject is interesting to you, yet I hold in mind you have not my freedom, but I would take the passing moments as they fly. I would sip the sweets of passing pleasure with you. I could be happy. I could enjoy the sweets that confiding interest might press upon my lips and when I have renewed my acquaintance in person with you as formerly, I might then utter what only my manner might acknowledge first'.* Anne commented on the letter: *'Pretty plain me thinks I may have her on my own terms'.* The very next day, June 3rd, 1824, Anne received a letter from another friend, Sibbella Maclean, who she had just spent a few days with at Esholt Hall, the home of another friend, Henrietta Crompton. In her letter,

Sibbella wrote: '*did you know how much you occupied my thoughts since I parted from you. Unconscionable as you are, you would be perfectly satisfied it seems as if I never knew you before, so much did my acquaintance and of course my affection increase during the two days at Esholt. If I am ever with you at Shibden, you may be sure I shall be at your elbow from morn till night, if you choose, from night till morn'*. Anne had the highest regard for Sibbella Maclean and considered her '*so elegant, had much propriety of manner*'. In 1828, during an extensive tour of Scotland together, they became lovers. Tragically, just two years later, Sibbella died of tuberculosis.

During the mid to late 1820's Anne Lister spent a lot of time living in Paris. She even rented a little apartment on the Rue St. Victor. Anne absolutely loved Paris. Its energy, liveliness and beauty so appealed to her. She employed her talent for spotting women who she could have fun with, and pursued a 'friendship' with a widow, Maria Barlow, who lived in Paris with her daughter. It fascinates me that women who most likely had only ever had sexual relationships with men, so readily fell in love with Anne Lister. Maria was older than Anne and, having been happily married, was surprised, possibly shocked, by her own sexual feelings towards Anne. On January 4th, 1825, Anne wrote in her journal: '*waited a few minutes, then the coast being clear, got into bed for 23 minutes to Mrs. Barlow, who made no objection. Took her right nipple in my mouth, then looked at it, and grubbled her well, she yielding to the finger more than ever and being evidently sufficiently excited, we were both in profuse perspiration*'.

Anne Lister's '*oddity*' also manifested itself in her adventurous spirit, her style of dress, the forthright manner in which she walked, all captured perfectly by Suranne Jones in the Gentleman Jack tv show. Anne certainly did not dress as would have been expected of a female member of the landed gentry living in the first half of the nineteenth century. She wore a high collar, usually with a cravat. She dressed in black, and when outdoors, wore a black, ankle length coat and a small black hat, in stark contrast to the fashion at the time which required ladies to wear large ornate bonnets. For those of you who are fans of the Gentleman Jack tv show, no, as far as I can tell, she didn't wear a top hat, sorry. At times Anne was 'mistaken' for a man. I have put 'mistaken' in inverted commas because I doubt very much that this was a genuine mistake. Anne, at 5 ft 5 inches tall, was 4 inches taller than the average woman at the time, but, weighing only just over 8 stone, it would have been perfectly obvious that she was female. Any comments likening Anne to a man would have been made with the specific intention of causing her distress or, at the very least, discomfort. On Sunday, June 28th, 1818, such an incident occurred on her way home, after she had attended a lecture at a local church. That evening she wrote in her journal: *'The people generally remark as I pass along how much I am like a man. I think they did it more than usual this evening. At the top of the Cunnery Lane as I went, three men said, as usual, "that's a man" and one added "does your cock stand?". I know not how it is, but I feel low this evening'.* Since it clearly saddened Anne that she was, at times, likened to a man, I suppose some may say she could simply dress and behave in a ladylike manner and so avoid the upset. But identity, specifically lesbian identity, does not work like that. Dressing as she did would have empowered her. No amount of abuse would have made her wear pretty dresses and behave as expected of a 19th century lady. To do so would have felt humiliating. Some may also suggest that, dressing and behaving as Anne did, shows that she wanted to be a man. I can assure one and all that nothing could be further from the truth either then, in the 19th century, or now in the 21st century. As a 6 ft 2 inch trousers wearing, and at times short haired, lesbian, I have had a few such experiences, particularly in my younger days. These days it tends to be confined to shopping in Sainsburys where at times I can be mistaken, from behind, as a man, usually by a little old lady wanting me to reach an item for her from a top shelf.

In 1823 two incidents occurred in which Mariana struggled to cope with her feelings of embarrassment related to Anne's *'oddity'*. The first incident, referred to as *'the three steps'* occurred on August 19th of that year. Mariana was travelling with her sister Louisa on the Mail Coach from Lawton Hall in Cheshire to York, via Halifax. The plan was that Anne would meet the coach in Halifax and travel to York with them, staying one night and then returning home the next day. However, Anne was totally overexcited at the prospect of meeting up with Mariana and decided to intercept the coach, on its way to Halifax, and surprise her. She walked for 10 miles, in the rain, to the Coach and Horses Inn, where she spotted the Mail Coach coming up the hill. When the coach stopped outside the inn, she bounded up the steps into the coach, talking nineteen to the dozen about her walk from Halifax, and plonked herself down next to Mariana who she was expecting would of course be delighted to see her. No so. The astonished looks on the faces of the other passengers and the comments from the coach driver wondering if the person who had just leapt up the three steps into the coach was a man, was too much for Mariana, who, clearly horror-struck, demanded an explanation for Anne's actions. Anne, devastated by Mariana's response to her arrival in the carriage, tried to excuse herself, but Mariana finished with *'you are going to vex me, hold your tongue'*. Mariana maintained that Anne had leapt up the coach's three steps in one action and this totally unladylike behaviour could potentially reflect badly on her. As someone quite likely to bound either into or out of somewhere (well in my youth, at least) my sympathies are instinctively with Anne, but I feel I should spare a thought for Mariana. She had a great fear of being the subject of gossip or rumour, which I think was understandable. For a woman in Mariana's position in society, visiting other people in her social circle, in their homes and having them visit her home, would have occupied a lot of her time, and been the main source of entertainment for her. Anne's unladylike behaviour had, by association, the potential to turn her world upside down. However, also understandably, Anne was absolutely gutted by Mariana's response.

The second incident occurred the following month in Scarborough, situated on the north-east coast of England, whilst Anne was on holiday with the Belcombes, who had been renting a house there for about two weeks by the time Anne arrived on the evening of Friday, September 12th, 1823. Dr. and Mrs Belcombe had already returned home to York leaving Mariana and her sisters, Louisa, Eliza and Harriet to continue their holiday. Anne had her own dressing room but as usual, she and Mariana shared a bed together. The next morning, Saturday, Anne described that night: *'soon grew tender and had a good kiss. In fact, we both said we had had three instead of one. Mariana's cousin had come in the morning. This we did not mind but put one of her napkins under us, awaked about seven, in about an hour, had another good kiss and got up at nine'.* By the way, Anne's phrase *'cousin had come'* meant her's, or her lover's period had started.

Saturday, September 13th, was a very rainy day so everyone stayed in and spent the day reading and chatting, although, they were visited by a Miss Goodricke to whom Anne Lister was introduced. Anne described that night and the following morning: *'Very good kiss last night, felt inclined for one this morning but obliged to get up and be disappointed. Mariana having been biliously inclined these last few days, took a dose of salts this morning and has a cup of tea in bed'.* With Mariana not feeling well, she and Anne remained at the house whilst the others either went to church or out into the town. Clearly by the afternoon, Mariana must have perked up a bit since Anne recorded in her journal: *'Mariana and I, left to ourselves, talked and made love when they were gone in the afternoon. She came up into my dressing room. We both became excited. She took off her gown and I my pelisse and lay down on the bed between the blanket and quilt at thirty five minutes past three. We had two good kisses and were dressed again and out of the house to go on to the sands in twenty five minutes'.* Anne described Sunday night: *'Mariana had been in bed an hour but roused herself to be affectionate. Perhaps about 12.30 a.m., every door and window in the house seeming to rattle, which disturbed us exceedingly. At first, we thought someone breaking into the house, but the continuance of the noises and the pattering of rain soon ushered in a tremendous thunderstorm. Very vivid, fast, succeeding flashes of lightning enlightened the whole room. After some time, came one or two tremendous peals of thunder, and the heaviest rain I almost ever heard. In the midst of all this, we drew close together made love and had one of the most delightfully long tender kisses we have ever had. Said she, in the midst of it, "oh don't leave me". Yet this renewed and redoubled my feelings and we slept in each other's arms perhaps till six, my linen still wet with perspiration. We then lay apart and slumbered till nine when we got up'.* It appeared that Anne and Mariana were getting on rather well, however, during their walk on the sands, on the Sunday afternoon, people had been staring at Anne. Mariana admitted that she observed this and that it had made her feel uncomfortable. Always very considerate of Mariana's feelings, when Anne got dressed on Monday morning, she made some concessions to please her. She covered her cravat with a frill and wore her velvet spencer jacket instead of her black cloth pelisse. Interesting that Anne was still determined to wear her cravat, even if she had to hide it. Later that day a note arrived at the house from Miss Goodricke inviting the sisters to a dance, but not including the friend (Anne) that the Belcombes had staying with them. Being snubbed socially was a big deal in polite society in the nineteenth century and Anne was mortified, particularly as she had been introduced to Miss Goodricke on the Saturday. But deciding to keep her feelings to herself, she pretended that she did not care. To add insult to injury, the following day, Tuesday, Mariana and Louisa paid a social call on Miss Goodricke and her friend Miss Moffitt. Anne found out that Miss Goodricke and Miss Moffitt had been told by a Miss Fountaine, of Bath, that Anne was masculine and had therefore decided that they did not want to know her. To improve her spirits, Anne set about writing up her journal for the previous few days and felt better for doing so: *'I seem to have opened my heart to an old friend. I can tell my journal what I can tell no one else'.* Referring to when she would inherit Shibden, and had money and status,

Anne wrote: *'may the day come when even outward circumstance my friendship may do some honour to those who have it, whenever the Misses Moffitt and Goodricke of their day may think it worth their while to pay me civility'.* Later, on Tuesday evening, Anne and Mariana were chatting: *'We touched on the subject of my figure. The peoples staring so on Sunday had made her then feel quite low. I expressed my sorrow and consideration for her. She knew well enough that I had stayed in the house to avoid her being seen with me yet said I, taking meal together, would you have me changed? "Yes" said she "to give you a feminine figure". She had just before observed that I was getting mustaches, and that when she first saw this it made her sick, if I had a dark complexion it would be quite shocking. I took no further notice than to say I would do anything I could that she wished'.* That night Anne and Mariana had a heart to heart, both getting upset, each comforting and consoling the other, and declaring their love for one another. Whenever Mariana appeared upset or sad, Anne's first thought was always what could she do to make her feel better. Although the three steps business and the Scarborough incident had hurt Anne deeply, she tried not to show it but did find it difficult to reconcile the thought that Mariana had felt embarrassed to be with her in public. Despite this, Anne still hoped that one day she and Mariana would live together.

As a young woman, Anne Lister had been happy to take whatever opportunity for sex came her way, and it seems that there was no shortage of women happy to yield to her charms. As she got older, her long felt desire to live with a woman she loved became even stronger. Mariana, of course was still married and her husband, despite being much older than her, was in robust health, so the prospect of Anne and Mariana living together was looking increasingly unlikely. Through her relationship with Sibbella Maclean, Anne had developed friendships with some members of the aristocracy including Lady Gordon, Lady Stuart de Rothesay, Lady Stuart and her great niece Vere Hobart, the daughter of the Earl of Buckinghamshire. Anne spent time in

London and on the continent with these friends. In the autumn of 1831, Lady Stuart asked her to spend the winter with Vere Hobart in Hastings, seemingly for the benefit of Vere's health. Anne had high hopes of a romantic relationship with Vere, but it was not to be. Although Vere was happy to kiss Anne, basically she was straight, and wanted to be in Hastings to give an admirer of hers, a Captain Donald Cameron, the opportunity to court her. Anne had undoubtedly been taken advantage of by Vere and, realising this, returned to Shibden in May 1832. Anne and Vere remained friends and, as per usual, continued to maintain a correspondence, seeing each other occasionally.

I have mentioned that Anne's adventurous spirit also contributed to her *'oddity'*. Besides living in Paris, she travelled extensively throughout Europe. She was very much drawn to mountain scenery and explored the Alps, and also the Pyrenees, where she was the first woman to reach the summit of Mont Perdu and the first person to officially reach the summit of Mont Vignemale. In fact, there is a mountain pass in the Pyrenees named after her: Collado de Lady Lister.

CHAPTER 4: MISS LISTER COURTS MISS WALKER

Just to put you in the picture, the start of this chapter corresponds to episode 1, of season 1, of the Gentleman Jack tv show. Those of you who have watched the show will occasionally notice, as you read from here on in, a few differences between my account of what happened and that presented in the show. Try not to be upset by this. The tv show is a dramatization, and the writer, Sally Wainwright, has, of course, the absolute right to work her magic and apply artistic licence whenever she so chooses.

Devastated that Vere Hobart had chosen to marry Donald Cameron, Anne decided to head back home to Shibden, calling on Mariana Lawton en route, probably in the hope of some comfort. She arrived at Lawton Hall at 7.35 p.m. on the evening of Monday April 30th, 1832. Her letter telling Mariana that she was coming to visit arrived ¼ hour before she did herself, consequently she was greeted by Mariana's husband Charles, Mariana being out. Later that evening, Anne and Mariana had the opportunity to talk. However, whilst Anne wanted to discuss the possibility of their having a future together, Mariana was only interested in talking about the people she had been socialising with. It certainly seemed that Mariana had now settled into her life as mistress of Lawton Hall. Anne wrote: *'She cannot leave Charles and he may live twenty years, then what am I to do?'* Anne stayed at Lawton Hall for one week then set off on Monday, May 7th, arriving at Shibden at 8.25 p.m. that evening. At this point in time, Anne's Aunt Anne, father Jeremy, and sister Marian were living at Shibden, Anne's uncle James having died six years previously, in 1826.

Anne Lister was now forty-one years of age and her dream of finding someone she could love, and share her life with, was as far away as ever. Although she was highly motivated in many areas of her life, I think her desire to find a lover, who would live with her, was by far the strongest driving force, and despite the setbacks and heartbreaks, she could never give up searching.

The next day, Tuesday, May 8th, 1832, after breakfast, Anne explained to her aunt the situation with Mariana: *'Said how Mariana was changed to me. I was no longer the first object of her thought, and it was therefore unlikely that we should come together'*. Anne told her aunt that she felt she must go abroad. Perhaps only the idea of travelling again could ease the pain of her disappointments. However, Aunt Anne was fearful of her travelling on the continent because of reported outbreaks of cholera and had suggested she consider remaining in England. In a letter written to Vere, Anne wrote: *'I must be some time here. You know how gladly I would flee away and be at rest or in motion elsewhere'*. An argument with her sister, Marian, that evening did not help matters. Although the argument was about the essentially trivial matter of whether their pew in church should be locked or not, I suspect it was indicative of the tension in their relationship. Anne: *'Well I wish I could avoid saying anything. We shall never agree. The less we see of each other the better. I like her less and I must get away somewhere. The money is the thing. I must invent something or other very shortly but off I must go'*. I suppose, during Anne's absence from Shibden, Marian had, perhaps quite happily, been keeping house for her father and aunt, and Anne's return had upset the status quo, even though in reality of course, it was Anne who was the mistress of Shibden, not Marian.

On the afternoon of Thursday, May 10th, there was a second dispute between the sisters. For some reason, Marian told Anne that she did not intend to leave her anything in her will. Anne wrote in her journal: *'I shall go and make my will and not name her'*. Later that afternoon, Anne wrote to Mariana: *'I am sick of the whole world and the sight of my will made, will give me more pleasure than anything else'.* Mariana's reply, which arrived on Monday, May 14th, was, despite Mariana being poorly with *'constant pain in the head, giddiness and sickness',* full of concern for Anne's low spirits: *'Do not despond Fred, you have yet I hope many comforts and blessings in store, friends who value and love you dearly and surely you ought not to be "sick of all the world" because some occasional contretemps arise'.* By the way, Anne and Mariana's pet names for each other were Fred and Mary, respectively. It was certainly kind of Mariana to try to make Anne feel better, but I think her letter shows that she did not have any real understanding of the heartbreak that Anne was experiencing. Anne's reply to Mariana confirmed this: *'From your sentence you ought not to be "sick of all the world" because some occasional contretemps arise", I fear you thought me peevishly impatient. But Mary, where the hope of 20 years is suddenly blighted in an instant, is that an occasional contretemps?'*

Anne Lister had not felt well for some time, but the quiet of Shibden (provided she kept out of Marian's way), the fresh air, spending time outdoors, including taking long walks, having long talks with her dear Aunt Anne, she found her appetite increasing, her health improving and her good spirits returning. So much so that by Friday May 18th, her mind refocussed on the task of finding a companion for life. She listed in her journal the names of some potential candidates: *'Miss Mackensie, Miss Thackray, Miss Hall, Miss Freeman, Louisa Belcombe, Miss Price, Miss Salmon, and Miss Walker of Lidgate'.* Interesting that Ann Walker was on her list. Although near neighbours, just two miles apart, the Listers and the Walkers did not have a close association. Anne Lister had met Ann Walker on several social occasions over the years, but on Friday, July 6th, 1832, an opportunity arose for them to become reacquainted. That morning, Anne had been out walking on the estate. On her return home: *'Miss Walker of Lidgate and her uncle-in-law and aunt, Mr. and Mrs. Atkinson, called for ¼ hour at 10.45 just as I came in. Received them and was very civil. Joked Miss Walker about travelling'.*

Like Anne Lister, Ann Walker was an unlikely heiress. She was born at the Cliff Hill mansion on the huge Walker estate in Lightcliffe on May 20th 1803, moving with her family to the Crow Nest mansion, also on the Walker estate, around 1809. Her parents, John and Mary, had five children, of which Ann was the second youngest. The first born was William, who died in infancy. Then came Mary, Elizabeth, Ann, and the youngest, John. In 1815, when Ann was aged eleven, her eldest sister, Mary, died aged just fifteen. In 1823, when Ann was twenty years old, both of her parents died, about seven months apart, and her younger brother, John, inherited the Walker estate. Ann, John, and Elizabeth continued to live at Crow Nest. However, in 1828, Elizabeth, married a Captain George Sutherland and moved with him to Scotland. The following year, John married, and around this time, Ann moved from Crow Nest to Lidgate House, where she lived alone (apart from her servants of course). Sadly in 1830, Ann's brother John died, aged twenty-five, whilst on honeymoon in Italy, which meant that Ann and her sister Elizabeth jointly inherited the Walker estate. I get the impression that the Crow Nest mansion was classed as her sister's property and the Cliff Hill mansion and Lidgate house were regarded as Ann's. With one of Ann's aunts, her father's sister, still living at Cliff Hill, Ann chose to remain at Lidgate House and this is where she was living when she became reacquainted with Anne Lister in 1832.

About a week after seeing Ann Walker at Shibden, Anne Lister decided to make a social call at Lidgate House. Anne Lister: '*sat ½ hour with Miss Walker and with her relatives, Mr. and Mrs. Atkinson. Saw all over the house. Miss Walker very civil and glad to see me*'. During the next few weeks, Anne Lister concerned herself with her potential travel plans and with the Shibden estate, including renovations to the Hall, improvements to the grounds, including an ornamental walk, and the possibility of increasing the estate's profitability by accessing its coal reserves.

On Tuesday, July 31st, Mariana arrived at Shibden having travelled from York. She was to stay just the one night before continuing on to Lawton Hall in Cheshire. She was still poorly, suffering from what Anne Lister described as *'inflammation of the left ear'*. If this was the same condition that caused her the pain and dizziness she described back in May, then she had been suffering for over two months. I suspect that Mariana may have had an inner ear infection, which has very debilitating symptoms and can last many months. That night Anne and Mariana shared a bed as usual. Despite Mariana being unwell, the two women were not going to miss the opportunity to have sex. Anne Lister: *'She could only sleep on the right side last night. It was well she was ready for me without any trouble moving. A pretty good kiss on getting into bed and another about an hour. After seeming to have had two good ones, said after the first she thought I had done her good, and in the midst of the second, said "how delightful".*

The next morning, Wednesday, August 1st, Anne and Mariana talked about Anne's intention to go travelling abroad and Mariana agreed to make enquiries to find a suitable manservant to travel with her. Unfortunately, Mariana made a remark that upset Anne, although Anne did not let her feelings show. Anne: *'If she saw me at all before my leaving England, should see me at Leamington, where they would probably spend the winter. I made no definite reply, thinking to myself she talks of if she sees me at all, but I avoided making any unpleasant remark and all went off well'*. Anne travelled a short way with Mariana and further conversation revealed that Mariana, believing she would not live long, and fully expecting her husband to outlive her, was feeling indifferent to pretty much everything.

Apart from a brief mention in connection with Ann Walker's steward, Samuel Washington, with whom Anne Lister had had some dealings, there is no further reference to Ann Walker in Anne's Lister's journal until Friday, August 10th, when she wrote: *'called on Miss Walker of Lidgate and sat 1¾ hour with her.*

Found her very civil and agreeable'. On this occasion, Ann went on to record some of their conversation in her journal: *'She said she had heard that Mrs. Kenny would not have been walking arm in arm with my sister but that she wanted her for another, Mr. Clarke. Said the thing seemed absurd but agreed that Marian was likely enough to be taken in. Miss Walker then said how deep the Kennys were. Mrs. Kenny would have been as intimate with her, Miss Walker, but she had fought shy thinking her very forward about it. Said how she disliked Doctor Kenny as a medical man. He asked queer questions and made odd remarks. She would never have him again. We got on very well together. Thought I as I have several times done before of late, shall I try and make up to her?'.* Well, they certainly seemed to have had a good old gossip!

One week later, on Friday, August 17th, Anne Lister called again at Lidgate to visit with Ann Walker. This time stayed for 2 hours: *'Talked of household economy. Got on very well. She consulted me about tenant right and told me all about the Priestleys and really made a too good story against them. He not really a man of business. Things went on better without him and neither he nor Mr. Edwards had not behaved like gentleman. Said how astonished I was. They, the Priestleys, knew all my family concerns. I meant to leave him my executor and all she said astonished and grieved me. In playing with it foolishly, broke a pretty ivory book knife Miss Catherine Rawson had given her. Very sorry. Miss Walker behaved very well about it. Said my getting consolation was that it would be a good excuse for my giving her one someday from Paris which I hoped she would value as much as the one destroyed. Yes! She should value it more. Thought I, she little dreams what is in my head, to make up to her. She has money and this might make up for rank. We get on very well so far and the thought, as I returned, amused and interested me. She gave me, home with me, the last Saturday's Penny Magazine'.* The following evening Anne Lister told her aunt about her visit to Lidgate to see Ann Walker but wrote very little about this conversation in her journal and made no further reference to Ann during the next two weeks.

Just a note about Ann Walkers relatives. Firstly, there were a lot of them! Besides the Atkinsons that I have already mentioned, there were many Priestleys, Edwards, and Rawsons, all interlinked through marriage over many years.

On Friday August 31st, Anne Lister called again on Ann Walker at Lidgate House. They sat talking for two hours then walked to Cliff Hill to call on Ann Walker's aunt. This visit to Cliff Hill had been at Anne Lister's suggestion and would have been her way of taking her friendship with Ann a step further. It was one thing to pay a social call on someone, but to go somewhere with that person, to an event or to make a visit on someone else, demonstrated an increased level of friendship. After this visit, Anne Lister wrote extensively in her journal about her developing relationship with Ann Walker: *'Miss Walker and I do certainly get on marvellously. She seems quite confidential and glad to see me. Told me of her plans of altering the Cliff Hill grounds etc. Miss Walker and I talked of her going with Miss Catherine Rawson to Wast Water Lake on Wednesday and of this place and that. She would like to see the Giant's Causeway and lake of Killarney. So should I. Said I would take her next month and she would have gone but for having promised to go to Wast Water! I hoped she would not be long away. To be back before the end of next month. She would like well enough to see Switzerland. Shall I get her there? Mentioned my being lost near Wast Water and begged her to think of me there. Yes, she should not forget me. Really, I almost think she has no dislike to me at any rate, who knows how it may end. I shall be wary this time. I shall really be glad enough when she is come back'*. Although Anne Lister was clearly worried about the possibility of being hurt yet again, I think this journal entry shows she was beginning to develop feelings for Ann Walker. After accompanying Ann Walker back to Lidgate after their visit to Cliff Hill, Anne Lister called on Mrs. Eliza Priestley, at New House, and sat talking with her for a couple of hours. Anne Lister: *'Said how well Miss Walker and I got on together. Had been at Cliff Hill together'*. Anne then started to open up to Mrs. Priestley, explaining how she felt: *'more unsettled than ever since the last 2 years. Death had broken in upon my plans. All my thoughts of a fixed companion frustrated. Must have someone. Difficult to choose again. She would and must be certain I meant poor Sibbella. Mrs. Priestley said all that would be easy when the time came. She mentioned Mrs. Lawton. Oh no I liked her very much but that was a different thing and made the same answer about Miss Norcliffe. All this was to throw Mrs. Priestley off the thought of Mariana, whom I know she must have fancied I had fixed on. I got on as usual, friendly as ever, tho' at first it struck me she thought of my seeing so much of Miss Walker. Perhaps the Priestleys will think of it by and by'.* The personal nature of this journal entry does seem to indicate that Anne had a close friendship with Eliza Priestley, although, Anne, of course, did what was necessary to *'throw Mrs. Priestley off'* knowing the true nature of hers and Mariana's connection, having promised Mariana never to allude to their relationship being anything more than common friendship.

A couple of days later, on Monday September 3rd, Anne Lister and Ann Walker made several social calls together, visiting several friends with whom they were both acquainted, including Ann Walker's cousins, the Edwards at Pye Nest, a mansion in the south-west of Halifax. Clearly the two women were happy to demonstrate to elements of Halifax society that they had become good friends. After the social calls had been made, they went to Throps to look at shrubs and flowers for their estates. Ann Walker had arrived at Shibden Hall in her carriage a little before midday to collect Anne for the outing and had chatted for a little while with Aunt Anne whilst Anne was getting ready. Ann Walker would, in time, become very fond of Aunt Anne.

Anne Lister was now writing increasingly detailed entries in her journal relating to her relationship with Ann Walker. Her description of the outing: *'Miss Walker and I got on very well. She was not for leaving to Pye Nest. Shewed me a queer huffy letter she had had from Mr. Edwards, would not call before November. I advised differently and we went, but I see there will be no cordiality again between them. She seems well enough inclined to consult me and tell me all. I am to choose shrubs for her and she for me. I begged her not to stay longer than three weeks or if she did not go so soon as Wednesday to be back on the twenty sixth and I would breakfast with her on the twenty seventh, at which she seemed pleased. Joked and said she had better go with me and be at Rome for Easter. Her refusal was weak enough to make me guess her going as possible. She does not seem to dislike me at any rate. Well, what shall we make of it? If she was fond of me and manageable, I think I could be comfortable enough with her'.* The Mr. Edwards, referred to was Ann Walker's uncle, her mother's brother.

So, in two separate journal entries, Anne Lister mentioned that Miss Walker *'does not seem to dislike me at any rate'*. This does suggest to me that the rejections by Vere Hobart and Mariana Lawton had knocked Anne's self-confidence and positivity. Was Anne genuinely unsure whether Ann Walker found her appealing or could it have been possible that Anne was starting to fall for Ann Walker and was worried that her feelings might not be reciprocated? In any case, some feelings were certainly developing because the next night, Tuesday, Anne Lister: *'incurred a cross thinking of Miss Walker, first time'*. Another *'cross was incurred'* on the Thursday night. By the way, *'incurring a cross'* meant that Anne had achieved an orgasm by masturbation.

On the following afternoon, Friday, a note arrived at Shibden from Ann Walker. Anne Lister: *'She goes on Monday with Miss Catherine Rawson. To sleep that night at Bowness, and the next, Tuesday, at Keswick and then, she says, see seven lakes before getting to Wastdale. I think we shall get on together. She feels satisfied at having called at Pye Nest and grateful to me for persuading her to do so. I wonder if I can at all mould her to my own ways'.*

The next day, Saturday, September 8th, Anne Lister called on Ann Walker at Lidgate. The visit was only for 10 minutes as Ann Walker was to be off in her carriage at noon to go to Huddersfield to collect Catherine Rawson and bring her back to Lidgate, prior to their departure for the Lake District on the Monday.

During the next two and a half weeks, whilst Ann Walker was on holiday in the Lake District, Anne continued to be busy with Shibden estate business, including extending her ornamental walk in the grounds of Shibden and with the completion of the building of her chaumière (a.k.a hut or moss house) started on August 24th. The chaumière was essentially a posh hut with a thatched roof that was to be a place where Anne could escape to for a bit of peace and quiet or whatever else she had in mind (definitely was not a shed!). Anne incurred a cross thinking of Miss Walker on two more occasions. I just want to highlight that it was usual practice for Anne to keep a detailed record of her sex life whether it occurred with another person or on her own. It was in no way disrespectful to the persons involved.

Anne Lister and Mariana Lawton continued their correspondence as they had always done, writing to each other every two or three weeks. In Mariana's letter, posted in London, and which arrived at Shibden on Tuesday, September 25th, she wrote of having found Anne a suitable lady's maid to take abroad with her, a young woman called Eugenie Pierre. Anne Lister: *'She talks of my probably settling abroad for some years.. this seems as if Mariana had no thought of ever being with me'.*

On Wednesday, September 26th, Anne Lister called at Lidgate to see if Ann had returned from her holiday: *'Yes! Last night. Sat with her from 12.50 p.m. to 2.20 p.m. She had brought me a presse-papier from the marble works at Kendal. Very civil. Our conversation quite confidential and we really get on very well. Yet she said she could not go to Italy'.* The next morning, Thursday, September 27th, Anne Lister set off at 7.30 a.m. to Lidgate to have breakfast with Ann. They sat talking all morning, but, at about half past twelve, just before they were about to out for a walk, Mrs. Stansfield Rawson and her daughter Delia paid a social call on Ann Walker. My understanding is that it was customary, for a current visitor to take their leave when a new visitor called. On this occasion Anne Lister decided to stay put: *'Miss Walker glad I had sat them out'*. After the Rawsons had departed, Anne and Ann had lunch, then walked to Shibden for Anne Lister to show Ann the ornamental walk she had been working on. They then went to Anne Lister's moss house, with Ann Walker being its first visitor. The two women spent two hours in the moss house, chatting: *'Miss Walker and I very cozy and confidential. On parting she said she knew not when she had spent so pleasant a day. I believe her. She sat in the moss house, hardly liking to move. Of course, I made myself agreeable and I think she already likes me even more than she herself is aware. She seemed pleased at my reminding her of our walk ten years ago by hilltop etc. when I had joked about her going abroad. Said it had always been my intention to make the offer more seriously as soon as I could. That she must remember I had always been in the same strain. That I had never joked anyone else in the same way and I hoped she would now understand that I was more serious than she supposed. She said her Uncle and Aunt Atkinson had said I should get her abroad but that she had told them "oh no it was all joke". Ah said I, then they understood me better than you did. She had told me, before, that she was always told I was not to be depended on. I successfully parried this, and she believed me and in fact she seems inclined to follow my advice implicitly. She consults me about her affairs. She said she would call on my aunt on Monday, I to meet her between nine and ten. I really did feel rather in love with her in the hut and as we returned. I shall pay due court for the next few months and after all I really think I can make her happy and myself too. Well said I to myself as I left her, she is more in for it than she thinks, she likes me certainly. We laughed at the idea of the talk our going abroad together would cause. She said it would be as good as a marriage, yes said I, quite as good or better. She falls into my views of things admirably, I believe I shall succeed with her. If I do, I will really try to make her happy and I shall be thankful to heaven for the mercy of bringing me home. We shall have money enough. She will look up to me and soon feel attached, and I, after all my turmoils, shall be steady and if God so wills it, happy. I can gently mould Miss Walker to my wishes and may we not be happy?*

How strange the fate of things seem if after all my companion for life could be Miss Walker'.

It appears Anne Lister's self-confidence and positivity had started to make a comeback. Also, since she and Ann became reacquainted, entries related to their relationship contained two brief references to money but repeated references to being happy. This shows that Anne Lister's top priority was clearly to find a life partner with whom she could have a loving, joyful relationship, and any suggestion that she was only interested in Ann Walker's money, is incorrect. Also, the extent of the repetition regarding the possibility of being happy and making Ann Walker happy rather suggests that Anne Lister was overexcited at the prospect. Of course, in the nineteenth century, there was a financial aspect to heterosexual marriage so it would be reasonable to assume that could also be the case for same-sex partnerships. However, from the time that Anne Lister inherited Shibden in 1826, the women with whom she was involved had either no, or very little, independent income, so making a financial gain from her relationships with those women was clearly of little importance to Anne. Interestingly, Ann Walker was the first person that Anne was involved with after 1826 who had an independent income greater than hers. Also interesting to note, is that it was Ann Walker who was the first to mention their marriage.

Next morning, Friday, September 28th, Anne Lister: *'Musing, before getting up and as I dressed, of Miss Walker. I think we should be happy together. I should gently lead her into my ways and soon be really attached to her to the exclusion of all care for anyone else'.* That morning Anne set out at 10 a.m. to her ornamental walk and worked at pruning the young oak trees for four hours. She then went to the hut supposedly for a rest, Anne: *'Incurred a cross thinking of Miss Walker. I shall think myself into being in love with her. I am already persuaded I like her quite well enough for comfort'.* A few minutes after Anne returned home, there was a knock at the door. It was Ann Walker. She was shown into the drawing room as it had been assumed that she was paying a call on Aunt Anne, even though their plan had been for her to pay a formal call on Aunt Anne on the Monday. After about half an hour, Anne and Ann set off back to Lidgate. It transpired that Ann Walker had actually come to consult Anne Lister about a problem with one of her tenants, and had sent a note, in advance, to Shibden to that effect. However, for some reason, Anne Lister had not received the note, hence the confusion. They then decided to go to the hut for a sit down and a chat, Anne Lister: *'Bordering on love making in the hut. Said I should certainly take her off with me. Hoped she could trust me, yes, she had the greatest confidence in me and our going together was actually agreed on, and we, afterwards, talked of it as a thing settled depending on our respective aunts, both of whom in a precarious way. Our liaison is now established. It is to be named to nobody but her sister and aunt and that not till a week or ten days before our being off. We shall now go on swimmingly and our courtship will progress naturally. She already likes me, perhaps she scarce knows how, and we shall both be in love seriously enough before our journeys. She looked happy'.* In the margin of the same diary page Anne wrote: *'like the day of engagement between Miss Walker and me'.*

The following day, Saturday, September 29th, Anne Lister had a long visit with Eliza Priestley at New House in Lightcliffe and later in the afternoon, she called on Ann at Lidgate and the two of them visited Ann's aunt at Cliff Hill. They returned to Lidgate and spent the evening together. Anne Lister: *'We now get on beautifully. I obscurely love making and she all smiles. Said I felt sure of my own happiness and I might be equally so of hers. Oh, she was sure of hers but had been thinking last night whether she could make me happy and be a companion for me. She said how happy she now felt and looked so as we sat on the sofa. In moralizing a little on how much we had both to be thankful, how happy we should be etc. She said yes, she had often looked at all her things and said what was the use of having them with nobody to enjoy them with her. She said it all seemed now like a dream to her. She is getting more and more affectionate to me and I really do begin to be in love'.* It was dark and quite late when Anne Lister set off from Lidgate to return to Shibden so one of Ann Walker's servants walked with her carrying a lantern. Partway home she met two of her own servants, Elizabeth Cordingley and Rachel Hemingway coming from Shibden. Apparently, Aunt Anne had been worried about her being out late so her sister Marian had sent the servants out to look for her. Anne Lister: *'Marian set on me on my entering the room that I must do so no more etc. etc. in that, sort of to-me-appearing dictatorial manner that I as usual could not stand it and it ended in Marian's crying and having a nervous fit, however all got round again at last'.* Anne then sat talking to her aunt until 11 p.m. She told her aunt about her developing relationship with Ann Walker and that she was very confident that they would go travelling and then settle down together. Anne also told her aunt about the likely extent of Ann Walker's income and Aunt Anne was well pleased with Anne's choice and prospects and said that her father and uncles would be pleased. Interestingly, the possibility of Anne and Ann settling together had, in fact, already occurred to Aunt Anne. I wonder whether Aunt Anne was just incredibly broadminded or maybe it was not that uncommon for two women from the same social class to live together during the nineteenth century, or perhaps she just knew instinctively what was required to ensure her niece's happiness.

Anne Lister repeatedly wrote in her journal about feeling increasingly in love with Ann Walker, about thinking that Ann Walker liked her, and about the possibility of them being happy together. Was she trying to convince herself that her life's dream might actually be coming true or was she getting ahead of herself?

Anne and Ann did not see each other the next day, Sunday, but met up again on the morning of Monday, October 11th, and spent the day together. Anne Lister told Ann that she had confided in her aunt about their intention to travel and settle down together and that she was very pleased. Anne Lister decided to delay their plan for Ann to pay a formal call on her aunt, planned for that afternoon, and set about trying to convince her that, after their travels, she should move into Shibden and find a tenant for Lidgate House. Anne Lister was always keen to get matters settled as soon as possible but, on this occasion, I think she was being premature. Ann Walker resisted Anne's best efforts at persuasion, and she explained that *'she had said she would never marry but that as she had once felt an inclination not to keep to this, she could not yet so positively say she should never feel the same inclination again. She should not like to deceive me and begged not to answer just now'.* Anne Lister said *'she was quite right. Praised her judiciousness. That no feelings of selfishness should make me even wish my happiness rather than hers. That I would give her six months, till my next birthday, to make up her mind'.*

The two women next saw each other when Ann Lister called at Lidgate at 10 a.m. on the morning of Thursday October 4th. Ann Walker started by giving reasons why she needed to continue to live on the Walker estate. Anne Lister: *'it was person, not place, I cared for. This said she seemed reconciled and satisfied. I said I would listen to no difficulty but the pre-engagement of her own heart. She declared it not engaged. I had my arm on the back of the sofa. She leaned on it, looked as if I might be affectionate and it ended in her lying on my arm all the morning and my kissing her and she returning it with such a long continued passionate or nervous mumbling kiss that we get on as far as we by daylight mere kissing could. I thinking to myself, well this is rather more than I expected, of course she means to take me'.* Although having agreed, just three days earlier, to a six month engagement, and also being in the middle of their first passionate encounter, Anne Lister could not resist the opportunity to try to push Ann into giving her answer sooner. Well, as it turned out, Ann Walker was no pushover. Anne Lister: *'She held out saying her mind was quite unmade up and I must not hope too much for fear of disappointment. Yet she asked me to dine with her at five and stay all night'.* Anne Lister agreed to return for dinner that evening but had to decline Ann's request to stay overnight because her father was unwell and her sister was away, staying with friends in Market Weighton. When Anne Lister returned to Lidgate at 5 p.m. Ann was wearing an evening gown and the dining room was set out ready for a formal dinner. I wonder, could it have been Ann Walker's intention to seduce Anne Lister? After they had eaten, and the servant had left the room, Anne Lister described what happened: *'drew near to each other and she sat on my knee and I did not spare kissing and pressing her, she returning it as in the morning. Yet still I was not to hope too much. She said I was infatuated, when the novelty was over, I should not feel the same and might not find her a companion for me'*. For Ann Walker to have been trying again to explain to Anne why she wanted to wait six months to give her answer, I can only assume that, as had happened that morning, once more in the midst of a passionate embrace, Anne Lister must have pressed her case for an earlier answer. They then left the dining room and sat *'most lovingly on the sofa'*, presumably in the drawing room. Anne Lister: *'We let the lamp go out. Long continued mumbling moist kissing. I prest her bosom then finding no resistance and the lamp being out, let my hand wander lower down, gently getting to queer, still no resistance'*. I think it was clear that Ann Walker wanted physical intimacy with Anne, but unfortunately Anne Lister ruined the moment by whispering *'she would break my heart if she left me'*. This resulted in Ann Walker crying and explaining she had been engaged to a man, who had died three months earlier and that she could not transfer her affections so soon. Oh dear, instead of enjoying potentially their first sexual encounter, Anne Lister ended up apologising profusely to a distressed Ann Walker. Anne Lister then left saying she would return the following day. When she got home, she wrote in her journal her thoughts on what had gone so wrong that evening. She was genuinely very puzzled at the events that had occurred, and I don't think she realised her mistake in keep pushing Ann to commit to her there and then instead of waiting for an answer at the end of their agreed six-month engagement. Perhaps she had assumed Ann Walker's readiness to engage in an increased level of physical intimacy meant that she intended to commit to her or maybe she felt driven by a sense of desperation having previously been let down by lovers who ultimately married men. Ann Walker, on the other hand, seemed sure that, in time, Anne would tire of her. She had previously said that if she did agree to settle down with Anne Lister, it would be a lifetime commitment, so I assume she felt such a big decision should only be made when she was certain it was the right thing to do. Also, I wonder if Ann Walker's eagerness for them to be more intimate was partly because she wanted some illicit fun but also maybe she wanted to know, for future reference, just how pleasurable sex with another woman would be. Either way, Anne Lister was surprised and a little put off by Ann's forwardness. After all, in the past, she had always found herself more attracted to women who resisted her advances, so it would be reasonable to assume that the reverse would also be true.

The next day, Friday, October 5th, Anne Lister arrived at Lidgate determined to be 'cautious' and 'gravish'. Basically, she was playing it cool. At first Ann Walker went to be affectionate to her, but, realising her manner, pulled back. She said she had not expected Anne Lister to come to Lidgate and she understood that Anne meant all was over between them. Anne Lister: *'I explained how sorry I was. Would have been the last to have intruded on her feelings under circumstances of such recent grief, but my being hopeless now, no reason that I should be always so, and we would leave things as they were so far that I would not let her give her answer now but wait the six months as agreed. She thought she could not feel regard enough for me and it would not be fair to me. I said my expectations were very moderate. I should be satisfied if she could always be to me as she was now'.* I get the feeling that Ann Walker had turned the tables on Anne Lister and was now the one calling the shots. Anne Lister: *'we then got much as yesterday but her back bad and she very languid as she lay on the sofa on my arm. I might have done what I liked. She gave me her mumbling kisses again and I seemed empassioned but still said I had no hope.*

She said she thought I had hope. I got up to go before four, but she asked me to stay and I loitered and said how little resolution I had. She said Catharine Rawson would suit me better, I said no. She took me up to her room. I kissed her and she pushed herself so to me, I rather felt and might have done it as much as I pleased. She is man keen enough. If I stay all night it will be my own fault if I do not have all of her I can'. Before Anne Lister left, Ann asked her to pay a call on her cousins, the Priestleys before they went to Harrogate on the following Tuesday and not to visit her at Lidgate until after the Priestleys had gone. Now knowing that her liaison with Anne was to continue, Ann Walker was obviously keen to prevent the Priestleys from finding out. Anne Lister now understood that Ann wanted to enjoy their physical relationship to the full without making a commitment until she was sure of her own feelings. Anne Lister: *'shall I or shall I not give in to fun with her?'* For Anne Lister, this realisation took the romance out of their relationship, and she felt *'cooled about the thing'*. Could Ann Walker be right to be concerned that Anne would eventually lose interest in her?

The next day, Saturday, October 6th, as requested, Anne Lister paid a social call on the Priestleys, however Mrs. Priestley was not at home, so she called on old Miss Walker at nearby Cliff Hill instead. Mrs. Priestley also called at Cliff Hill and she and Anne Lister left together, then walking and chatting for three quarters of an hour. Their conversation did get round to talk of Ann Walker with Mrs. Priestley commenting on Anne Lister being good friends with her and visiting her every day. She also said that a friendship with Anne would be a very good thing for Ann Walker. Anne explained that they were indeed good friends but that she did not call on her every day. Mrs. Priestley invited Anne to breakfast with her on the following Monday.

The next afternoon, Sunday, October 7th, Anne Lister called again on Mrs. Priestley to say she would not be able to breakfast with her the next day, Monday. It seems she had a prior engagement to breakfast with old Mrs. Rawson which presumably had slipped her mind. Mrs. Priestley commented that she had not seen Ann Walker in church that morning and that she feared she might be ill, since she noticed that the blinds were down at Lidgate when she passed by. Anne said she would call at Lidgate and inquire after Ann Walker, but Mrs. Priestley proposed that she would go too. They arrived at Lidgate to find that Ann Walker was absolutely fine, so Mrs. Priestley left after a few minutes leaving Anne and Ann alone. They soon got to discussing their relationship again and agreed that the plan for them to be each other's companion for life was off the table for the foreseeable, and instead, they would live at their own residences and essentially be friends with benefits. Anne Lister: *'it seems I can have her as my mistress'*. They certainly didn't waste any time, Anne Lister: *'she kissed me and lay on my arm as before, evidently excited. I kissed and pressed very tenderly and got my right hand up her petticoat to queer but not to the skin. Could not get thro' her thick knickers, for tho' she never once attempted to put my hand away, she held her thighs too tight together for me, I shall manage it the next time. She asked me to spend the whole day and stay all night on Tuesday. If she really continues to excite and amuse me, well and good, I will take her on her own terms'.* That night, one of Anne's own servants called at Lidgate with a lantern to walk her home to Shibden. Unfortunately, he mistakenly thought Anne was spending the evening with the Priestleys, so called at their house first. Anne knew that this was potentially a costly mistake as it was likely that the Priestleys would wonder why Anne was with Ann Walker till such a late hour.

The following morning, Monday, October 8th, Anne Lister went to Stoney Royde to breakfast with her friend, old Mrs Rawson. After breakfast she went to the see how the development of Halifax's Philosophical and Natural History Museum was progressing. She then paid a social call on a Mrs. Veitch and afterwards walked to Lidgate, where Ann Walker was pleased to see her. The purpose of Anne's visit was to change their plans for Tuesday to the Thursday on account of her period having started that morning. Anne only intended staying a few minutes, but Ann Walker wanted her to stay longer so they dined together, then, as usual, *'kissing and pressing'* on the sofa. Then, shockingly, at four o'clock, Mrs. Priestley burst into the room, both unexpected and unannounced. Ann Walker had put the blinds down and perhaps Mrs. Priestley had noticed this as she was passing by and decided to investigate or maybe she was getting suspicious of Anne and Ann's relationship and had decided to pay a call on Ann Walker to find out what was going on. Anne Lister: *'I had jumped in time and was standing by the fire, but Ann looked red, and I pale, and Mrs. Priestley must see we were not particularly expecting or desiring company. She looked vexed, jealous, and annoyed, and asked, in bitter satire, if I had where I was ever since she left me there. No said I, I only ought to have been'.* Mrs. Priestley then declared that Anne Lister's staying out late at Lidgate was causing her aunt a *'host of miseries'*. Anne Lister: *I laughed and said I really did not intend doing so again. "Yes" she replied angrily "you will do the same the very next time the temptation occurs".* Mrs. Priestley accused Anne of having refused breakfasting with her, not to go to Stoney Royde and breakfast with Mrs. Rawson, but to go to Lidgate to be with Ann Walker. She then stormed out in a suppressed rage. Anne Lister: *'Miss Walker laughed and said we were well matched. We soon got to kissing again on the sofa. At last, I got my right hand up her petticoats and after much fumbling got thro' the opening of her drawers and touched, first time, the hair and skin of queer. She never offered the least resistance in any way, and certainly shewed no sign of its being disagreeable. She liked my attentions and the first night of my being there will give me all I am able to take'.* At 6.25 p.m., Anne Lister set off from Lidgate to return home to Shibden. It was raining heavily and there was a strong driving wind against her. As she left Lidgate, Ann lent her a tartan cloak to keep out the worst of the weather. She got home at 7 o'clock, and after changing her clothes, had dinner, then told her aunt all (well almost all) of the goings on at Lidgate that day.

Well now, the big day (and night), Thursday October 11th, had arrived, and began with Anne Lister arriving at Lidgate at 7.45 a.m. Ann Walker came down from her dressing room a few minutes later and they enjoyed a long leisurely breakfast together. Afterwards, Ann Walker sought Anne's advice on various matters, one of which was a request for funds from one of her cousins, and together they wrote a suitable letter in response. After dining at 2 p.m. they sat on the sofa *'lovemaking and kissing'* as usual. After a while they got to talking. Anne Lister had already begun making improvements to Shibden Hall and the surrounding estate and she now told Ann of her other planned improvements should Ann move in with her. Clearly she was trying to make Shibden more appealing. To be fair to Anne Lister, there was a good reason why, if they were to live together, it should be at Shibden. Anne Lister's heirs were her distant Lister cousins in Wales as per her Uncle James' wishes, however, because eventually she would own Shibden outright, she would be able to settle Shibden on Ann Walker for life, so if Anne Lister predeceased her, which was likely being as she was 12 years older, Shibden would continue to be Ann Walker's home. You might think, in the event of Anne's death, Ann Walker could just move back into one of the properties on the Walker estate if she so chose. Unfortunately, it was not that simple. These large houses were too costly to be left standing empty, they had to be rented out. The practice at the time for renting such properties involved long term leases, 10 years for example. So, it was important, if the two women were to live together, that, should one die, the other could still continue to live in their shared home. However, the complex nature of Ann Walker's shared inheritance of the Walker estate did not permit her to give a life interest to Anne Lister were they to live together in one of the houses on the Walker estate. This may seem a rather morbid conversation but, in those times, life was pretty precarious and, if they were to end up living together, these were important matters and needed to be discussed. As evening approached, Anne and Ann returned to their lovemaking. Anne Lister: '*As it became dusk, we crept closer and I, without any resistance, got for the first time, right middle finger up her queer at three separate times. She nothing loth but evidently excited, liking it and wet and taking it altogether as if she had learnt her lesson before in this way too, as well as in kissing. She whispered that she loved me*'. By the way, '*she nothing loth*' means she showed no reluctance. Anyway, I think you can probably guess how Anne Lister interpreted Ann's whisper. Yes, of course, she assumed it meant that Ann wanted to live with her, because again she pressed her case for them living at Shibden and again it resulted in Ann bursting into tears. Well, all this put paid to them spending the night together, and, as Anne Lister set off home, Ann reiterated that she must '*not to hope too much*'.

Anne Lister returned to Lidgate to see Ann a couple of days later, on Saturday, October 13th, in the afternoon. There were already three visitors at Lidgate, Mrs. Dyson, and Mrs. and Miss Salmon, who left about a quarter of an hour after Anne's arrival. Ann Walker was not feeling well so Anne tried to persuade her to see her doctor, Dr. Belcombe in York, to which she agreed. It almost seems as if the upset of Thursday was forgotten. They carried on as usual discussing business matters and travel, with Anne Lister recounting anecdotes and observations from her travels on the continent. Then, Anne Lister: '*She lay down and I leaned over her kissing her as usual. After tea got more affectionate but on gently putting my hand up her petticoats she whispered don't and I desisted. She said I did not know how she had suffered from it the other night, had not got the better of it yet. She was very tender there. I talked soothingly and affectionately*'. Anne Lister stayed at Lidgate till just before 10 o'clock when her servant John Booth arrived to walk her back to Shibden. About a half hour before Anne's arrival, her sister, Marian, had also returned to Shibden from her stay at Market Weighton.

The following Monday, October 15th, in the morning, Ann Walker arrived at Shibden in her carriage and she and Anne Lister went off on their travels, shopping and making social calls.

The two women got back to Lidgate at 5.15 p.m and dined at 6 p.m. They spent a cosy evening together and, on this occasion, Anne Lister was to stay all night, although they would sleep in separate bedrooms. They both went upstairs at 10.15 p.m. Anne Lister: *'I undressed in half hour and then went to her room. Had her on my knee a few minutes and then got into bed, she making no objection, and staid with her till twelve and three quarters, grubbling gently. Right middle finger up almost all the time. Made two or three attempts to get myself quite near her but somehow could not manage it and she seemed so tender and able to bear so little (I think she was more intact and innocent and virgin than I had latterly surmised) that I contented myself with handling her gently and love making. She whispered to me in bed how gentle and kind I was to her and faintly said she loved me or "else how can you think" said she "that I should let you do as you do". On leaving her, my night things so wet, obliged to take them off and sleep in my dressing gown'.*

The next day, Tuesday, October 16th, Ann Walker was not feeling well and spent most of the day lying on the sofa. She *'felt sickish, had pain in her back and felt great heat and soreness about her queer'.* Apparently, she had irregular periods, and suffered greatly during menstruation, and also for about a week prior. She thought that her period was coming but also seemed to think that being intimate with Anne the night before also contributed to her discomfort. Anne Lister nursed, comforted, and consoled Ann all day. They made the decision that they would go to York the following Monday for Ann Walker to have a consultation with Dr. Belcombe and hopefully get to the bottom of her health problems. Dr. Belcombe was Anne Lister's doctor, and a close friend. He was also Mariana's brother. Anne Lister stayed with Ann till 6.25 p.m. that evening, then walked home to Shibden.

Anne Lister called at Lidgate to see Ann the next morning, Wednesday, October 17th, to make plans for their trip to York on the following Monday for her to see Dr. Belcombe. Ann Walker was still feeling unwell but wanted to call at Cliff Hill to see her aunt, so Anne walked with her then continued, on her own, to Shibden.

The following morning, Thursday, Anne Lister arrived at Lidgate at ten past eight to have breakfast with Ann. After breakfast they *'sat cozying as usual'* and got to discussing their relationship. Anne Lister: *'She was now convinced I loved her. Thought, at first, I liked but not love and mere liking was not enough. Something more required for living together. She owned she loved me. I made strong love and really felt it. She said she should not mind her cousin coming on while we were away. Should not mind being ill if I was with her. I had right middle finger moderately and gently, she making no resistance, but say how kind and gentle I was with her. She lay on my arm on the sofa as usual, no objection to my going tomorrow. In fact, surely, she has no thought but of taking me'.*

Anne Lister left Lidgate at 2 p.m. having estate business to deal with. After the remarks made by Ann Walker that morning, she was now feeling increasingly confident that the two of them would settle together at Shibden. That evening she wrote to Mariana, although she only put the letter in the post on Saturday, October 20th. Anne described the contents of the letter: *'mentioned my being in York for a few hours on Tuesday with my neighbour, Miss Walker, whom I had persuaded to go over to consult Stephen [Dr. Belcombe]. Begged Mariana not to name it as my taking Steph such a patient would not be taken well hereabouts if known. Did not mention her [Miss Walker] in any way so that Mariana could surmise anything particular'.*

The following afternoon, Friday, October 19th, Anne Lister arrived at Lidgate at 2.30 p.m. to find that Ann was not at home. She had gone to visit her aunt at Cliff Hill, so Anne Lister called there, and they walked back to Lidgate together. They dined together, and Anne Lister stayed at Lidgate till quite late that night. Ann Walker's period had started that morning and she was feeling rather poorly, but despite this all was going well, Anne Lister: *'Miss Walker consulted me and made me stay and talked and treated me exactly as if her mind was, in reality, made up to take me and I felt almost sure and not two people could get on more lovingly as we'.* Anne Lister had read to Ann the letter she had written to Mariana the previous night, and, similarly, Ann Walker read out the letter she had written to her cousin Miss Atkinson. Anne Lister described the two of them as getting on *'just like a married pair'.* So confident was she feeling that, later on that evening, she made a joke about them having to be just good friends if they decided to live separately. Ann Walker's response was not quite what Anne expected: *'Her mind was not made up. She did not think she should have suffered so much, that there would have been so much difficulty. If she was really married it would be different, would be easier'.* Anne thought to herself: *'I see how it is. My difficulty in getting to her on Monday night and my being able to do so little was not what she expected or relished'.* It seems that Anne Lister had tried to have sex with Ann Walker in the way that she and Mariana usually did, that is by scissoring with their vulvas in contact, and it had not gone well. Hardly surprising though, given Ann Walker's inexperience, she probably had no idea what she was meant to be doing. Although Ann Walker's words were probably not intended to be particularly hurtful to Anne, unfortunately they most certainly would have been, given that Anne had, on more than one previous occasion, written in her journal, about her concern that she may not be able to satisfy Ann Walker sexually. Anne Lister left shortly after this conversation, arriving back at Shibden at 11.20 p.m.

The following afternoon, Saturday, October 20th, Anne Lister arrived at Lidgate at 3.00 p.m., an hour later than was planned, and feeling out of sorts with Ann but determined not to show it. She attempted to explain to Ann why she thought that Ann was mistaken in thinking that having sex with a man would be easier than with her. Ann Walker listened attentively while Anne *'explained the size of men'.* She then went on to tell Ann that if she ultimately decided that she did not want them to live together as a married couple, she would have to give her up entirely. Anne

Lister left Lidgate at 6.20 p.m. believing that Ann *'would like to keep me on so as to have the benefit of my intimacy without any real joint concern'.*

The mixed messages coming from Ann Walker in their conversations over the previous few days had the effect of making Anne Lister doubt her own mind regarding their future together. She was starting to question what she herself wanted and wondered if she should go off on her travels abroad regardless of what Ann's final answer about their future together might be. She was, of course, committed to taking Ann to see Dr. Belcombe, and, as planned, arrived at Lidgate on Sunday evening to spend the night there before travelling to York the next morning, Monday. They set off to York in Ann Walker's carriage at 11.35 a.m. on Monday October 22nd, and arrived there, at the Black Swan, at 4.55 p.m. They had dinner and then Anne Lister sent a note to Dr. Belcombe to let him know they were there. Dr. Belcombe called to see them at 8.30 p.m. and stayed for an hour. Anne and Ann retired at 10.55 p.m. with Anne Lister *'grubbling her till two'.*

Dr. Belcombe called at the Black Swan again the following morning, Tuesday, for a second consultation and then again in the evening. His diagnosis of Ann Walker's health problems was not particularly sympathetic: *"Nothing the matter with her but nervousness. If all her fortune could fly away and she had to work for her living she would be well. A case of nervousness and hysteria. No organic disease. But going abroad would do her good'.* I do wonder, since her back pain was worse during her period, surely they would have been better visiting Dr. Belcombe when she was menstruating. But then again, I cannot imagine that any 19th century doctor would have the slightest idea of how ill a woman can be during, and prior to her period.

Anne and Ann spent Wednesday and most of Thursday in York. They did a lot of shopping but also visited York Minster. Anne Lister paid social calls on some of her friends on her own, although she did introduce Ann to one friend, Mrs. Duffin. They set off home late on Thursday afternoon, arriving back at Lidgate at 9.40 p.m. During the journey Anne Lister told Ann more about her own financial situation and the alterations she was planning for Shibden. The nature of their conversation again suggested to Anne Lister that Ann did intend to commit to their future together, although again she did not explicitly say so. Anne Lister did keep getting this impression from their conservations only to discover subsequently that Ann had not yet made up her mind. Unfortunately, this was about to happen yet again. Anne Lister spent the night at Lidgate. Her diary entry the following morning, Friday, October 26th: '*Grubbling till late last night and gave her, as she owned, pleasure, tired as she was. At it again before eight in the morning and left our bed sheets (she came and slept with me) quite wet, our night linen being ditto. Unluckily, so pleased with the success of last night grubbling, ventured to take off my drawers and try to get to her. Did not succeed, in despair about it. Owned that I had no business to think her fairly my own till we had been really and properly together, and this led to doubts and fears on my part. She talked of not deciding till the third of April*'. That afternoon, Anne and Ann walked to Cliff Hill to visit Ann Walker's aunt, who handed Ann Walker a black edged letter with a black seal on their arrival. As Ann read the letter it fell from her hands. The letter was from a Miss Bentley who had written to inform Ann of the death of her friend Mrs. Ainsworth, who had been killed in a carriage accident. Ann had mentioned her friends, the Ainsworths, to Anne Lister on at least two previous occasions. She was expecting a visit from them in the New Year and had explained to Anne Lister that she would not be able to go travelling abroad with her until after their visit. Anne Lister immediately took Ann back home to Lidgate and sent a note to Shibden telling her aunt that she would not be home that day. Anne Lister observed that Ann was '*much affected*' by her friend's death. Anne Lister: '*It instantly struck me she would, in due time, succeed her friend and be Mrs. Ainsworth, however, she has just said "well, now there is no obstacle to our getting off in January"*'.

The following day, Saturday, October 27th, Anne Lister stayed with Ann at Lidgate till about two o'clock. Anne Lister: *'lay in bed grubbling and love making till our linen was almost as wet as yesterday morning. Breakfast at 12, talked till 2'.* Anne Lister then visited old Miss Walker (Ann Walker's aunt) at Cliff Hill and walked to Shibden to see her aunt, returning to Lidgate for dinner at 6.05p.m. and spent the evening *'comfortably cozy'*. She stayed at Lidgate that night and spent the whole of Sunday with Ann Walker. Mrs. Priestley called at Lidgate in the afternoon and stayed for a short while. In the evening Anne and Ann talked about the Ainsworths. It transpired that Ann Walker had planned to consult Mrs. Ainsworth about the propriety of her leaving her own property and moving into Shibden with Anne. Anne Lister spent Sunday night at Lidgate with Ann and the following day they took a long walk, called at Cliff Hill, and then, having met Mrs. Priestley, walked a short way chatting with her until it started to rain. Later in the afternoon, Ann Walker showed Anne some of her financial documents relating to her income and her tenants' rents. They had dinner at six o'clock, tea at eight o'clock, and again Anne Lister stayed the night.

The following day, Tuesday October 30th, Anne Lister wrote a long letter to Isabella Norcliffe, then, at 11.30 a.m., Anne and Ann went out with Ann Walker's gardener to look over the Cliff Hill plantation. They had dinner as usual at 6 p.m., took tea at 8.30 p.m., and retired at 11.30 p.m. after a bit of grubbling.

Before breakfast the next day, Wednesday, October 31st, the two women talked things over. Anne Lister: *'got her to shorten the time of waiting for her final answer from 3rd April to 1st January. She seemed satisfied this would be better. Should be settled before we set off the end of January for the continent. She seems less and less likely to say no, in fact, we talk and act as if yes was all but said'.* After breakfast, they went for went for a walk, then spent an hour with old Miss Walker at Cliff Hill. Hemingway, one of Anne Lister's servants at Shibden, arrived at Lidgate with a note from Jeremiah Rawson regarding arrangements for a meeting he wanted to have with her to discuss coal mining at Shibden, and also, a letter from Mariana, in which she wrote that she hoped Anne's friend, Miss Walker, was better. After tea that evening, Anne and Ann spent time studying maps of Italy and Switzerland, as they planned the trip to Europe they intended to take from the end of January (1833) to the autumn. On returning to England, they intended to go to Scotland for a month to visit Ann Walker's sister, Elizabeth Sutherland, and her family. They also discussed the possibility of making Lidgate their permanent home, even to the extent of considering what it would cost them each year to live there '*in sufficiently good style*'. This is an interesting change from Anne Lister's previous insistence that they should live at Shibden.

The following day, Thursday, November 1st, Anne and Ann called on Mrs. Priestley for about twenty minutes. Anne Lister noted in her journal that Mrs. Priestley '*talked exclusively to Miss Walker*'. Anne Lister had had seemingly pleasant conversations with Mrs. Priestley since the occasion when she interrupted hers and Ann's lovemaking on the sofa at Lidgate, so it is potentially ominous that she was now conspicuously ignoring her. That afternoon, Anne Lister had planned to go back home to Shibden, however, shortly before she was due to set off, Ann Walker received a letter from Mr. Ainsworth, the husband of her friend who had tragically died in a carriage accident. Ann Walker begged Anne to stay until she had read the letter. She told Anne that, in the letter, Mr. Ainsworth asked her to '*not forsake him as a friend*' and begged her '*to write to him without mentioning to Miss Bentley (his sister-in-law) his having written*'. Both women realised immediately that Mr. Ainsworth had designs on Ann Walker. Seeing how much the letter had upset Ann, Anne Lister sent a note to her aunt at Shibden saying she intended to stay at Lidgate another night. For some reason, Ann Walker would not allow Anne to read the whole of the letter, nor would she explain why. Anne Lister knew that the approach by Mr. Ainsworth would lead to an offer of marriage and explained to Ann Walker: *'that she must now decide between Mr Ainsworth and me, and ought to make up her mind before she sat down to write to him. Convinced her of this and it ended in her resolving to give me her final answer on Monday, to write to Mr Ainsworth on that day and shew me her letter'.* After tea they sat together on the sofa, both of them distraught, with silent tears trickling down their cheeks, Ann Walker *'torturing herself with all the miseries of not knowing what to do'* and Anne Lister realising that it was most likely that, yet again, a woman she loved, and hoped to share her life with, would choose to be with a man rather than her. Ann Walker told Anne that she now realised how attached she was to her, and, also, that she *'felt repugnance to forming any connection with the other sex'.* She also promised Anne that the following morning she could have *'a lock of queer's hair'.* Anne Lister: *'We fretted ourselves to sleep last night. She lay on me as usual to warm her stomach and then lay in my arms, but I was perfectly quiet and never touched her queer, the tears silently trickling from my cheeks down hers'.* In a futile attempt to find comfort, Anne Lister repeatedly told herself that she did not care what Ann finally decided, but her tears told a different story. As Anne Lister was about to head home to Shibden that morning, Friday November 2nd, Ann *'hung upon'* her and *'*c*ried and sobbed aloud at parting, saying "well I hope we shall meet again under happier circumstances". "Ah"* said Anne Lister, *"any circumstances would be happier than suspense".*

Anne Lister was very confused by the mixed messages she was getting from Ann. She thought that Ann's conduct and manner surely meant that she would choose her, not Mr. Ainsworth. It may seem strange to our 21st century minds that there was any debate to be had, because, of course, Ann Walker should choose the woman she had grown to love rather than the husband of a friend. But, in the 19th century, propriety was everything, and few people had Anne Lister's courage to follow their own heart. Anne Lister arrived back at Shibden at 12.10 p.m. to find that two items, she and Ann had ordered whilst shopping during their trip to York, had arrived at Shibden, a pair of boots for her and a new seal for Ann Walker. That afternoon, Jeremiah Rawson came to see Anne Lister to discuss coal mining leases on the Shibden estate. The following morning, Saturday, November 3rd, Anne Lister awoke early but felt so bilious she decided to stay in bed. Her period had started that morning although I suspect that the billiousness she felt was partly due to the stress she was experiencing. Feeling better in the afternoon, she walked into Halifax and called at Rawson's bank and also the office of hers and Ann's solicitor, Mr. Parker. She mentioned to Mr. Parker the circumstances regarding one of Ann's tenants, a Mr. Collins, whom she and Ann had observed selling hay stolen from the Walker estate a few days earlier whilst they were out walking. Anne got Mr. Parker to write a letter in Ann Walker's name threatening Collins with legal action which she took with her. On getting home, she wrote a letter to Ann explaining what she had done and advising her to sign and seal the letter, written by Mr. Parker, and have it delivered to her tenant Mr. Collins by one of her servants or her estate manager, Mr. Washington. In her letter, Anne also wrote that she was anxious to hear that Ann was feeling better. She then parcelled up her letter with Mr. Parker's letter, and the new seal, that had arrived the previous day, and gave the parcel to her servant, John Booth, to take to Lidgate, which he duly did. On his return, John brought a note for her from Ann Walker, in which Ann described receiving the new seal: *'it is more precious to me than you have an idea of, words are powerless to express my thanks'*. In her note, Ann Walker said she was feeling better although was still very nervous. Anne Lister: *'now is this or is not, like a person who is going to refuse me? What will be the end of it? Does she or does she not know her own mind already? Or will she really be undecided till the last moment?'* And, as Anne often did, gaining comfort from her religious faith: *'with the blessing of heaven I can be satisfied and happy either way'*.

Ann Walker's distress caused by the death of her friend Mrs. Ainsworth, her anger at receiving that inappropriate letter from

Mr. Ainsworth, and the pressure from Anne Lister to make the decision, regarding their future together, within the next few days, was, not surprisingly, all too much for her. Fearing that making a conspicuous commitment to Anne Lister might result in being ostracised from her relatives and Halifax society, and, also knowing that Anne had said, if she refused her, their friendship must end, meant that Ann Walker was, most definitely, between a rock and a hard place. She had a wretched weekend, unable to eat, and very probably unable to sleep. She believed, that in her present mental state, she was incapable of making a life-changing decision and, if a decision had to be made then it should be God that made it. So, on the following morning, Monday, November 5th, she sent a basket containing a note, a little purse, and some grapes to Shibden Hall. In the purse, she had put two slips of paper. On one piece was written 'yes' and on the other 'no'. In the letter to Anne Lister, she explained that in her present state of mind, she could not make a decision about her future, and, if Anne still required a decision, she should take a slip of paper out of the purse and whichever word appeared, was the answer. The basket was delivered to Shibden Hall at 11.00 a.m. Anne Lister, of course, was expecting Ann's letter to contain the final answer to her offer of marriage. I think it is fair to say that Anne had never fully understood why it was such a difficult decision for Ann Walker to make. Well, she read the letter, and at 11.10 a.m. she was off to Lidgate. Anne Lister arrived at Lidgate, determined to stay calm and behave well. She found Ann Walker in a nervous state. They kissed and were '*affectionate as usual*'. Anne returned the purse containing the two slips of paper to Ann Walker and told her that she *'could not leave to the decision of chance what ought only to be decided by her own heart'*. Ann Walker was taken aback by this remark. In her mind the decision would have been made by God not by chance. Anne Lister explained to Ann that she was taking her answer as a 'no' and if Ann then decided the answer was a 'yes' she was to return the purse to her containing only the 'yes'. Ann Walker begged Anne for more time to make her decision and Anne explained that she intended to be off on her travels abroad after rent collection day on January 2nd, 1833, so agreed that Ann Walker could have until January 1st to make her decision. Ann Walker admitted she had wanted to suggest they went back to their original intention of simply travelling together but knew that would be unfair on Anne. Anne Lister responded: *'there had been too many endearments and too great a tie between us for me to go back to what I had been'*. She then read the letter that Ann Walker had written to be sent to Mr. Ainsworth and proposed a change to its conclusion which Ann Walker readily adopted. The letter was very polite and kind, and *'thanked him for his kindness to her during the life of her much lamented friend'*, but also made it clear to Mr. Ainsworth that any communication between them would have to be done via his sister-in-law Miss Bentley. Thankfully, Ann Walker felt much better after seeing Anne. However, Anne Lister only felt that she herself had fully regained her composure once she had written of the day's events in her journal. The experiences of the day had created doubts in her mind: *'I have asked myself once or twice, is this a sort of spell breaker? Should she even say yes at last, should I value it as much as if it had come more freely. Had it been earlier, it had been kinder. Better be an end of it at once?'*.

The following day, Tuesday, November 6th, after running a few errands in Halifax, Anne Lister called at Lidgate. She had said she would call on the Wednesday, but it seems she just could not keep away. Ann Walker was in good spirits and very glad to see her. Anne Lister: *'I kissed her but in a common way and she did not push herself to me as yesterday and was more guarded. She will not give me much reason now either to hope or despair'*. Anne Lister stayed with Ann for half an hour: *'I left her with no pleasant feeling, saying to myself damn her, it is a narrow and perhaps lucky escape. I don't think her answer will be yes and the more easily reconciled I am the better'*. It seems Ann Walker was relieved that their friendship appeared to be continuing but Anne Lister was clearly bitterly disappointed, and now believed that they would never live together, and that she had to find a way of reconciling herself to this situation.

The next morning, Wednesday, November 7th, Anne Lister again went to Lidgate to see Ann and found her in an anxious state and in tears. Ann Walker talked of having been indiscreet with Mr. Ainsworth and that if she were to marry him it would be out of a sense of duty. She told Anne that Mr. Ainsworth had taught her to kiss but that they had not been as intimate as she and Anne had been. Anne Lister explained that she was under no obligation to Mr. Ainsworth because he had taken advantage of her. Then to Anne Lister's surprise, Ann declared that there was now no obstacle between them. She asked Anne Lister to take her, saying she hoped Anne would find her to be faithful and constant. A moment later, Mrs. Priestley called and stayed for a quarter of an hour. At 1 p.m. Anne Lister's father and sister called to tell her that the craftsmen had arrived at Shibden to work on the library passage. Anne Lister needed to return to Shibden to supervise the work but just before she set off, Ann gave her the purse containing the slip of paper on which was written 'yes'. I wonder what caused such an unexpected change of mind on Ann Walker's part. Could it be that she felt she needed protection from Mr. Ainsworth's advances, and, who better to be protected by than Anne Lister. The two women had planned to breakfast together the following morning but Anne Lister, clearly overexcited, decided to head back to Lidgate and sleep there that night. Before heading back to Lidgate, she wrote her reply to Mariana's letter and had dinner with her family. In her letter to Mariana, she promised to visit her before leaving England to travel abroad in January but also mentioned Ann Walker: *'my friend was much pleased with your brother. Hope he will be of service. She has plenty of faith in him. Was going on admirably well till the afflicting news of the sudden death of her most particular friend'.* Anne Lister arrived at Lidgate at 6.20 p.m. to find Ann in a nervous state but very glad to see her. A package had arrived from Mr. Ainsworth and its contents had distressed

Ann Walker. The package contained an account of the last day of Mrs. Ainsworth's life as well as a note marked 'private' in which Mr. Ainsworth described Ann Walker as *'his affectionate Annie'*. Anne Lister: *'He wrote that he was a friend to her in affliction and calling upon her to be one now to him and concluding with a call upon God to bless her as the prayers of her own Thomas Ainsworth. He had said too that she was the only one he could rest upon and that he would send her the drawing room scrapbook'*. Anne Lister was suspicious of the content of the letter and said as much: *'I remarked that this last expression was what he could only have used to a woman who had gone all lengths for him'*. Ann Walker appeared indignant at this remark. She had not yet posted the letter she wrote to Mr. Ainsworth on Monday, and together, Anne and Ann, made changes and additions to include a response to receipt of Mr. Ainsworth's parcel that afternoon: *'had read the detail of the last day of her friend's life with deep interest and returned the details according to his desire. Was much obliged by his offer of the scrapbook but positively declined accepting it'*. The two women had a pleasant evening *'and got on very well'* despite Ann Walker feeling poorly, suffering with pain at the back of her neck. They had tea at eight o'clock and went upstairs at 10.15 p.m. This was the first night they slept in the same bed together. Anne: *'Slept in my drawers as usual but grubbling at intervals and talking and kissing till after one. She seemed satisfied tho' as I told her mind would waver at times for long to come'*.

The next morning, Thursday November 8th, Ann Walker decided to give Anne more detail about her indiscretion with Mr. Ainsworth. Anne Lister: *'She said she was not worthy of me. Ought not to have decided till I had had proof she might be trusted. She had been much to blame. Declared things had never gone to extremities but said he had asked her to yield all assuring her it would not hurt her that no harm would be done and then he should be sure of her. Luckily, she refused. He had vowed pathetic contrition and she had forgiven, but then it first happened last April twelve month and she had been staying at his house since and the thing had been reiterated in spite of all her resolutions and his contrition worked on her as before. All she regretted was that she had not done as she had now some month ago. While Mrs Ainsworth lived, she wished to have made some reparation to her, but she felt she was in his power. He had charged her never to breathe the thing that it would be ruin to him but adding that indeed she could not as it would commit her equally'.* So it seems that whilst Ann Walker had some intimate contact with Mr. Ainsworth, she did not have sexual intercourse with him. Anne Lister did her utmost to be *'consoling and soothing'* to Ann and this seemed to do her good. I think Anne Lister recognised that Ann was very much the innocent party in what had gone on and felt angry and hostile towards Mr Ainsworth saying: *'I should never endure the sight of him'.* Interestingly, Ann Walker wore a carbuncle ring that Mr. Ainsworth had given her. I do not think she wore it out of any feelings of allegiance to Mr. Ainsworth, I think she just really liked the ring, a further indication of her innocent nature. However, when Ann Walker told Anne about the ring, Anne took it off her finger *'saying she should neither see nor hear of it more'.* Anne Lister then reassured Ann saying: *'I would have got you out of this scrape at all rates whatever had been your answer to me'.* They talked until 2.15 p.m. when Ann Walker's friend, Miss Harriet Parkhill, arrived. A few minutes later Anne Lister departed.

The following morning, Friday, November 9th, Anne Lister set off early to Lidgate arriving at 7.35 a.m. and, not surprisingly, found that Ann was still in bed, feeling nervous and unwell, but glad to see her. Anne Lister stayed with Ann while she washed and dressed and *'talked and reasoned her into being to all appearance better'.* After breakfast, Miss Parkhill, went to Cliff Hill to see old Miss Walker. Ann Walker, still feeling poorly, told Anne that she was wrong to say 'yes' to her. Anne Lister had said she wanted to contact her jewellers to purchase a turquoise ring for Ann, but Ann begged her not to. So just two days after agreeing to marriage with Anne Lister, Ann Walker had changed her mind. Anne Lister was back home at Shibden by 2 p.m. supervising the work being done on the library passage. Interestingly she did not appear to be too disheartened by what Ann Walker had said. It seems that she anticipated that Ann would waver in her decision and she herself was now confident that she was able to successfully reason Ann into both raising her spirits and keeping her on board with the plan to live together. Later that afternoon, she wrote a note to Ann aimed specifically at cheering her up that evening: *'You cannot count upon being much out of my thoughts. Reasoning will do you good for reason is on your side and even-handed justice will be more lenient to you than you are to yourself. May comfort soon break in upon you more abundantly than you now dare hope, and may you soon feel that tho' the spirit may be bruised, it neither is nor ought to be nor can be so broken, as you fear. There bends no reed so low, but it may rise again. Who that has that hope, which human power nor gives nor takes away, who that has that hope can ever feel forlorn, forsaken or disconsolate. God bless you, ever affectionately and very faithfully yours, AL'.* Anne's servant, Hemingway took the letter to Lidgate. She returned with a letter Ann Walker had received from her brother-in-law, Captain Sutherland that she wanted Anne Lister to read and also a note from Ann herself: *'I had in reality just finished a note to you, written in real despair, intending to send it with Captain Sutherland's letter by James when I received your affectionate note. My love, I will not disappoint you by sending what I had written but beg you not to write for the ring tonight. I must not and I cannot take it my love, till I have fewer torments of conscience than I endure at present. I cannot say that I feel stronger this evening and so weak as I am, it would be madness in me to leave the kingdom. I must talk seriously with you on this subject tomorrow. Yours faithfully and affectionately. AW'.* That evening, after dinner, Anne Lister wrote a note to Ann in which she advised her what do regarding the letter from Captain Sutherland. She added her kind words of comfort to help Ann feel better: *'and lastly you know how well I can and do enter into all your feelings on that one especial subject which engrosses us both. I have even forewarned you to expect what you tell me of. Excess of sorrow is in the very nature of things its own remedy. Our mind and nerves will be stronger by and by. Even conscience is not always strictly just, she may be too lenient or too severe or lulled to sleep or tossed in feverish restlessness. We cannot judge ourselves. We are too mistrustful or too confident too fearful or too presumptuous. We walk in a vain shadow, but as I cannot believe you to deserve the torments of conscience, neither can I believe that they will endure with you beyond a season and that a short one. We will talk over any plan most likely to re-establish your health by whatever or where so ever you find this blessing, I shall be equally grateful to heaven for the boon. Affectionately and very faithfully yours. A.L.'*

The following morning, Saturday, November 10th, Anne Lister set off at 8.10 a.m. to Lightcliffe to have breakfast with Mrs. Priestley. En route, she called at Lidgate to drop off her note for Ann Walker and then continued to New House and spent the morning chatting with Mrs. Priestley, who, not only had some knowledge of Mr. Ainsworth's approaches to Ann Walker, but also had formed an opinion on the matter. In her conversation with Anne Lister, Mrs. Priestley praised Mr. Ainsworth and was sure that he and Ann Walker would be a suitable match. Anne just went along with Mrs. Priestley, who then described the now deceased Mrs. Ainsworth as *'very plain and much marked with smallpox and filled up the pitting with rouge. Fifteen or twenty years older than her husband, who married her for money'*. Anne Lister spent Saturday afternoon and evening at Lidgate with Ann and Miss Parkhill. She read the Morning Herald and the York Herald while Ann and Miss Parkhill had dinner at 2 p.m. Ann Walker was still feeling poorly and spent the afternoon either in her easy chair or lying on the sofa. After tea at 6 p.m. Anne and Ann played several games of backgammon. Then, whilst Ann Walker wrote her reply to Captain Sutherland, Anne Lister sat talking for a while to Miss Parkhill, who retired to bed just after 10 o'clock. Anne and Ann went upstairs at 10.35 p.m. That night, Anne Lister: *'two long and good grubbles. She spoke during it, as she often does. Said she felt it was better than usual etc.*

In fact, it was longish and hardish work to me, first with right, then left hand, and she sleeps all night on my arm or more on me, so that I sleep nor much nor well'.

The next morning, Sunday, November 11th, Anne and Ann talked of their plan to travel abroad in the New Year. Ann Walker was very much against leaving the country until she felt very much better. Anne Lister asked her if she meant to keep her promise for them to be together. Ann Walker replied *"yes, if I am not bound to Mr. Ainsworth".* When Anne Lister then asked if Ann was pleased to have her, she replied *'yes, but you shall not be here tomorrow'.* Ann Walker then went to church, probably with Harriet Parkhill, and Anne Lister returned to Shibden. I think I understand the turmoil of Ann Walker's mind. It seems that she believed her intimacy with Mr. Ainsworth gave him some moral entitlement to her now that his wife was dead. This belief may well have had some religious basis. She was emotionally and sexually attracted to Anne Lister but was concerned with how Halifax society would view the propriety of her moving in with her. And, it seemed, she did not truly believe that Anne Lister would not abandon her at some time in the future. The fact was that Anne and Ann could not be legally married to each other. So unlike marriage to a man, a vow of commitment from Anne Lister had no legal basis, and Ann Walker pledging her future to her, would therefore be a huge leap of faith with a significant associated risk. It must have felt impossible for her to resolve this level of mental conflict, and her efforts to achieve this would have pushed her anxiety to an unbearable level, hence her feeling so poorly. It is, in fact, difficult to see how Ann Walker's situation could have been resolved. Anne Lister was also conflicted, but being more experienced, was better able to cope. Anne Lister was very kind and caring towards Ann and, I think, had become very fond of her and also felt protective towards her. Anne Lister wanted a companion for life that she could love and cherish, but at the same time, she had an adventurous spirit, wanted to be off travelling and felt driven to enjoy the present to the full without fearing what the future might hold. She had no way of knowing just how long she would have to wait for Ann Walker to resolve her torments of conscience before they could start their life together. Although she was feeling impatient with the situation, she did not show it. She tried to counsel Ann Walker and rally her spirits, and appeared successful in this endeavour, only to find Ann as ill as ever the next time she saw her. Anne Lister's conversation with her aunt when she returned to Shibden at 11.30 a.m that Sunday morning does suggest that the length of time she would wait for Ann to recover her spirits and positively commit to her was finite: *'I just talked to my aunt as if Miss Walker's being so poorly and unable to get about would never suit me and, as if I might wish to be off our agreement, and then should not fail to make some good and sufficient excuse and be at liberty again. My aunt determined not to fret about me, sure I would manage things as I liked and as suited me best'.* Despite being busy with refurbishments to Shibden Hall and working to develop the profitability of the Shibden estate, Anne Lister still had it in her mind to be off travelling abroad in the New Year with or without Ann Walker.

Before breakfast on the morning of Monday, November 12th, a letter arrived from Mariana in which she enquired about Miss Walker. Being quick on the uptake, Mariana had realised that Anne Lister and Ann Walker were more than just good friends. It was clear from Mariana's letters that she had been quite happy for Anne Lister to travel, and even settle, abroad, so much so that she was even helping to find suitable servants to travel with her. But there was no way she would be happy if Anne was to be traveling with a potential lover. So, even though Mariana's health and spirits had significantly improved over recent months, she was once again complaining of being unhappy and not expecting to live long. Anne responded in the way she had always responded to Mariana being upset, she became emotional and felt intensely protective towards her.

At 1.10 p.m. that afternoon, Anne Lister received a note from

Ann Walker ending their relationship. Ann Walker: *'I have received a letter which you shall see but we must meet on different terms. Oh that I had taken you at your word last Monday and, as you said, finished the matter on that day. I should then have spared you this additional bitterness. I did hope, when my word was once given to you, that I should have felt at rest and satisfied but, in reflection on all you have said, and trying to turn it to my own advantage, I cannot satisfy my conscience and, with such suffering as I have endured since Wednesday, I feel I could not make you happy. That I should only bring misery upon you for misery I am sure it would be to you to see me in this state I have been in for several days. It was this sort of wretchedness that was expressed in my note on Friday. It was these miserable feelings that prompted my request. For your own sake fly, whilst it is yet in your power and believe that I will never intrude myself in any way upon you (unless it is your wish) whenever you revisit the neighbourhood. November 12 eight hundred and thirty two'.* Now, if Anne Lister truly believed it would be best for her to be at liberty from Ann, this note was surely her opportunity. However, it was an opportunity she chose not to take, I think, most probably out of sympathy and concern for Ann, who was clearly suffering terribly. Anne Lister immediately walked to Lidgate to find Ann *'lying on the bed in tears'.* She *'kissed her and soothed her'*, and within a few minutes Ann had recovered sufficiently to go downstairs and have lunch with Miss Parkhill, while Anne Lister read Mr. Ainsworth's latest letter. She was annoyed with the content of the letter, in which Mr. Ainsworth begged Ann Walker to *'take the scrapbook as a friend'* and asked if he could send her a narrative of himself. Playing on Ann Walker's sympathy he wrote *'if this business should be the death of me, I will pray for blessings on you'*. Anne Lister then went downstairs and *'agreeablized and amused both Miss Parkhill and Miss Walker'.* Once lunch was over, Anne Lister said that there were business letters for Ann to answer and so Miss Parkhill left them. Ann Walker wanted Anne to write a letter to Mr. Ainsworth that would bring to an end his interest to her. Before she would write the letter, Anne Lister wanted to know exactly what was going on. Anne Lister: *'I had asked if it was her heart that had changed towards Mr Ainsworth. No, it was all her conscience. She owned she was not in a fit state to judge fairly and tho' she had felt great affection for him, yet she did not know it was now, all seemed dead and if she felt at liberty, she did not know or think he was quite the man she should choose'.* Anne Lister then asked *'what would you have done had I not been here?'* Ann Walker explained that she would have gone to London and brought back some of her friends to stay with her and basically kept a low profile until it had all blown over. Before she wrote the letter, Anne Lister decided to try a different approach to ease the burden of worry on Ann's mind. She pointed out that since Ann had already made a promise to her, she was not at liberty to marry Mr. Ainsworth or anyone else. Ann agreed that she could not marry without Anne Lister's consent. Anne Lister explained that this gave her power over Ann which *'I was determined to use in her service. She would be better by and by, and more able to judge for herself and then she might try again, but now I should not let her'.* By taking away Ann Walker's freedom to choose, Anne was able to stop the question as to who she should choose from constantly going round and round in the poor woman's head. It was a very clever change of tack on Anne Lister's part, and it worked: *'She brightened up and owned how much better she was'.* They then agreed on the letter to be sent to Mr. Ainsworth: *'Sir I am commissioned by Miss Walker to acknowledge immediately the receipt of your letter and to inform you that she has given me, for the future at least for some time to come, the surveillance of all her letters and parcels. I am sir your obedient servant, Anne Lister'.*

The following day, Tuesday, November 13th, a parcel arrived at Lidgate from Mr. Ainsworth, containing the scrapbook and the narrative of himself. Ann Walker immediately sent the parcel to Shibden for Anne Lister to deal with, along with a note from herself: *'I scarcely believed the parcel would come, but here it is, and you will perceive carriage paid. You will do for me about this as you think best in returning it. I am better this morning thanks to you my love for it. My heart cannot give utterance to what it would say to you on this subject but if I do recover my health, I shall ascribe the blessing under the mercy of providence to you. Faithfully and affectionately yours A.W'.* Anne Lister wrote the following note: *'I am requested by Miss Walker to return the parcel unopened as it must have been sent off before your receipt of my letter of yesterday'.* Anne then set off to Lidgate, taking the note with her. She arrived at 2.25 p.m. and found Ann Walker in much better spirits, having dinner with Miss Parkhill. When Miss Parkhill left them alone for a while, Ann Walker sat on Anne's knee. Anne Lister kissed her from time to time and spoke words of comfort and encouragement. Anne Lister showed Ann the note she had written to be posted with Mr. Ainsworth's parcel, which Ann approved. Ann said that she used to feel affection for him but now this had gone. Anne Lister stayed for a couple of hours then headed home to Shibden, made up the parcel to be sent to Mr. Ainsworth and gave it to John, one of her servants, to take to the post office. Interestingly, on writing up her journal that evening, Anne included the following: *'I wonder what will be her feeling towards me six months hence? Will she let me leave her behind me? Yes, my own mind is quite reconciled to this. I seemed to have ceased to think of, or wish for her as the future companion of my life, but we now get on better together than we have ever done before'.* Perhaps Anne genuinely felt as she had written, or maybe she was again trying to prepare herself for probable disappointment. Either way, the support and care she gave to Ann Walker during this difficult period was extraordinary.

The following morning, Wednesday, November 14th, Anne Lister arrived at Lidgate at about ten o'clock. Miss Parkhill went to Cliff Hill to visit old Miss Walker, and Anne and Ann walked to Stump Cross Inn and back, about four miles in an hour and a half. Ann Walker's physical energy clearly returning now that her anxiety had lifted to some extent. As they walked, they talked of Mr. Ainsworth. Anne Lister asked Ann if he had touched her and she answered that he had done so repeatedly.

'He had told her that she would have suffered less from the real thing, it would have been much easier'. Anne Lister reminded Ann of what they had agreed: *'I said she was not fit to be left to herself which she admitted. "Yes" said she, she would do as I liked. I then said I should see what was best. She was to remember I had pledged myself to nothing, was at liberty and unpledged to any decision. My present idea was not to leave her. She must really consider herself no longer at her own option but must really do as I wished, to which she fully consented'.* I think Anne Lister had realised that telling Ann Walker that she was not permitted to make any decisions gave her the greatest release from her anxiety. Ann Walker and Miss Parker had dinner together at 2 o'clock and Anne Lister sat with them in the dining room, eating only a little. After dinner the postbag was delivered. Anne Lister opened the bag and saw it contained two letters, one for one of Ann Walker' servants and the other addressed to herself from Mr. Ainsworth. Anne Lister kept Mr. Ainsworth's letter hidden. When she was about to head for home, Ann Walker went with her to the door, and she took the opportunity of their being alone to tell Ann Walker about the letter. Anne Lister did not let Ann read the letter but did give her an idea of what it was about and how she intended to reply. Anne Lister again reiterated that the matter was out of Ann's hands as she was not a free agent. This time Ann Walker smiled, I am sure knowing and appreciating what Anne Lister was trying to do to help her. In his letter, Mr. Ainsworth asked Anne Lister to have pity on him and not expose him. He begged her permission to send a box to Ann Walker containing some things he believed his wife would have left her had she lived to add a codicil to her will. He excused his first letter to Ann Walker as being written under the effect of opium. Anne Lister left Lidgate at 3.55 p.m. She took her time, went via her walk, spent some time in the moss house and arrived back at Shibden at 5 p.m. Before having dinner at 6 o'clock, Anne wrote her reply to Mr. Ainsworth's letter: *'Sir, I have just received your letter and am sorry that considering all the circumstances of the case I cannot consent to your sending the box you mention. I very earnestly hope that you will*

understand the propriety and the necessity of abstaining from any further communication with my friend or myself as the best and only means of preventing that exposure which it is so desirable to avoid to a gentleman and a clergyman. I trust it is unnecessary to add more. I am sir, your obedient servant. A. Lister'. The letter was addressed to Mr. Ainsworth's sister-in-law, Miss Bentley, in Salford.

The following day, Thursday, November 15th, Anne Lister was up early and out on the Shibden estate between 8.30 a.m. and 10.30 a.m. supervising work being done to change the route of the brook. She did not go to Lidgate as she wanted to catch up with her correspondence, writing letters to her friends Lady Stuart de Rothesay, Lady Vere Cameron and Mrs. Norcliffe. However, the next day, Friday, Anne Lister spent about three hours with Ann Walker. They went for a walk down the Cliff Hill fields, and Ann Walker began to talk of the possibility of her going abroad with Anne in January. They then walked to Ann Walker's stables in Lightcliffe to organise the repainting of her carriage and also called on old Miss Walker for about 25 minutes. Anne Lister headed back home to Shibden at 1.15 p.m. It was certainly beginning to seem that Ann Walker was on the mend. Anne Lister spent most of the afternoon out working on the estate with various workmen but when she got home at 5 p.m. she found a package on her desk sent from Ann Walker and containing correspondence from Mr Ainsworth that had arrived at Lidgate that afternoon. Anne did not record the details of his letter, just described it as foolish. She knew he must have sent the letter before he had received her last letter, which she decided would therefore act as her reply.

The next day, Saturday, November 17th, Anne Lister called at Lidgate at 12.15 p.m. but, finding Ann Walker not at home, called on Mrs. Priestley, who it appears was still very much good friends with her. Anne returned to Lidgate at 1.55 p.m. to find Ann and Miss Parkhill having dinner. After dinner, Anne and Ann had an hour alone, drank tea, and were affectionate with each other. It appeared that Ann Walker had now started to become anxious about Anne going abroad and feeling that she, herself, may not be up to going with her. That is the problem with anxiety, when one issue is sorted, it jumps to a different one. When Anne and Ann rejoined Miss Parkhill, they found that she was in a bad mood. Up to this point, Miss Parkhill had found Anne Lister to be both engaging and amusing, but, for some reason, it seems she was turning against her. Anne Lister speculated that Miss Parkhill might be feeling that she had too much influence over Ann Walker or perhaps she thought that she should be paying more attention to her.

Anne Lister did not go to Lidgate the following day, Sunday, but did call to see Ann later in the afternoon of Monday, November 19th, when Ann and Miss Parkhill had returned from a trip to Huddersfield. Anne and Ann spent an hour alone together upstairs. Although they had planned to spend the night together at Lidgate, Anne Lister felt that it was best that she did not, given Miss Parkhill's growing hostility towards her. Ann Walker said that she had written to her sister for advice on whether she should travel abroad and then declared she was still not sure if she had done right by not marrying Mr. Ainsworth. She also said that if she did not marry Mr. Ainsworth, she would not marry any other man. The conversation was clearly a disappointment to Anne Lister, but she described herself as having behaved handsomely about it. She thought perhaps she should visit Lidgate less often in future.

Well, Anne Lister must have changed her mind, because the next day, Tuesday, November 20th, she was on her way to Lidgate at four o'clock that afternoon. En route, she met Ann Walker's postboy who gave her a note. In this note, Ann Walker invited Anne Lister to dinner and to stay overnight at Lidgate on Wednesday and also said *'you know how glad I shall be to see you and remember how truly happy you will make me if I can be useful to you in any way in your enterprize au secret'*. The *'enterprize au secret'*, I understand, referred to Anne Lister's request to borrow some money from Ann to help her purchase some property on the Godley Road. Anne Lister continued on her way to Lidgate and stayed there talking to Ann and Miss Parkhill for three quarters of an hour. As she got up to leave, Ann Walker took her into the dining room and was affectionate to her, *'more than usual'*. Anne Lister explained that she thought it best if she did not come to dinner or stay overnight, or even come for breakfast, during Miss Parkhill's visit. She managed to persuade Ann Walker of this, and they agreed that Anne Lister would not visit again until Friday.

So, Anne and Ann did not see each other again until Friday, November 23rd. Anne Lister arrived at Lidgate at ten thirty that morning and stayed with Ann for about two hours, Miss Parkhill having left the two of them alone. Ann Walker was now doubting whether she should have told Anne about Mr. Ainsworth, thought she should have waited before pledging herself to Anne, and, also said she could not go abroad, because she could not leave her aunt. Anne Lister told Ann, if she wanted, she would have no difficulty in getting rid of her, but Ann replied that was not what she wanted. Ann Walker's doubts and melancholy were becoming a considerable strain on Anne Lister. She knew now that her efforts to ease Ann's anxiety had no lasting effect and she thought of returning the purse, containing the 'yes' releasing Ann from her pledge and going off on her travels abroad.

Although the two women did not see each other the following day, Saturday, when Anne Lister went to her study, after being out working on the estate all day, she found on her desk four throat cravat frills from Ann Walker, making a total of six that she had made for her.

Anne Lister called again at Lidgate at 1.45 p.m. on Sunday, November 25th, to find Ann looking low and disconsolate. A ring had been sent to her, presumably by Mr. Ainsworth, that had belonged to his wife, and this had pushed her deeper into depression. Ann Walker again talked of it being her duty to take

Mr. Ainsworth as her husband. Anne Lister: *'she will have him after all. I spoke with indignation as usual and she of duty and all that. I said whatever she had done to him, she had not behaved very well to me. I had had two promises of which she had evaded the one and broke the other. She said she was more than ever determined not to go abroad'.* Interestingly, or indeed surprisingly, despite expressing totally opposite viewpoints, the two women then got down to a bit of grubbling. Either during or after the grubbling, Ann Walker said that she thought that Mr. Ainsworth had smaller hands than Anne, who responded with *'he had done it more roughly than necessary to spoil her as much as he could without the real thing'.* Ann Walker agreed then hastily added that he had grubbled her first. Anne Lister found it difficult to believe that Ann's feeling duty bound to marry Mr. Ainsworth arose because he had grubbled her first. Anne Lister: *'in spite of all her declarations to the contrary, I begin to suspect he really has deflowered and enjoyed her'.* I can see why Anne Lister's suspicions were aroused but it occurs to me that perhaps Ann Walker was worried about refusing to take Mr. Ainsworth because she feared he might expose her for allowing him to be sexually intimate with her. Anne Lister left Lidgate a little after five o'clock after having apologised to Miss Parkhill for keeping Ann from her for so long. An unpleasant incident occurred on Anne's way home: *'Near German House, an impertinent fellow with a great stick in his hand asked if I was going home and made a catch at my queer. "God damn you" said I and pushed him off. He said something which I took as meaning an attack, "do" said I "if you dare. I'll soon do for you"* and he walked one way and I the other. I did not feel the least frightened'.

Still not wanting to give up on Ann Walker, the next day, Monday, November 26th, Anne Lister wrote to Dr. Belcombe, in York, asking for advice regarding Miss Walker's nervousness which she admitted she was finding much more difficult to manage than she had expected. She added that she could *'neither understand nor guard against'* Miss Walker's frequent relapses.

The following morning, Tuesday, November 27th, a letter arrived at Shibden for Anne from Mariana in which she described having put her affairs in order, still convinced that she would not live long but assuring Anne that she felt better than the last time she wrote. Mariana said she would come to Shibden if that was what Anne wanted but would rather not on account of Anne's sister, Marian, making her feel unwelcome. Mariana: *'it is not comfortable to visit where one is only tolerated'.* Anne Lister: *'[Mariana] tells me I am far better off without a companion than if I had one who did not suit me… Mariana's thought of ever being with me is quite gone by'.* That day Anne Lister called at Lidgate at noon to find that Ann was no better. Once again she *'tried to rouse her into more ease of mind'* with only limited success. I suppose that for as long as Ann Walker believed she had only two options open to her, either to marry Mr. Ainsworth or to make a conspicuous commitment to Anne Lister, she would never be able to ease her anxiety. Both options had their pros and cons. Marriage to Mr. Ainsworth meant approval from society for being the wife of a clergyman but also meant loss of control of her fortune to a man known to marry for money and also a requirement for heterosexual intercourse for which she felt a repugnance. A conspicuous commitment to Anne Lister meant she would be living with someone whose company she loved whilst retaining control of her own wealth but also meant she may be the subject of hostility from Halifax society and her own relatives. I wonder, had she realised that she had the third option of not choosing either, for the time being at least, perhaps her mental health might not have spiralled out of control. Then again, perhaps she had thought of this third option, but the thought of once again being all alone was unacceptable to her. Ann Walker asked Anne to call again on Thursday as she was intending to make some house calls in Halifax on the Wednesday. However, on the Thursday morning, a note arrived at Shibden for Anne from Ann Walker which said *'We are going to Halifax this morning, the day was too unfavourable yesterday. May I hope to see you on Saturday?'* Anne Lister replied: *'thank you very much for your note. I shall hope to see you on Saturday. Affectionately yours A.L.'*

The next morning, Friday, November 30th, Anne Lister was up at 7.45a.m., and 15 minutes later, James, one of Ann Walker's servants, arrived at Shibden with a note for her telling her that Ann Walker was not well. Anne immediately sent James off to ask Mr. Sunderland, a medical man, to go to Lidgate to attend to Ann Walker. James was then to return to Shibden to collect a note to take back to Lidgate for Ann. In her note Anne Lister explained to Ann that she had a business appointment that morning and so could not get over to Lidgate until noon. The note also contained words of comfort. Anne arrived at Lidgate at 11.50 a.m. to find Ann Walker in bed with a fever and being attended to by Mr. Sunderland. Anne Lister put Mr. Sunderland in the picture about Ann receiving treatment from Dr. Belcombe and asked Mr. Sunderland to consult with Dr. Belcombe on the matter, to which he agreed. Anne Lister then sat by Ann's bedside. Anne Lister: *'She had been fretting all yesterday and last night because she thought, from my note of yesterday, that all was over, and I had made up my mind to end the thing between us and she could not bear to part with me. She said, if I had gone away, she should never give up the hope of our coming together some time'.* At first, Anne Lister found all this totally confusing, but then Ann explained that her note of the previous day had concluded with 'affectionately yours' rather than the usual 'affectionately and faithfully yours' and it was this omission that had caused her distressed state. Anne Lister: *'She had never felt drawn so close to me as since Tuesday and now thought that I could make her happy and had prayed for us to be happy together. I did not say much but asked why with these feelings she refused me. She owned that she always thought she should refuse the man she might marry merely to try his affection. She asked if I would be her executor. I neither said yes nor no but rather declined than otherwise but said that all this seemed as if she really cared for me. "Oh yes" she never knew before how much. In fact, she does not like to give me up but said that she should sink when I went, and nothing could raise her. Said she had never felt for me as she did now. Should have no confidence in Mr. Ainsworth. Should not be happy with him'.* Ann Walker also admitted that Miss Parkhill was jealous and had been making mischief. Anne Lister endeavoured to have a calming influence: *'I behaved very kindly but did not press her to decide. Bade her think of it till the first of January and we would go to York afterwards. She had doubted that I would go to York. Said I would do all I could for her as long as I could'.* By two o'clock, Ann Walker was feeling much better and no longer felt the need to stay in bed. Miss Parkill, it seemed, had gone off in a huff. Anne Lister stayed till about four o'clock and then headed back home via her ornamental walk, having spent a while talking to some of the men working on the Shibden estate. Despite Ann's declaration of affection, Anne Lister knew that it was just as likely that the next time she was at Lidgate, Ann would be again saying that she must marry Mr. Ainsworth, such was the tumultuous state of her mind and her emotions. Having had a reply from Dr. Belcombe, that evening after dinner, she wrote her reply to him, and also completed her letter to Mariana.

Anne Lister was, at this time, very much embroiled in negotiating leases for the mining of coal on the Shibden estate. It was a complex business and seemed to be taking up a lot of her time. Never-the-less, she was back at Lidgate at 11.50 a.m. the next morning, Saturday, December 1st, to see Ann. Anne Lister: *'She thought I seemed indifferent yesterday, how the thing terminated between us, whether she should be with me or not. I parried this very gallantly, saying that actions were more than words and I did not act like one who was indifferent'.* Another medical man, a Mr. Day, had been to see Ann Walker and had concluded that having a very weak spine was the source of her health problems. Anne Lister did not at stay at Lidgate for long. It seems that Ann Walker was feeling under considerable pressure to keep Anne and Miss Parkhill apart, so Anne thought it best if she kept away for a while.

There was no communication between the two women on the Sunday or Monday, but on the morning of Tuesday, December 4th, Anne wrote the following note to Ann Walker and instructed her servant, Hemingway, to take it to Lidgate: '*I am anxious to hear how you are. Do send word by the bearer and let me hear from you every other day at least, by the postboy. As unless I can be of the smallest service, I fear I shall not see you till after Monday. Faithfully and affectionately yours, A.L.*' Ann Walker replied saying she was feeling better, but that Mr. Sunderland would not allow her go outside. She said she did not know when Miss Parkhill was leaving but begged Anne to go to see her the next day. It seems that Ann Walker was growing tired of Miss Parkhill, as her note contained the line: '*She is not to dictate to me who I am or am not to receive*'.

The next day, Wednesday, December 5th, was already going to be a busy day for Anne Lister. She was seeing Mr. Holt, who had been advising her regarding coal leases, and now he was to look over the estate with her to assess the possibility of sinking pits on Shibden land. So, Anne sent a note to Ann Walker to say she could only come to Lidgate later in the afternoon. Ann Walker replied begging her to go as early as she could and saying '*I will not ask you to stay all night and indeed if I did I scarcely think you would*'. Anne arrived at Lidgate at 5 o'clock to find Ann Walker alone. The two women had dinner and spent a cosy evening together. At nine o'clock Miss Parkhill returned accompanied by Miss Emily Rawson. It was raining heavy, so Anne Lister decided that she would stay the night. She shared a bed with Ann Walker, and they talked until 2 a.m. '*Said she should not suffer for me, so declared I would not grubble her. She excited as she lay on me and I pretended great difficulty in keeping my word. I felt her over her chemise and this all but did the job for her. She owned she could not help it and that now she had got into the way of it and did not know how she should do without it. Thought she should be getting wrong with somebody when I went away. Oh, thought I, this plain *enough, yet still she talked of her sufferings because she thought it wrong to have this connection with me'.* This conversation must have been so confusing for Anne Lister. It was less than a week since Ann Walker had declared that she could not bear to part with her, never felt so close to her, and prayed they would be happy together. However, now she was talking about their connection being wrong. So, for some reason, she had got the idea that their sexual relationship was immoral. Up to this point, such a thought had not appeared to have even crossed her mind. It seems that Anne Lister was right to take Ann's declaration of devotion, on the previous Friday, with a pinch of salt. Anne Lister was off back to Shibden the next morning, Thursday, December 6th, at 9.55 a.m., having a busy day ahead of her dealing with estate and coal related matters.

Anne Lister next called at Lidgate at 1.30 p.m. the following afternoon, Friday, December 7th, with a gift for Ann; a book of prayers that she had sent for from London and which was bound in crimson Moroccan leather with silk fly leaves and gilt edges. Anne Lister's record of hers and Ann's conversation focuses on a discussion regarding their travelling abroad together. Ann Walker was adamant that she would not travel abroad, and Anne Lister was equally determined that they should. The conversation resulted in Ann Walker bursting into tears and Anne Lister leaving after just half an hour.

The following day, Saturday, December 8th, Anne Lister arrived at Lidgate at 10 a.m. and *'sat with Miss Walker, tête á tête, in the dining room till 12'.* They discussed a plan to go to York together for three or four weeks the following month. Ann Walker rightly or wrongly, thought that this was a ploy to then make her travel abroad which she again said she did not want to do. I am sure, in two hours, they had other, less contentious, topics of conversation but, understandably, Anne Lister does not record what she would describe as *'chit-chat'*. However, having said that, I am beginning to suspect that neither of them was now getting much joy from the other's company. Ann Walker repeated her concern that their connection was wrong and, also said she could not make Anne happy. It appears that they just kept going round in circles and clearly were making no progress. I assumed after transcribing this last journal entry that the writing was on the wall for their relationship only to discover that they had planned for Anne Lister to go to Lidgate for tea on Monday and stay all night. Very contrary!

On Sunday, December 9th, a letter arrived at Shibden from Mariana telling Anne of the sudden death of her housekeeper at Lawton Hall. Mariana wanted Anne to write an inscription for a headstone for the housekeeper's grave, which Anne duly wrote and sent off in that day's post. Mariana also mentioned that she had found *'a remarkably handsome, fine looking young man'* who was a native of Lawton, and who she thought might be a suitable groom to travel with Anne on the continent.

Anne Lister arrived at Lidgate at ten past six in the evening of Monday, December 10th, to have tea with Ann and her friend, Lydia Wilkinson, who had arrived that day, Miss Parkhill, thankfully, having gone home. They had a pleasant evening and went upstairs at 10 p.m. Ann Walker showed Anne to a room above the kitchen and stayed with her for an hour talking. Ann Walker explained that she had heard from Mrs. Plough, one of her aunts, who was in need of her help, and, as a consequence, she was not able to go to York as planned. Perhaps it was a genuine reason or maybe it was an excuse not to go. Ann Walker then started again talking about hers and Anne's connection being wrong. Anne Lister: *'I reasoned gently but with some gravity and dignity and she asked me to sleep with her'.* They went to Ann Walker's room and *'without any persuasion and forgetting all the wrong, she lay on my arms all the night and had three good long grubblings. In fact, I was obliged to pretend sleep after it struck two or she would have gone on. We awoke at seven and talked till eight. Now that she seems me inclined to be off, she wants to be on again. Said no more about the wrong but began to think she was throwing away her happiness and said she could not bear to part with me'.* Anne Lister was undoubtedly becoming weary of Ann's frequent changes of mind and, on this occasion, she decided that something had to be said: *'told her of her inconsistency and indecision and asked gently how I could possibly trust her?'* Anne Lister makes no record of Ann's response in her journal so perhaps she simply did not give an answer. They agreed to see each other again on Thursday. On getting back home to Shibden, a little after midday, Anne sat talking to her aunt: *'told her that I knew not how things were for now. Again, that I wanted to be off. Miss Walker seemed fretting to bring it on again'.*

Anne Lister arrived at Lidgate at 3.45 p.m. on Thursday: *'Miss Walker very glad and much affected at seeing me. She thought it all at end between us and was overcome. Gradually consoled and said that if she really could not bear to part with me and could decidedly make up her mind, I would do all I could and reverse my intention even at the eleventh hour'.* Again, there was no record of Ann Walker's response to Anne's offer, but she did ask her to look over some of her estate accounts and stay all night, which she did. Anne Lister: *'Talking and pressing and lovemaking till after three. Then slept to near eight and then talked till after ten. Insinuated that our present intercourse without any tie between us must be as wrong as any other transient connection. She seems to think refuting me is refusing her best chance of happiness and is more likely than ever to accept me'.* At twenty past one that afternoon, they walked to the moss house on the Shibden estate and sat there talking for an hour. *'She said "yes" again. It should be binding. It should be the same as a marriage and should give me no cause to be jealous. Made no objection to what I proposed, that is her declaring it on the bible and taking the sacrament with me at Shibden or Lightcliffe church'.* So, Ann Walker had again agreed to commit to a future with Anne, who, when back in her study at Shibden and writing up the details of the day's events in her journal, asked herself: *'Am I foolish to risk it again?'*

Anne Lister was back at Lidgate at eleven thirty the next morning, Saturday, December 15, to find Ann being attended to by Mr

Day, a medical man. Once he had left, the two women walked to Cliff Hill. They then walked back to Lidgate so that Ann Walker could have some lunch, but Anne Lister continued on to New House to call on Mrs. Priestley. There then followed an incident which was to put a further strain on Anne's friendship with Mrs. Priestley. When Anne arrived at New House, Mr. and Mrs. Priestley were having dinner, so John, one of the Priestley's servants, showed Anne to the drawing room and asked her to wait there for an hour, after which Mrs. Priestley would come to her. Well, there was no way that Anne would want to be sat for an hour when she could be back at Lidgate with Ann Walker, so instead, she followed John to the Priestley's little sitting room, where Mrs. Priestley *'jumped up angrily saying "I admit nobody here".* Mrs. Priestley came out of the sitting room and took Anne back to the drawing room, where Anne apologised and declared that it was not John's fault. I suspect Anne just wanted to excuse herself and head back to Lidgate, but clearly Mrs. Priestley had some reason for not wanting anyone in her sitting room, perhaps it was untidy, and she was embarrassed. Anyway, Anne Lister was astonished and annoyed at the manner in which Mrs. Priestley had spoken to her. When Anne arrived back at Lidgate, Ann Walker was in the process of copying her letter to her sister, Elizabeth, to ask for advice about her moving in with Anne Lister at Shibden. *'If her sister approves, she will do it and it is to be as a marriage between us'.* Ann Walker then read a letter that had arrived from Miss Bentley with a melancholy account of Mr. Ainsworth, but this did not appear to upset her for long. Anne Lister: *'She was melancholy for about an hour but then recovered her spirits amazingly. Sat on my knee while I grubbled her with my left middle finger. She owned she loved me, seemed more satisfied and happy than usual'.* At 5.50p.m. Anne Lister set off for home: *'thought I as I returned, well it may or may not be. I will think or care little about it till it is finally settled one way or the other, and either way will do'.* Clearly, she was far from convinced that she could trust Ann not to have another change of mind. In fact, all her journal entries suggesting she did not care about the outcome have convinced me that the opposite was most probably the case. She was so driven to find a companion for life, and I wonder if she thought Ann Walker was her last chance, that the prospect of potential disappointment was something for which she had to be well prepared.

Anne Lister was back at Lidgate at ten o'clock on the morning of Monday, December 17th. She found Ann Walker *'not quite so well today, had been miserable again about Mr. Ainsworth'.* Not really what you would want from the woman who just two days ago said she loved you and agreed to marry you (admittedly subject to her sister's approval). Anne Lister: *'She seemed wavering, and I said the thing seemed now as uncertain between us as ever. Talked a little sentiment and argued against Mr. Ainsworth and pressed her hard to decide. Then I brought her round to say she would try to cheer up and that I left her now in the same mind as I did the last time, that is that if her sister approved there would no longer be any obstacle between, and she would say a positive decisive yes'.*

Anne Lister's next visit to Lidgate was two days later, on the afternoon of Wednesday, December 19th. She found that *'Miss Walker had been miserable again, as usual'.* Regarding Ann Walker's letter to her sister, Anne wrote: *'I said I saw she would be no more inclined to decide even when the answer came, than now. My manner shewed that I was not quite pleased. I said the additional length of unnecessary suspense was not fair. Had she known half the uneasiness she gave, I was sure she could not have found in her heart to act as she did. She sobbed and cried and said I made her very nervous, both today and Monday. I expressed my great sorrow at this and at my not even having the consolation of believing that her seeing me did her good'.* They talked of the letter Ann had written to her sister. It seems that Anne Lister had written down what she thought Ann should include in the letter. However, it transpired that Ann had written the question about her moving in to Shibden in a different way to what Anne Lister had suggested. Realising that this change was more likely to illicit a "no" from Elizabeth Sutherland than a "yes", she was not pleased and left at

5.15 p.m. saying to herself *'I should not go again in a hurry'*.

Anne Lister saw Ann as wavering between Mr. Ainsworth and herself and was hurt by this, after all, surely, she was a better catch than he was. However, I think that part of Ann Walker's reluctance to move into Shibden came from her strong attachment to the to the huge Walker estate that she had been brought up on, which she and her sister had inherited, and where she was mistress of half of all she surveyed. However, her relationship with Anne Lister over the previous five months had given her a taste of the comfort and joy to be had from sharing her life with another person. She had previously mentioned that if she did marry Mr. Ainsworth, they would live at the Cliff Hill mansion, on the Walker estate, and she would ask him to change his name to hers. So, the appeal of Mr. Ainsworth was based on his providing companionship and her being able to continue to live on the Walker estate. Being Anne Lister's companion for life would have required her to risk being ostracised by Halifax society and leave her beloved home. Yes, of course, she had stronger feelings for Anne Lister than Mr. Ainsworth, but in the nineteenth century, marriage was not necessarily based on love, fondness was often considered sufficient. Put like this, it becomes easy to see that the choice between Anne Lister and Mr. Ainsworth was, in fact, finely balanced, and this explained the waverings of Ann Walker. Could she have considered the third choice of continuing to live at home alone? I think, before she met Anne Lister, Ann felt very much alone in the world having lost both parents, a sister and her brother, and her only surviving sister having moved to the north of Scotland. Ann desperately did not want to be alone again. Although she wanted to continue her relationship with Anne Lister, this came at too high a price. However, continuing their relationship whilst living at their own properties was not enough for Anne Lister; she did not want them to be just friends with benefits, she had enough of those already. It was hardly surprising that Ann Walker's mental health was showing signs of considerable strain, she was in an impossible situation and could see no way out.

For all Anne Lister's talk of not going to Lidgate again in a hurry, she called the very next day, Thursday, December 20th, but only for 25 minutes. Anne Lister: *'we might have had a scene, but my calm dignity of manner kept it off. She evidently supposes, from my manner, that I mean all to be off between us and so I do'.* I suppose, it does rather beg the question, if it was all off, why did Anne Lister keep going to Lidgate? Although she did not call at Lidgate the next day, Friday, she was there again at 2.30 p.m. on Saturday, December 22nd, and, on this occasion, stayed for an hour and a half. There was the usual talk of Mr. Ainsworth, and Ann Walker not wanting to leave her home, but there was also some grubbling, while Ann Walker was sat on Anne Lister's knee. Despite this, Anne Lister: *'I left her with less care than ever, and more resignation being rid of her. I am better without her'.*

Anne Lister did not venture out the following day, Sunday, on account of having come down with a cold. But the next day, Monday, December 24th, she called at Lidgate at 4.45 p.m. on her way home from Halifax. Anne Lister: *'Miss Walker was at her door, just returned from distributing things at the school. Very glad to see me. Asked if I had got her note'.* It transpired that Ann Walker had sent a note up to Shibden for Anne but, having come directly from Halifax, she had not yet seen it. Obviously, Anne did not read the note till she returned home, but I include it here now to show Ann Walker's line of thought: *'I have considered and reconsidered all you so kindly said to me on Saturday and however painful it is to me to tell you, yet I must tell you, that as my convictions with regard to its being right and against my duty remain, I think we had better not meet again till I have received my sister's letter'.* As I have previously mentioned, Ann Walker had started to believe that the sexual part of her relationship with Anne was morally wrong and was suffering guilt in this regard. I have heard it suggested that this shows that she felt homophobic towards herself, however I am not altogether convinced of this. I think she felt just as guilty at having allowed Mr. Ainsworth to touch her sexually and thought that these guilty feelings would only be assuaged by marrying him. However, Ann Walker had immediately regretted sending the note and despite all her concerns about morality, asked Anne to stay the night. And despite thinking all was off between them, Anne Lister agreed. Despite the many difficulties their relationship seemed to be generating, there was clearly an incredibly powerful attachment between the two women. They had a pleasant evening, including dinner at 6 o'clock, then tea a little later, conversation, which Anne Lister described as cheerful chit-chat, and went upstairs at 10.10 p.m. *'Did not sleep much last night, smothered as usual under four great blankets. Grubbled her a little, did not do it well enough, or she was not much in humour for it, so lay still. She thought me asleep, but I was not. About two turned round and grubbled her again, rather better than before, but still not well. She said it had not been so agreeable to her for the last few times. She thought I was nervous, and she said she did not think it right, wished we could do without it. At breakfast I referred to her scruples and wishes and said I would try not to care for her in that particular way and promised her that if I once seriously tried, I would succeed, but I was not quite sure whether we should be the happier for my success or not. Sat talking all the morning, combatting her scruples and really thought I had made some impression and done her good till going away and asking her to write and tell me how she was tomorrow. She said "oh no" she should be no better and burst into tears, and I left her thinking I never saw such a hopeless person in my life. How miserable said I to myself, thank God my own mind is not like hers. What could I do with her?'*. Anne Lister left Lidgate about one o'clock and headed back to Shibden via her walk and stayed for a while at the hut (the moss house). Once inside, *'knelt down and prayed and thanked God as well as I could for ten minutes then sat down in the hut and tried to sleep'*. She arrived back home at 3.35 p.m. and read Ann Walker's note. Anne Lister: *'Poor girl what a miserable state of mind, and all for nothing'*. I am sure you have realised that this was, in fact, Christmas Day. However, Christmas was not celebrated in those days as it is now. It was usual to go to church on Christmas Day but nothing more. It would be another eleven years before Charles Dickens wrote 'A Christmas Carol', and a further five years before Prince Albert popularised the Christmas tree.

Anne Lister was back at Lidgate at about half past one the next day, Wednesday, December 26th, and, finding that Ann Walker was out, walked to meet her on the road to Crow Nest and they returned to Lidgate together. They spent a pleasant enough afternoon together, Ann Walker had dinner and a little later they took a walk to Whitehall and back, the weather being dry, although cold. On their return, Ann Walker's *'scruples seem abated'* so they enjoyed a bit of grubbling. They talked of going abroad on the last day of January if Ann Walker decided "yes", and, if "no" Anne Lister suggested they travel together as far as London, a plan which Ann Walker seemed pleased with. At about six o'clock, just before Anne Lister headed home to Shibden, Ann showed her a note: *'She said she had been looking at the first note she ever had from me which she had carefully kept, and it was dated the seventh November 1828. This date seemed to have made a great impression on her. In fact, tonight she was quite inclined for going and seemed to think more seriously of her word and the tie between us, but I attached, in reality, no importance to all this, well knowing that tomorrow she might be all on the other side the question'.* It was only a friendly note responding to an invitation to Crow Nest but it was very sweet that Ann Walker had kept it safe these four years.

Anne Lister was back at Lidgate, two days later, at 3.55 p.m. on Friday, December 28th. Ann Walker was out but returned in her carriage a few minutes later. She had been to Halifax but prior to this she had called at Shibden, and finding Anne Lister was out, had sat talking to Marian and Aunt Anne. She had sent off a letter to Miss Bentley the previous day, and a reply received on this day, gave a bad account of Mr. Ainsworth which, had made her miserable. Ann Walker certainly seemed to be getting out and about, and also appeared to be eating well, from which I conclude, that at this point in time, her anxiety was at a manageable level.

The following day, Saturday, December 29th, Anne Lister did not go to Lidgate, but at half past eight in the evening, a note arrived at Shibden from Ann Walker: *'I have had a letter from my sister saying everything that is kind, but she strongly recommends our trying the plan before we decide. She fancies your departure for the continent is not finally fixed and she advises our taking lodgings in York for the winter, going to visit her in the summer and then if we are both in the same mind make a tour on the continent next year. She adds that she believes I think at this present time that I shall never marry but that it is very probable my sentiments will change. I have not courage to make my promise stronger. I dare not trust myself to say more. December 29, 1832'.* The letter from Ann's sister, Mrs. Sutherland, was clearly very disappointing for Anne Lister: *'Well surely it is settled now, and she will waver no more. I will be off as soon as I can. How little Mrs. Sutherland guesses the real truth, and how coolly she plans for us. Her plan would never do for me, have all the pother for nothing. Merely to take care of her till Mr. Ainsworth was ready for her. I am not quite so simple as that'.* The next day, Sunday, December 30, Anne talked to her aunt about her relationship with Ann Walker and said: *'I now thought the thing as much off as if it had never been on'.*

Anne Lister next called at Lidgate at about half past four the following afternoon, Monday, December 31st. She found Ann Walker as *'miserable as ever'.* She asked Ann Walker to thank her sister for her judicious advice, but also explained that her sister's plan was not feasible, although I am sure Ann Walker was already aware of this. Anne Lister: *'Miss Walker fretted and cried and sighed and said she should not live long. I proposed returning her notes and having mine. She said she had burnt all that were material and wished to keep the rest. I begged to see them and then had no objection to her keeping them. She begged me not to send back her history of Paris, it would be of no more use to her, and she wished me to keep it. Our going to York apparently at an end. Parted in tears both of us, I saying I never did or could understand her'.* This seemed pretty final, with both of them now convinced that the possibility of a future together was gone forever. Anne Lister was back home at Shibden in time for dinner at quarter past six. She was not feeling well and after dinner slept on the sofa till nine o'clock. This was, of course, New Year's Eve, and Anne added to her journal her concluding remarks for 1832: *'Well! Here is the end of another year! How different this New Year's Eve from the last! Tho', in each case, unsuccessful love making. What will be the leading event of the next 12 months? Quite off with Mariana, Vere married and off at Rome. What I have never been before since fifteen, absolutely untied to anyone. I never stood so alone and yet I am far happier than I was twelve months ago. In fact, happier than I have been of long, I am used and reconciled to my loneness'.*

During the past week, one of Anne Lister's horses had become very ill, and the next day, Tuesday, January 1st, 1833, she had to make the difficult decision to have one of her workmen shoot the poor creature to put it out of its misery. Despite such an unpleasant experience, but also knowing that Ann Walker would most likely be in a distressed state, she decided to go to Lidgate. She was right, Ann Walker was tearful when she arrived. For a little while Ann Walker was out of the room, and Anne Lister saw a letter to Ann's sister lying on the table. Ann had written to her sister *'to say all was at end between us and she should not go to York'.* She had also arranged for one of her cousins, Catherine Rawson, to come and stay at Lidgate with her the following week. When Anne Lister got back home to Shibden, she too was in a distressed state: *'I think she will get over the loss of me. How can she have much real feeling for me and do as she does? May she do better but seeing her always unhinges me. I was low and in tears at dinner and could not get her out of my head and why? Low and tearful. Till at last I incurred a cross about her as I sat, and this set me into a more reconciled and cheerful train of thought'.* Well, I suppose you have to find comfort wherever you can.

Although both women knew it was just a matter of time before Anne Lister would be off on her travels abroad and they would be separated, the bond between them remained very strong. Despite, or perhaps because she felt unhinged whenever she saw Ann Walker, Anne Lister could not keep away from Lidgate, returning there on the afternoon of Thursday, January 3rd. Anne Lister: *'Both in tears and owned ourselves wretched. She not knowing what to do'. Grubbled her. Said "it was a comfort to me", was happier for it. We could never go back to common acquaintanceship. She owned it a comfort to her at the time but remorse afterwards'.*

So a bit of comfort sex for them both but with Ann Walker still believing it to be wrong, although not sufficiently wrong to require abstinence. Anne Lister stayed for dinner and tea, and then walked home, her way lit by moonlight. Although Anne Lister was still very much drawn to Ann Walker, she was also hurt by her rejection. She felt that she was being taken advantage of, believing that Ann Walker wanted her for sex and for her advice, particularly regarding financial and estate matters, but did not actually want her.

Anne Lister returned to Lidgate both on Friday and Saturday, the 4th and 5th of January, respectively. Just as on Thursday, the two women talked and grubbled, but as usual, Ann Walker was very despondent. On the Sunday, Anne Lister wrote to Dr. Belcombe. She was at a loss as to how she could help Ann Walker: *'I never exactly understood before what nervousness meant and God grant that I may know no more of it in any case which concerns me much! It is dreary to combat sickness without disease and misery without reason'.*

When Anne Lister arrived at Lidgate at 4.15 p.m. on Monday, January 7th, Ann immediately asked her to stay all night. Anne Lister: *'Told her that if she asked me to stay, she must understand I should take it as a confirmation of her promise. She tried to evade this, but I said I would not stay unless she said yes to our living together, and she did say so and I staid'.* They had dinner, then tea, talked of travelling, played backgammon, said prayers, and went upstairs to sleep in Ann Walker's bedroom at 10.25 pm. Anne Lister did not sleep well: *'before six heard her moaning and groaning. On my inquiry, she said she had done wrong, her promise was from a wrong motive, from the fear of being left. Nothing but misery. I could not cheer her'.* As Anne Lister walked home that Tuesday afternoon: *'well surely this is the last act in the melodrama. I shall be off and think no more of her'.* Just after dinner at Shibden that evening, one of Ann Walker's servants arrived with a note from her: *'When I left you this morning, I little thought how soon I should take up my pen. I do it as a last hope and in utter misery. What I said last night I bitterly regret. My promise was made from a bad motive, from a want of confidence in God. It is this that is the source of all my misery and wretchedness. It is not only death in this world but a far worse death that I fear. I wanted to tell you this today, but I could not. I dare not wait till tomorrow for every hour is of consequence. If ever the prayers of so true a friend may avail for another, may yours be heard for me this night, that the gate of mercy may not be for ever closed upon me, for I am wretchedness itself. A.W. I will walk to your hut tomorrow if the day be fine at ten o'clock'.* Anne Lister's first thought on reading the note: *'Why said I to myself, this explains all, the poor girl is beside herself'.* She now understood that the torment that Ann was suffering was caused by her feeling that her faith in God was not sufficiently strong. Anne Lister's instinct was to try to help and comfort Ann. She immediately sent a note back to Lidgate: *'I am very glad you have written. I quite enter in to all your telling me. I hope tomorrow will be fine and then I shall count upon seeing you at ten in the morning. Be assured of my saying and doing everything in the world I can to cheer and console you. Yours in haste. A.L.'*

I think at this point I should tell you what I have learned about Ann Walker's issues with mental health. I think it is very likely that Ann had an inherited susceptibility towards experiencing heightened levels of anxiety. I also wonder if the death of her sister Mary, when Ann was just 11 years old, was the trigger for her chronic anxiety. Mrs. Eliza Priestley told Anne Lister in August 1828: *'Miss Ann Walker's illness likely to be insanity. Her mind warped on religion. She thinks she cannot live, has led a wicked life etc. Had something of this sort when she was seventeen but slighter. The illness seems to be, in fact, a gradual tendency to mental derangement'*. Assuming Mrs. Priestley's recollection was accurate, Ann Walker had a serious mental breakdown when she was seventeen and again when she was twenty-five. Now, in 1833, she was having a third breakdown, aged 29. All three breakdowns manifested in a fear associated with religion, specifically on whether she would ultimately go to Heaven or Hell. In 1823, Ann's parents died within months of each, when she was just twenty years old. That was a lot of bereavement to be endured at a relatively young age. There is something else that may have contributed to Ann's suffering so badly from anxiety. In Anne Lister's diary entry for Tuesday, July 9th, 1822, she recorded comments made by Mr. William Priestley about Ann Walker's father: *'They were not surprised at Mr. Walker's conduct, his family saw enough. Mr. Priestley said he had been spoilt all his life and I think it was Mr. Priestley who said he was sometimes like a mad man in his passion. Mr. Priestley said he blackguarded his wife and daughters'*. So, Ann Walker was verbally abused by her father when she was a child and, the fact that it was common knowledge, suggests that it must have occurred on numerous occasions. Obviously, there is no way of ever knowing the details of the verbal abuse directed at Ann Walker by her father, but just suppose it was religious in nature. This could explain why feelings of extreme anxiety triggered an intrusive thought that convinced her she would go to Hell when she died. It seems to me that Ann Walker's religious based intrusive thoughts had returned as a direct result of the high level of anxiety she experienced as a result of the death of her friend Mrs. Ainsworth and the resulting attention from Mr. Ainsworth. The phrase that Ann Walker used, *'from a want of confidence in God'*, suggests to me the intrusive thoughts she experienced in her three mental breakdowns all had the same origin, which was the commonly held Protestant belief, at the time, that it was the strength of one's faith in God that got you into Heaven rather than your actions. I think it is highly likely that when Ann Walker was experiencing extreme anxiety, the intrusive thought that popped into her head was that her belief in God was not sufficiently strong enough to prevent her from going to Hell. It therefore follows that, although Ann Walker believed that her sexual intimacy with both Mr. Ainsworth and with Anne Lister was morally wrong, she did not believe that these acts were themselves sufficiently wrong to result in her going to Hell, hence explaining why, despite her scruples, she could not resist the opportunity of a bit of grubbling.

The next morning, Wednesday, January 9th, a letter arrived at Shibden for Anne Lister from Mr. Ainsworth. The main purpose of Mr. Ainsworth's correspondence was to return fifty pounds that Ann Walker had given him as a donation to help pay for improvements to his church. However, he felt he should return the money on account of his having given up his position at the church. His letter certainly gave the impression that he had now given up his pursuit of Ann Walker. Anne Lister hastily read Mr. Ainsworth's letter, then set off to the hut. She met Ann Walker on the way and they continued to the hut together. Anne Lister: *'She was in tears, had no hope for this world or the next. Reasoned with her, as well as I could. Said her belief was wrong'.* The two women talked for nearly two hours, and gradually Ann Walker became more composed. They then walked to Shibden Hall where they had wine and sandwiches and sat talking to Aunt Anne. Anne Lister then took Ann upstairs on the pretext of showing her the new library passage. A great believer in the beneficial effects of sex, Anne Lister took Ann on her knee and *'grubbled her well and longish, and she appeared to enjoy it and looked happier, and said she was much better and was sorry she had written last night. Had she not written then she should have let her promise remain. I had told her of having heard from Mr. Ainsworth and she said she wished I had not told her, thought he ought not to have returned the money, it was given for charity'.* They went downstairs at two o'clock and then walked back to Lidgate. Anne Lister: *'said how happy we might have been, what good going abroad would have done her. She might set her note of last night aside if she liked. She hesitated so I said "well then let it stand". Asked if I might give her a ring, yes if I pleased'.* Anne Lister set off home to Shibden at five o'clock as Ann was expecting a visit from a Mrs. Carter. Being in Anne Lister's company, plus a grubbling session, had brought about an improvement in Ann's spirits. Unfortunately, and not surprisingly, as soon as she was alone, her intrusive thoughts about death and Hell immediately returned. At two o'clock the following afternoon, Thursday, January 10th, a note arrived at Shibden from Ann Walker: *'Not well in body or mind. I will try to gain comfort and consolation from what you said tho I fear it is almost hopeless. If you can come either for an hour or to stay all night, I shall be indeed glad to see you, but do as you think best. A.W.'* Anne Lister, now aware of just how serious Ann's mental illness had become, was starting to think that she should write to Ann's sister, Elizabeth, in Scotland, to inform her of the situation. On receiving Ann Walker's note, she wasted no time in getting over to Lidgate. I would just like to take this opportunity to comment on just how kind and caring Anne Lister was towards Ann Walker. In fact, in my transcribing of her diaries, I have come across numerous occasions which demonstrate just how supportive and considerate and emotionally aware a person she was. When Anne arrived at Lidgate, Ann Walker was not there. She had gone to Cliff Hill, so Anne went there to collect her, and they went for a little walk, then headed back to Lidgate. Anne suggested they play backgammon, but Ann Walker just wanted to her to read passages, out loud, from the Bible. It is interesting that during the first few months of their courtship, Ann Walker seemed to have minimal interest in religion, apart from sometimes going to church on Sunday. When they went upstairs to bed that night, Ann Walker continued to read prayers, until eventually, Anne insisted she got into bed. Even then Ann Walker's mind was too distracted for sleep. At about three o'clock, Anne Lister suggested Ann keep repeating the Lord's prayer until she dozed off. The following morning, Friday, January 11th, Anne Lister stayed at Lidgate with Ann for as long as she could but had to leave at about ten o'clock with so many pressing estate matters needing to be dealt with. It was half past five before she was back at her desk at Shibden where she found a letter from Captain Sutherland, thanking her for taking Ann to York to see Dr. Belcombe. She replied immediately to Captain Sutherland's letter describing in detail, Ann Walker's mental illness. The following afternoon, Saturday, January 12th, a note arrived at Shibden from Ann Walker: *'Had comfortable sleep till twelve last night then, till three, misery again. It is these hours of the night I so much dread and they make me feel afraid of going to bed. Oh my very very dear friend, if I could have more faith it would enable me to support better other afflictions... Believe me, yours most gratefully and affectionately, A. Walker'.* Later that afternoon, Anne Lister arrived at Lidgate to find Ann sitting with her cousin Catherine Rawson, who had come to stay. She sat talking to both women then had a chat with Ann in her bedroom. She asked Ann what she meant in her note by *'other afflictions'* and Ann replied that it was the prospect of Anne Lister going abroad. Ann also told Anne Lister that, the previous night, she was sharing a bed with Catherine, but was disturbed by something at midnight and jumped out of bed, frightening Catherine. Anne Lister: *'advised Miss Walker to sleep in her own bed and to have a lamp by her and some gruel, kept hot upon it, for her to take on awakening in the night. Said she had better not have the clock strike as it alarmed her, and I took off the striking weight'.* Anne Lister headed home at 5.25 p.m.

The following day, Sunday, January 13th, Anne Lister was busy with estate business, but soon after getting home at 5.05 p.m., a note arrived from Ann asking her to go to Lidgate. She was at Lidgate by 5.50 p.m. and had dinner and later tea with Ann and Catherine, and they retired at 10.25 p.m. Anne Lister: *'Had made Miss Walker give up Mr. Days ointment and have her back clean washed with hot water last night, and sleep with me over the kitchen. She came to me and grubbled her at first and once afterwards in the night. She awoke for a few minutes twice then slept again, had really a good night. Not so I, whose sleep was long in coming and disturbed and never sound. There was too much fire and she clung to me too closely, but it is evident I do her more good, and have far more influence than anyone'.* As usual, Anne Lister did not get a good night's sleep at Lidgate, but knowing how much Ann was comforted by her presence next to her in bed, she accepted this. That morning, Monday, January 14th, she walked a little way with Ann and Catherine, then continued to the Shibden estate to meet up with her workmen to supervise the many improvements and developments she had on the go. She was one busy woman! She got home at 5.30 p.m. had dinner and spent the night in her own bed.

The following day, Tuesday, January 15th, Anne Lister worked on estate business all day, and the next day, Wednesday, January 16th, she was again very busy out on the estate despite her period having started. A note arrived from Ann Walker on Wednesday afternoon asking her to go to Lidgate, but at five o'clock, just as she was thinking of going there, James Holt arrived at Shibden with coal leases to be reviewed and also to discuss the possibility that the Rawson brothers had been stealing Shibden coal. Once Mr. Holt had left, Charles Howarth called to discuss the hall refurbishments. Anne Lister decided that there was no way she could get to Lidgate so sent a note to Ann Walker saying so and promising to be there the following morning.

When Anne Lister arrived at Lidgate at 11.30 a.m. on the morning of Thursday, January 17th, she found that the doctor, Mr. Sunderland, was there having been called to attend Ann. Mr. Sunderland told Anne Lister, that *'Miss Walker's bodily health better but there is so little excitement of the mind'.* The two women then had a long talk in Ann's bedroom. Anne Lister: *'despairing as usual and I tried to cheer her as well as I could'.* They talked of the possibility of going to York to see Dr. Belcombe the following week. Anne Lister then walked a while with Ann and Catherine, then took her leave when they went in to have dinner.

The next morning, Friday, January 18th, Anne Lister was out early on the estate, cutting and pruning alder bushes. Unfortunately, she slipped and fell into the brook, the water up to her hips, so she headed home. When she got back to Shibden she found a letter from Mr. Ainsworth waiting for her. She described it as a *'long ringmarole letter'* but she did not bother to describe its contents in her journal except that he had promised it would be his last. She was back at Lidgate at five o'clock the following evening Saturday, January 19th. Anne Lister: *'Miss Walker low as of late but always better on seeing me and while I am there'.* Anne made no record of having told Ann Walker that she had received another letter from Mr. Ainsworth. She clearly thought it was better not to mention it, given Ann's response to his previous letter. She had dinner with Ann and Catherine at 6.30 p.m. followed by tea and retired at 10.10 p.m. Anne Lister: *'Slept with me over the kitchen without fire and Miss Walker had an excellent night, slept uninterruptedly after my grubbling her well but not too tediously and all at once. I slept or dozed better than usual but so that I heard her if she stirred'.*

The following morning, Sunday, January 20th, they had breakfast at 9.20 a.m. and afterwards Anne Lister spoke with Catherine, whilst Ann was out of the room: *'Miss Rawson kept me this morning saying Miss Walker would be worse as soon as I was gone. We had a little tête-à-tête after breakfast and both spoke openly of Miss Walker's being not herself, I begging Miss Rawson not to name it at home but let it be all hushed up as much as possible'.* Anne Lister headed back to Shibden at 11.35 a.m. having persuaded Ann not to attend church on account of the heavy rain.

The next morning, Monday, January 21st, Anne Lister was busy in the morning seeing Samuel Washington, Charles Howarth and then James Holt on estate business. At twelve thirty, Ann and Catherine called at Shibden, having walked from Lidgate.

Ann Walker was tired, so Anne took her upstairs and she lay down for half an hour. Anne Lister took the opportunity of having another chat with Catherine who said *'how uneasy and unhappy she was about Miss Walker, who was quite out of her mind'*. Catherine thought that Mrs. Priestley had hinted at Anne Lister going to speak to her about Ann Walker. Anne Lister, however, told Catherine that this was not a good idea, and that she was in fact hoping to hear from Captain Sutherland, and, if she did not, she would take Ann Walker to see Dr. Belcombe in York. Anne Lister walked back to Lidgate with Ann and Catherine and on arriving they found that a letter had come from Ann's sister, Elizabeth. In the letter, Elizabeth explained that Captain Sutherland was coming to Yorkshire on business and suggested that Ann went back with him, staying, for a week or two, with his mother in Edinburgh *'for the benefit of medical advice'* before travelling on to Inverness to be with her. Anne Lister persuaded Ann to write and accept her sister's offer and they put off their plan of going to York. They had dinner at 7 p.m. then tea and had a *'tolerably cheerful evening'*, with Anne and Ann retiring together at 10.50 p.m. The following morning, Tuesday, January 22nd, Anne Lister: *'Slept with me as on Saturday, and, after a nice not tedious grubbling, had as good a night. Meant to have been up early but she kept me first grubbling her and then talking of her going. Said I would see Captain Sutherland once but might then get out of the way and go to Langton. Thought she had better not write to me, better not begin a correspondence. I could hear of her from her sister, for being abroad and uncertain of the fate of letters, must be careful, must begin with "my dear Miss Walker" and end with "very truly yours". She said she would do whatever I liked, but had said before, she would rather write to me than anybody. Twenty minutes in her room before dressing so that not ready till 11.30 a.m'*. Anne, Ann, and Catherine had breakfast at 11.45 a.m. After Catherine had left them alone, Anne Lister: *'Sat over the breakfast table talking to Miss Walker in favour of the Scotch plan about which she was hesitating. Said she ought to go for my sake for, if we were to be eventually together, it could be brought about so much better'*. Ann

Walker then said she would make Anne happy by agreeing, there and then, to go abroad with her. However, Anne Lister knew, from experience, that what Ann agreed to one day, would be reneged on the next, and besides, it was obvious that she was not well enough to travel abroad. I think she also knew that she and Ann had reached stalemate, and that some significant change would have to occur, for example Ann going to Scotland to stay with her sister, for them both to move forward with their lives. I believe it was out of kindness that Anne Lister chose to give Ann hope that one day they could be together under happier circumstances: *'told her, if in a year's time, she thought she could not live without me, then she must send for me back again, thus going, her hope that all is not, or needs not, be quite at an end between us'.* The three women then took an hour's walk together, after which Anne Lister returned to Shibden to supervise work being done on the hall chimney.

Anne Lister was as busy as ever the next day, Wednesday, January 23rd. On Thursday morning a letter arrived at Shibden from Mariana confirming that she had paid an advance of £4 to Thomas Beech, the groom she had engaged to travel abroad with Anne. The lady's maid, Eugenie Pierre, that Mariana had also found, had already corresponded with Anne regarding her travel plans. That afternoon Anne Lister called at Lidgate at 3.10 p.m. and chatted with Ann and Catherine for three hours. She found Ann appearing to be getting worse: *'she fears evil spirits at night and dare not sleep'.* When Anne Lister returned to Shibden that evening she wrote a letter to Captain Sutherland: *'Dear Sir, I am sorry to say I do not think Miss Walker's health improving and the sooner she has first rate medical advice the better. Nothing could be more kind or judicious than Mrs. Sutherland's letter which arrived on Monday and I am anxious for you to hasten your journey as much as possible. I see as much of Miss Walker as my own engagements will permit and I am sure you will believe that my anxiety about her is very great. She told me this morning she could not go on long as she does at present and seems herself aware that time ought not to be lost. I had fixed to take her to York as today but gave it up in consequence of Mrs. Sutherland's letter. It is desirable to get off from here. No friend could be more kindly attentive and judicious than Miss Rawson who has promised to stay till your arrival but she is hardly old enough to be left without the assistance of some more experienced person and I lament that it is not in my power to be constantly with them. Mrs. Sutherland will be as little uneasy as possible as I have really great hope that care and skilful medical treatment will by and by do all that is required. I am anxious and shall be very glad to see you, and, with my kind regards to Mrs. Sutherland, believe me, dear Sir, very truly yours. A. Lister'.*

Anne Lister was back at Lidgate at 2.10 p.m. the following day, Friday, January 25th. Anne Lister: *'Miss Walker had had a bad night and was very poorly. As to her mind, more despairing and beside herself. Very soon went with her to her room. She lay down and I sat by her talking and reasoning which did her good for the moment while it lasted, but no longer. Saw Miss Rawson for a little while alone in her room. Miss Walker frightens her'.*

A letter arrived at Shibden from Mr. Ainsworth, the next morning, Saturday, January 26th. He had changed his mind about leaving his church and wanted the money back he had returned to Ann Walker. He also seemed to be hoping for another chance to court Ann Walker and asked for Anne Lister's advice on how he should proceed. Anne must have been so irritated by this man. She politely replied: *'Sir your letter of the twenty third instant reached me this morning. I regret that you should have so hastily returned the subscription in question as, under present circumstances which I do not feel at liberty to explain, it does not seem to me advisable to communicate to my friend the content of your letter. You ask my advice, the difficulty of giving it is so great that I am really under the necessity of declining it. I am sir, your obedient servant. A. Lister'.* Anne went to Lidgate arriving at five o'clock that evening. The three women had dinner then tea, but it appeared that Ann's condition had worsened. Anne and Ann slept together in the orange room with the fire lit: *'no grubbling and she did not sleep so well, a little disturbed, but I kept her in bed and she slept'.* The next morning Catherine went to church, but Anne Lister persuaded Ann to stay at home and they read prayers together then went for a short walk. Anne Lister: *'poor Miss Walker, more despairing and beside herself than ever'.* I think that Anne Lister was keen that Ann did not go to church just in case anyone became aware of her troubled mental state. I suspect she feared that unscrupulous relatives might take the opportunity to have Ann Walker committed to an institution in order to get their hands on her inheritance. Indeed, I think it is reasonable to assume this was also the reason she asked Catherine not to mention Ann's mental health problems to her family.

Anne Lister next called at Lidgate in the early evening of Tuesday January 29th only intending a short visit. However, Ann Walker wanted her to stay all night and she was not able to refuse. After dinner at 6.15 p.m. Anne and Ann played backgammon and Catherine read prayers. Anne Lister: *'No grubbling, she in too low spirits for anything of that kind. She had rather a disturbed night and therefore so had I too'.* The following morning, Wednesday, January 30th, with so much estate business needing her attention, Anne Lister had planned to go back home to Shibden after breakfast, but Ann did not want her to leave so she stayed, and instead the three women took a walk together. Afterwards, before Anne Lister headed home to Shibden, Ann asked her to burn her promise, that was the purse containing the answer 'yes', then immediately changed her mind. Ann's mind was indeed in turmoil. When Anne Lister arrived back at Shibden at 4.55 p.m. she found a letter on her study desk from Dr. Belcombe. Besides corresponding with Ann's brother-in-law, Captain Sutherland, Anne had also written to Dr. Belcombe to create a back-up plan in case the plan for Ann to go to Scotland did not work out.

Late the following afternoon, Thursday, January 31st, a note arrived at Shibden from Ann Walker begging Anne to go to Lidgate. Just before the note arrived, heavy snow had started to fall, and when Anne told her family she was heading off to Lidgate, her Aunt Anne got very upset, fearful of her going out on *'such a night'*. Anne had no choice but to send her servant, John Booth, to Lidgate saying she was very sorry she could not go but promising to be there the following day. John Booth returned with another note from Ann saying that she was not surprised at Aunt Anne's objection but that she had sent off the note before the snow had started to fall. In her note Ann Walker added: *'I will try to get over the night tolerably and pray that the evil I fear may not come upon me, but it is very different without you, how I long to see you'*. Anne Lister's thoughts on receiving the note*: 'poor soul, she is quite beside herself and cannot stand all this long'*.

The next morning, Friday, February 1st, two letters arrived at Shibden for Anne Lister, one from Mr. Ainsworth and the other from Elizabeth Sutherland. Mr. Ainsworth wanted to know if Ann Walker was courting, and if not, could Anne Lister advise him of how he should proceed. Anne Lister: *'I have often thought, and think more and more, he must be beside himself'*. The letter from Elizabeth Sutherland was a request for Anne to take Ann Walker to Edinburgh to consult a Dr. Abercrombie and for Captain Sutherland to collect Ann Walker from there rather than having to travel all the way to Halifax. Anne Lister was shocked by this request and wrote back immediately explaining that it was not something she was able to do. I suspect that Anne may well have felt that Elizabeth Sutherland was out of order making such a request. Anne was so busy with all the work she was having done at Shibden, and with having to go back and forth to Lidgate, as well as having family commitments, that I think she was probably feeling under considerable pressure. Anne Lister: *'what pother I have had for my folly about this poor girl'*. Anne arrived at Lidgate at 5.15 p.m. *'Miss Walker very glad to see me, in cheerful spirits, a great deal better and had been so all day. Wants to go to Dr. Belcombe and not to Scotland'*. They slept in the same bed together as usual, and Ann Walker got a good night's sleep.

The following morning, Saturday, February 2nd, *'Miss Walker as much better as yesterday' and writing a letter *'to her sister to say how much better she was and that she would wait a few days determining about going to Scotland'.* Anne Lister was very dubious about this sudden and unexpected improvement in Ann's spirits and suspected that it would not last for long. She had realised that Ann wanted to stay at Lidgate for as long as she remained at Shibden. Ann Walker was desperate to have Anne with her, caring for her, and loving her, but was unable to fully commit to their relationship. Despite knowing this, Anne Lister had tried her very best to find a way to improve Ann's mental health, but in this she had failed, and she knew it. She believed that Ann needed expert medical care, but she also knew, if she took on the responsibility of getting her the treatment she needed, she would be in the role of Ann Walker's carer for the foreseeable future, and, given Ann's refusal to commit to her, and also her own plans to travel abroad, this was something she did not want. At some point that morning Anne Lister had had a private conversation with Catherine: *'I had told Miss Rawson there were more capabilities about Miss Walker than she Miss Rawson thought, but I now feared her mind would not hold out. Miss Rawson said she used to think me all that was disagreeable and how wrong she was. She said what good I had done her and wept over the injustice she felt she had done me'.* After a walk with Ann and Catherine, Anne Lister set off from Lidgate at two o'clock, sauntered back along her ornamental walk and arrived back at Shibden about three o'clock to find a letter from Mariana: *'It was the cheerful, satisfied way in which you spoke of the future, my dearest Fred, which pleased me so much in your letter of the 18th. I have been so long accustomed to hear you express yourself differently, that it did truly cheer me to find that you could fancy more ways than one of being happy. I have long wished to wean you from dwelling too intently upon an event which to me every year seems less likely to happen'.* The event that Mariana referred to was, of course, Anne being able to live with a woman she loved. Clearly Anne must have informed Mariana that she would be traveling abroad alone, and this knowledge had significantly improved Mariana's spirits.

The following morning, Sunday February 3rd, Anne Lister wrote again to Mrs. Sutherland: *'My conviction is unchanged that no time ought to be lost in placing your sister under the care of a skilful medical man, accustomed to the various shades of mental suffering. Dr. Abercrombie is, of course, such a person and will have no difficulty in understanding the case'.* That afternoon, a note arrived at Shibden from Ann Walker with a letter she had received from her sister, the previous day, stating that Anne Lister was to go with her to Edinburgh and that they should be off the following Tuesday with Anne Lister making all the necessary arrangements. I assume Elizabeth must have been sent the letter before receiving the letter from Anne Lister. Anne then sent a note over to Lidgate telling Ann not to be nervous, that she would see her the following day and that they *'would manage things beautifully'*.

The next morning, Monday February 4th, Anne Lister was at Lidgate by twenty past eight. She and Ann constructed a letter to Elizabeth requesting that Captain Sutherland come to Lidgate and that she would be ready to travel next Monday or Tuesday week. Anne Lister described another quiet chat she had with Catherine: *'Talked with Catherine, who again wept over the injustice, had been told I was the most dangerous person and the worst enemy'.* Catherine had clearly become fond of Anne Lister and was still feeling very guilty about her previous opinion of her. Although Anne Lister wanted to head back to Shibden in the early afternoon, Ann begged her to stay, so she remained at Lidgate till just after five o'clock.

Anne Lister was back at Lidgate the following evening, Tuesday, February 5th, and stayed overnight, only getting home late afternoon the following day. She did not go to Lidgate on the Thursday but returned on Friday evening and again stayed the night. On the Saturday morning, Anne and Ann walked to Shibden Hall to collect the purse containing the 'yes' that Ann Walker wanted to burn that night. When they got back to Lidgate later that afternoon, a letter had arrived from Elizabeth confirming that Captain Sutherland would be at Lidgate on Friday, February 15th, to collect Ann Walker. Anne Lister: *'what a godsend to have things settled. Well, there it is at last, a prospect of my being free of all this once again'.* That night: *'above half hour in Miss Walker's room, hesitating whether to burn the purse or not. She not liking to see me do it, at last threw it in her fire, purse and 'yes' in it. I glad enough to get rid of anything like a tie. She seemed, after all, very composed after it and I went quietly back to my room'.* Later, as usual, Ann Walker joined Anne in her bed: *'both very quiet last night. She jumped up and ran away twenty minutes before me this morning [Sunday] saying afterwards that she felt that if she had staid she should never get away'.* After breakfast at 9.50 a.m. Anne Lister told Ann that she had had more correspondence from Mr. Ainsworth but had not mentioned it to her. Ann Walker said she wished Anne not to mention Mr. Ainsworth *'as she had not thought of him lately'.* She also told Anne not to mention Mr. Ainsworth to Captain Surtherland. Anne Lister stayed with Ann all day, primarily to keep her from going to church. They read prayers in the afternoon and Anne Lister again stayed the night. During the evening, Ann Walker's spirits improved, and the three women had a philosophical discussion on religion which seemed to do Ann good. Anne and Ann again slept in the same bed together and had a quiet night. The following morning Monday, February 11th, Catherine said she could not stay till Friday and decided to go home that day. I suppose the strain of being with Ann Walker must have taken its toll on her. After she had left, Anne and Ann walked to Shibden Hall and sat eating sandwiches and drinking wine with Aunt Anne, Marian, and Jeremy. They got back to Lidgate at 3 p.m. then out again to look over Ann Walker's plantations at Cliff Hill. On returning to Lidgate, they sat together till seven o'clock. Anne Lister: *'she is now sorry for having said "no". Said she had been a foolish little thing and seemed low at the thought of parting'.* Anne Lister insisted she had to return to Shibden that evening: *'Miss Walker wanted me to stay but I said I could not, in fact, staying all night never suits me. I do not sleep really well, and my bowels always get wrong, so they have been the last 3 mornings that I have been there. Besides all at home is neglected'.* Anne Lister was back home at Shibden by 7.30 p.m. Despite not sleeping well at Lidgate, and the resulting disruption to her bowels, Anne Lister stayed with Ann the next four nights.

The next afternoon, Tuesday, February 12th, Anne Lister arrived back at Lidgate at 4 p.m. and she and Ann then walked to Shibden Hall where Ann Walker sat with Aunt Anne whilst Anne Lister finished some correspondence. Just before six o'clock, Anne and Ann walked back to Lidgate where they had dinner and later tea. Anne Lister: *'we slept in her own room over the drawing room and not in the orange room as of late'.* The following afternoon, Wednesday, February 13th, the two women paid a social call on Mrs. Priestley and then went to see old Miss Walker at Cliff Hill. They then went for a long walk and were back at Lidgate for dinner at six o'clock. Anne Lister: *'Quiet last night and this morning. She says she does not like the thought of their coming or her going'.*

The two women spent most of Thursday packing the many items that Ann Walker wanted to take to Scotland, although they were visited for about half an hour by Mrs. Dyson and two Misses Edwards of Pyenest. Anne Lister: *'touched her last night and this morning but not to amount to regular grubbling'.* The next day, Friday, was meant to be the day that Captain Sutherland arrived from Scotland, but he had been delayed slightly and was not now expected until the following morning. In addition to packing, the two women were 'siding' which I assume meant that many items had to be put away into storage given that Ann Walker could be in Scotland for some time. They both went out at 4.20 p.m. with Ann Walker going to Cliff Hill to see her aunt and Anne going home to Shibden to *'see them all'.* They were both back at Lidgate by 6.30 p.m. having dinner. That evening Ann Walker was busy writing *'3 letters and 4 notes',* whilst Anne went through some accounts for her. Anne Lister: *'grubbled a little last night and touched and handled her this morning'.* They had breakfast at eleven o'clock on Saturday morning, and just after they had finished, Captain Sutherland and his mother arrived. Ann Walker continued to be busy packing and siding, and Captain Sutherland's mother went to her room to write letters, so Anne Lister took the opportunity to further explain to Captain Sutherland the details of Ann's mental illness and the need for her to see a suitably qualified medical man. Mrs. Priestley paid a social call at two o'clock, Captain Sutherland went into Halifax and Anne Lister headed home to Shibden.

Anne Lister was back at Lidgate, the following afternoon, Sunday, February 17th, at 4.20 p.m. She found the Sutherlands' company particularly tedious, *'thought I, well poor girl, what a set she is getting amongst'*. They all retired at 11.15 p.m. Anne and Ann believed this would be the last night they would spend together. Anne Lister: *'grubbled her last night, she on the amoroso and wanted to be nearer to me, that is have my drawers off, but I thought it better not. She would sleep in my arms and snored so shockingly I could scarce bear it. She seemed as if she was going to leave all she liked best and could scarce have enough of me. Poor girl, she could hardly leave me in the morning, and this made us so late. She was a little on the amoroso again. I touched and handled her, grubbled a little, but would not do much'*. After breakfast, Ann Walker and Captain Sutherland went to Cliff Hill and, Anne found herself sat chatting to Captain Sutherland's mother, who quite openly talked of the possibility of her nephew, Alexander Mackenzie, marrying Ann Walker to pay off his debts and help support his mother and sister. Anne Lister replied: *'I said I thought Miss Walker would not marry to pay anyones debts, nor ought she'*. No wonder she was unimpressed with the Sutherlands. When Ann Walker returned from Cliff Hill, she was busy over one thing or other. Anne Lister described her as *'very low at going, said she would rather go with me. Knew she should be miserable there as she was before. Felt as if she should never come back yet smiled and rallied when I joked her about running after me. She seemed quietly bent on being back before June when she thinks I am to be off'*. Ann Walker gave Anne a little bronze taper-stick and a bible as parting gifts. Anne Lister saw them off at 1.15 p.m. Ann Walker and Captain Sutherland's mother sat inside the carriage, and, Captain Sutherland and James Mckenzie, Ann's servant, sat in the rumble seat at the back. Anne Lister's overwhelming feeling as she walked home was one of relief. She had begun as Ann Walker's friend, then became her lover, but ended very much as her carer, and was now, well and truly, exhausted by the whole affair. That night she looked at the little Bible Ann Walker had given her. On the fly leaf next to the Bible's title page, Ann Walker had written *'February 18th, 1833, Psalms 91.11'* and on the back (at the end), *'A.W. to A.L.'*. When Anne Lister turned to this reference, it read *'For he shall give his angels charge over thee to keep thee in all thy ways'*. Anne Lister: *'the sight of this affected me, poor girl, what a pity she has not more mind to be happy herself and make others so'*.

Their powerful desire to be with each other, the considerable amount of time they spent together, and their obvious joy when in each other's company, has convinced me that Anne Lister and Ann Walker loved each other very much. Ten and a half months would pass before they were to see each other again.

CHAPTER 5: SEPARATED

So, what were Ann Walker and Anne Lister up to during the 10½ months they were apart? Did they miss each other, did they keep in touch, did Ann Walker's health improve, and did Anne Lister go off travelling abroad?

On Saturday, March 2nd, 1833, twelve days after Ann Walker's departure to Scotland, a letter arrived at Shibden from Captain Sutherland. He wrote that on their way to Inverness they had stayed in Edinburgh for four days and were out of doors the whole time, during daylight hours. *'Miss Walker had declined taking medical advice and Captain Sutherland had thought it best not to urge it. More judicious to persuade her she wanted nothing but air and exercise'*. Still reeling from her experience of caring for Ann Walker, Anne Lister: *'I don't want to be in her way soon again, I have had enough of it'*.

Although Anne Lister was still very busy with estate business, refurbishments at Shibden Hall and arranging coal leases, she was also making plans for her travels abroad. At this point, she had it in mind to be off from Shibden early the following month, April. She had continued her correspondence with Eugénie Pierre, who was living in Brighton, and who she hoped would be her lady's maid whilst she was travelling in Europe, having already, with Mariana's help, secured the services of a groom, Thomas Beech. Anne's other major concern was the money she would need for the trip. The bulk of her income came from the twice yearly rent paid by her tenants on the Shibden estate although this was shared with her father and aunt. The next rent day was July 1st and she knew she would have to plan her finances carefully in order to be able to fund her travel plans. In the meantime, Anne had received a letter from Mariana confirming that Charles' plan for him and Mariana to move from Lawton Hall to Leamington had now taken place and she was very busy getting things sorted.

On Wednesday, March 13th, a large box was delivered to Shibden by Samuel Washington. When Anne Lister saw that the box was from Scotland, she assumed it was from a friend of hers, Miss Breadalbane McLean, from the Scottish Highlands. Anne had one of the men working on the hall refurbishments open the box to find it contained a round rosewood table and a note to Aunt Anne saying *'Miss Walker hopes Mrs. Lister will do her the favour to accept the small table which she trusts may prove a useful appendage to her work. Miss Walker begs to present her very kind regards to all the family at Shibden Hall'*. Anne Lister: *'My aunt thinks Miss Walker means not to let me escape her. This I owned would be the natural interpretation of the table if sent by a person knowing the world, but from Miss Walker, I know not what to make of it. She may mean it as a sort of acknowledgement of all my attention and kindness'*. The next day Anne Lister wrote a letter to Ann to thank her for the table. She described her letter as *'kind but perfectly judicious and proper'*.

On Saturday, March 30th, a letter arrived at Shibden for Anne from Ann Walker, some two weeks after she would have received the thank you letter from Anne regarding her gift of the small rosewood table for Aunt Anne. Apparently, Ann Walker had delayed her reply in the hope of being able to tell Anne that she was feeling better, but sadly this was not the case, her spirits were as low as ever, so much so, in fact, that she had been unable to muster the energy to show any interest in her sister's children. Her receipt of Anne Lister's letter had cheered her up and she described it as being *'like a sunbeam'*. Unfortunately, but not surprisingly, the improvement had been temporary. Ann Walker: *'any progress that I make one day, I lose the next, and my fears accumulate upon me'*. In her letter, Anne Lister had asked Ann to knit her some woollen knee-caps to which Ann had replied *'Whatever you ask me to do I consider as an especial favour conferred on myself.*

I have written for the worsted and in knitting your knee-caps, I will try what I can do and write you a note in the parcel'. In response to Anne Lister's promise to remember her, Ann Walker wrote: *'I cannot forget you, nor can a few weeks or months obliterate remembrance of the past'.* Anne Lister was unsure how to respond to the letter. She felt very sorry for Ann: *'I really feel for and pity her'.* She wanted to be supportive but was also concerned that it might not be beneficial to Ann to keep getting letters from her. In the end she decided to think about it and trust that *'providence orders all things rightly'.* She wrote in her journal that night: *'Nor Miss Hobart nor Miss Walker nor Mariana were for me. I must wait and see what heaven vouchsafes'.*

Three days later, Tuesday, April 2nd, Anne Lister visited old Miss Walker at Cliff Hill. Old Miss Walker had been planning to write to Elizabeth Sutherland so Anne asked her to include a message from her saying that she had received Ann Walker's letter but had not made up her mind what to do about it and that whatever she decided *'would be from no want of kindness or feeling'*.

Anne Lister's original plan to be off on her travels in early April had not materialised, mainly on account of coal related estate business that required her personal attention, but also because she had not finally made up her mind exactly where she was going to go.

On Monday, April 29th, Catherine Rawson paid a social call at Shibden to see Anne. Catherine had had a letter from Ann Walker, which she described as *'rather incoherent'* and from which she had concluded that Ann was no better.

By early May, Anne Lister's travel plans had come together. Her friends with international connections had sent her many letters of introduction to people all over Europe, including as far as Russia, so she had plenty of choice regarding where she could travel to and be sure of a welcome reception into society. She had arranged for her groom, Thomas Beech, and lady's maid, Eugenie Pierre to arrive at Shibden on May 6th, with the intention of travelling to York the following day. The next morning, Tuesday, Anne was up at six o'clock finishing her packing and covering all the books she wanted to take with her. She had breakfast with Aunt Anne at noon then read the two letters that had arrived at Shibden that morning from Mariana. The first to say that her husband's nephew, William Lawton, had had a dreadful accident and had suffered the amputation of one arm. The second to say that William had died. Mariana had become very fond of William and was clearly distraught, and Anne was very concerned about her. Once the horses and coachman had arrived at Shibden that morning, Anne was able to set off at 12.40 pm to travel to York in her own carriage, accompanied by her two new servants. Her plan was to spend two or three weeks in York, return to Shibden for a few days, meet up with Mariana, then begin her trip to the continent. The party arrived at the Black Swan Inn, in York at 6.50 p.m. Anne then went off to the residence of Dr. Belcombe and his wife Harriet, and dined with them and their guests, one of whom was Charlotte Norcliffe, Isabella's sister. Dr. Belcombe, being Mariana's brother and a close friend of Anne's, was often just referred to as *'Steph'* in her journal. When Anne left the Belcombes at eleven o'clock that evening, Steph walked with her back to the Black Swan Inn and went in for a little while to continue their chat. He had had a letter from Elizabeth Sutherland asking him whether he thought it might be too cold in Inverness for Ann Walker. Apparently, Ann Walker was feeling the cold and did not want to stay there. Steph had replied advising *'giving it a fair trial'*. *'Oh! oh!'* thought Anne *'I see the poor girl is tired of it already'*. Anne asked Steph if he thought it was likely that Ann Walker could be cured. He replied *'Yes! Chances equal or rather more than that in her favour'*. Anne told Steph that she was *'interested about her'* and *'should not mind 6 months trouble if likely to succeed'*.

The next morning, Wednesday, May 8th, Steph called at the Black Swan to see Anne Lister. He had obviously given some thought to their conversation about Ann Walker the previous night. As part of his medical practice, Steph had a property in the village of Thorp Arch, near Leeds, where his patients sometimes stayed whilst under his care. He told Anne that he thought *'he could manage about Miss Walker'* and that he *'could have her at Thorp Arch very comfortably for a fortnight and then see how she was'*. As their conversation continued, without being too explicit, Anne opened up to Steph about her friendship with Mariana. She told him that she had intended to provide *'more than amply for Mariana'*, by leaving her a life interest in all her property, had she moved in with her at Shibden. She explained to Steph that realising the chance of the two of them moving in together had gone had caused her considerable grief, which she had only felt able to share with her aunt and Charlotte Norcliffe. She also told Steph that she *'was dull without having some interest'* meaning, of course, that she needed a special woman in her life that she could love and care for. As their conversation came to an end, Anne said *'I would rather have Miss Walker than someone of higher rank and more worldly'*. As Steph left, he laughed and said *'you are an odd person!'*. The conversations Anne had had with Steph, that morning and the previous evening, had got her thinking about Ann Walker. In fact, judging by the letter she then wrote to Ann, her brain was in overdrive! I am including here the whole of the letter as I found the energy with which it was written to be quite extraordinary: *'Thank you very much for your letter which I can only regret you not writing in better spirits. I have thought often and much and anxiety about you. You told me my last letter was like a sunbeam – may this letter be like another sunbeam and a brighter one. I determined not to write till I was off from Shibden and am now writing in the very room where you and I were so comfy together in October. If you could recall that time, would you? Consider four and twenty hours. Judge for yourself if you can, if not ask your sister's advice and take it. I still think that health and happiness are within your reach, and, as I trust, by more ways than one. I have seen much of your aunt and we are such good friends, I do not fancy her opinions would oppose my own. I go to Langton tomorrow (direct to me at Mrs. Norcliffe, Langton Hall near Malton, Yorkshire) and intend staying a fortnight, after that I must return to Shibden for 2 or 3 days and shall then make the best of my way to the continent but in the meantime you may accommodate your plans to mine or mine to yours, if you please. I told you at parting that I would meet you on your return, if you wish it. If you have energy enough to determine, I will take you up at your sister's own door at Udale and, as during the present building operations it is impossible to accommodate extra people, I could or rather I mean we could sleep at Inverness. I think you would like Eugenie and find my manservant all we want. If you dare give a fair trial, I am sanguine as ever about your entire recovery. Write in answer whatever you think but better write it soon. Rouse yourself while there is yet time, remember that the sun is rising some while before we see him, and that when human ills seem without remedy, it is not because that remedy really fails to exist but simply because we know not how to find it. My kind regards to your sister and Captain Sutherland and be your answer to my letter what it may be. Believe me ever sincerely interested in your welfare and ever faithfully and affectionately yours. A.L. Am I not to have the kneecaps?'* It appears that the combination of Ann Walker having expressed the wish to leave Inverness and having described Anne Lister's letter as being like a 'sunbeam', along with Steph's suggestion that a cure for Ann Walker's nervousness was a possibility, had given Anne Lister a glimmer of hope that she and Ann might have a future together. Was it false hope, and was Anne Lister setting herself up for yet another disappointment? Clearly, despite the stress and trauma of the previous six or seven months, Anne still did not want to give up on Ann Walker.

After visiting friends in York, Anne Lister set off in her carriage on the afternoon of Thursday, May 9th to travel to Langton Hall, the home of the Norcliffes, accompanied by Charlotte Norcliffe. Anne was very fond of Mrs. Norcliffe and Isabella, of course, and very much enjoyed her visits to Langton Hall. On Wednesday, May 15th, a parcel arrived for her that had been forwarded from Shibden Hall. The parcel was from Ann Walker and contained two pairs of woollen kneecaps that she had knitted for Anne. The parcel also contained a note from Ann Walker that was dated April 24th so had been sent from Inverness three weeks previously. Ann Walker: *'I cannot tell you anything really favourable of my own mind. I am getting quite stout, but I feel that I am not improving in health of mind and evils seem to increase upon me. I have not yet been able to form one resolution as to my return home tho' my aunt says she wishes it, but I dread the idea of returning to greater evils. All your predictions, or I ought to say your warnings, appear to have been realized in me and I get deeper in the mire every day. If you saw me now, I am sure you would say I was changed, and you would observe it with regret and I begin to fear that my hopes of meeting you again, renewed in heart and body to which I have hitherto faintly clung, will never be fulfilled. My sister and Captain Sutherland beg me to say everything that is kind from them, with their very kind regards, accept all that friendship can offer from myself. Pray let me hear from you, for I shall not forget you and whatever befalls me you will hear of either from myself or your aunt, thro' her at least I can gain intelligence of you'.* Anne Lister was of course aware that Ann's note was not a reply to her last letter but it did show that Ann was *'no better in mind, and surely there neither is nor perhaps ought to be any prospect of our being together'.*

The following day, Thursday, May 16th, Ann Walker's reply to Anne's last letter arrived at Langton Hall. Ann Walker: *'If any further proof had been wanting in addition to those I had previously received of your fidelity and real goodness of heart, there would not be one more decided than is given in the truly kind letter I received on Saturday. I have given the subject every consideration and even asked my sister's advice, who says she could not bear me to leave the kingdom till I am in better health, but of this I can assure you that she, who of course is ignorant of the extent of your goodness to me, is most truly alive to your kindness. I can therefore only add, with every grateful feeling, that I will no longer be an obstacle to the fulfilment of your plans. May every blessing and every prosperity this world can afford attend you. The kneecaps I dispatched a fortnight ago, I am only sorry that for want of worsted I could not get them off sooner. Do not forget to let me know about the socks for I must still claim it as my privilege to finish them and frills. I trust that neither time or clime will cause me to forget the real friend I have found in you'.* Anne Lister described the letter as *'a very civil end of the thing',* realising that her love affair with Ann Walker was now over.

Six days later, on Wednesday, May 22nd, Anne Lister wrote to Ann to thank her for the woollen kneecaps she had sent. In the letter, Anne also outlined her own travel plans and included an assurance to Ann Walker that she would be pleased to be of use to her in any way she could. I would describe the letter as both kind and caring, but with a feeling of finality about it. I think Anne Lister was now keen to get on with the rest of her life.

Having enjoyed her stay at Langton Hall with her close friends, Isabella and Charlotte Norcliffe, on Monday, May 27th, Anne Lister, accompanied by her servants, Eugenie and Thomas, set off from Langton Hall and returned to the Black Swan in York. The party stayed at the Black Swan for three nights to give Anne the opportunity to spend time with her many York friends. On Thursday, May 30th, she booked her two servants into lodgings and travelled on the Mail Coach back to Halifax, arriving at Shibden at two thirty in the morning of Friday, May 31st. It had been Anne's original intention to stay at Shibden for just a few days but there was so much estate business to sort out, in particular coal related matters, it was not until Sunday, June 16th, that she returned by the Mail Coach, to York, and was reunited with her servants. Again, Anne spent a few days visiting with friends, then set off in her carriage with her servants on Wednesday, June 19th, and travelled to Leamington, Warwickshire, to spend some time with Mariana Lawton, who had been keen to see Anne before she travelled to the continent. Mariana and her husband, Charles, had left Lawton Hall and rented Claremont House in Leamington. Mariana had been very disappointed with the move because she was much happier living at Lawton Hall. I do not know why Charles decided he wanted to live in Leamington, but it may have been because Mariana's 'friendship' with a Mr. Willoughby Crewe, one of Charles' relatives, had continued and perhaps he wanted to keep her away from him. Anne and her servants arrived at Claremont House just before ten o'clock that night. Anne had some tea and cold boiled beef and was shown to her room, where she chatted to Mariana for a little while.

Anne stayed at Claremont house for two weeks. She and Mariana walked a lot and talked a lot, did a bit of socialising, and had sex every night. Mariana's twelve-year-old niece, known as little Mariana, was also staying at Claremont House.

Mariana and Anne's conversation became more illuminating as each day passed. On the first day, whilst out walking, and I suspect in an effort to elicit some tenderness and affection from Mariana after the strain of the many months of caring for Ann Walker, Anne tried to make her jealous by suggesting that she had a fancy for Harriet, Mariana's sister. This backfired somewhat, as Mariana showed absolutely no interest, resulting in Anne bursting into tears and Mariana telling her not to be pathetic. Later that day, Anne told Mariana that she had spoken to Steph and Charlotte Norcliffe about the decision Mariana made, about a year previous, that she and Anne would never live together. Mariana's response was that Anne *'was always a blab'*.

The following night, Anne Lister: *'undressed, got into bed and had Mariana with me half hour till 20 past 11 and grubbled as before, she quite wet and nothing loth. She hinted today she might be with me after all, but I took no notice, it is off and so be it, I can amuse without entangling myself'.* If Anne had correctly understood what Mariana had hinted, this would surely have been a very unexpected development.

Whilst Anne and Mariana were out walking on Saturday, June 22nd, Anne Lister: *'Talked of Marianas inconsistency towards me. I believe she half repents it but thinks she has not lost me yet'.* The following day, Anne told Mariana about her offer of marriage to

Ann Walker. Anne Lister: *'she said how odd I was and seemed a little confounded at finding how nearly she had lost me and as if she could not quite well bear the thought of it.... Upstairs at 10, talk, then in bed and had a tolerable kiss and a grand grubble afterwards'.*

On Wednesday, June 26th, Mariana brought up the subject of Mr. Willoughby Crewe. Mr. Crewe was a cousin of Mariana's husband, Charles. He had two sons but was not married so I assume he was a widower. In the diaries, I have come across his name mentioned occasionally by Mariana. It appears that he had always been rather attentive to her, and it was quite possible that she saw him as a potential husband once Charles had died. Anne Lister: *'she said she was not happy. A relief to have told me. I smiled and said it was a good sign and she would be happier by and by. She said all I did was right, nobody so likely to make anyone happy as I was... ...she was uneasy both about me and Mr. Crewe. I joked and asked her tonight if she liked me nearly as much as him, " yes" ...bade her cheer up ....on her telling me this morning that she really cared for me, I said I should now try her regard before believing it. Perhaps she is sorry for what she has done for I give no hint at bringing things on again nor do I feel much inclined. Let her take Willoughby Crewe'.*

The following morning, Thursday, Anne Lister: *'I jumped to let in Mariana, who came and sat talking a few minutes. [Mariana] had had a bad night from indigestion pain, dreampt she saw Willoughby Crewe in a pond with his head in the mud, his heels sticking up and somebody had put his hat on them ...she said it was my behaving so well that vexed her. She had a letter from him this morning, very proper one, but plain what he feels at heart tho' never the smallest impropriety'.* That afternoon, Anne Lister: *'Talking till 4 about Willoughby Crewe and myself. It seems she did not know till now how much she cared for me and in fact all her unhappiness is that which she gives up, she must do wrong to one of us. Convinced her I had not been the one to change. It was evident she would gladly have all on again between us but said she did not think I should ever like her so well again. I answered that I would not say that but her regard for me would now require some proving and, when she pressed me rather hard, I said I did not believe she knew her own mind and that I should think it not right to take any advantage of her feeling at this moment. If she remained the same a year hence, it would be another thing, best to try the effect of absence'.* I think it was now pretty clear that Mariana wanted the option of living with Anne, at some point in the future, to be back on the table. The puzzle was why should Mariana have had such a complete change of mind? Well, Anne Lister was about to find out. Anne Lister: *'as long as William Lawton lived, she [Mariana] thought only of him. In fact, she hoped he would marry little Mariana and then she would not have wanted either Willoughby Crewe or me'.* Ooops! I think Mariana may well have let the cat out of the bag. William Lawton, who I am guessing may have been in his late teens, was to have been Charles Lawton's heir, so Mariana's comment, does suggest that his death impacted, in some way, on her own financial security.

On Friday evening, after dinner, Anne Lister: *'Mariana entered on the subject of our break off. Altogether excusing herself, not done from caprice but from a fear of our not suiting. She says my aunt thought she had behaved ill. Yes, said I but my aunt only echoes my own sentiments. Mariana said both my aunt and Charlotte Norcliffe had only heard my story. Begged her to tell her own. Mariana enlarged on all she used to suffer at the oddity of my appearance, my being so like a man. Then entered into and defended, the Blackstone edge business. It was over hearing one of the postboys saying I was a man in petticoats that set her wrong. I said not much but how astounded I had been to find myself second to William Lawton. Tis now quite evident how much she wanted to bring all on again but, tho' I am very kind, I always avoid this. She owned the other day that, if William had not died, she should not have cared so much to get me back. She has not got me yet'.* Just for information: the Blackstone Edge business occurred ten years previously and was then referred to as the 'three steps business', and, post boys, are men, not boys.

Saturday evening, after dinner, Anne Lister: *'Mariana is evidently anxious to know whether I will take her back or not but I avoid saying "yes" tho' I do not say "no". She says she likes Mr.Crewe next after me and, if I won't take her, she shall not hesitate to take him. I shall leave it to its fate and not bind myself to her in a hurry. The person who had not confidence enough to trust me was not fit for me, on which she kissed me and said I was right, and said she was very fond of me. Asked me if I loved her answered "yes" but tho' she has often called me 'my own' I have never once done the same to her'.*
It seemed that Mariana was becoming increasingly keen to re-establish the plan that, when Charles died, she would move into Shibden with Anne. However, given that it was only just over a year since Mariana had made it clear that she intended to *'live and die where she is'*, that being Lawton Hall, it was not surprising that Anne was not prepared to commit herself. I have added the condition, 'when Charles died' in Mariana's plan even though I haven't read this in Anne's diaries, because I think it can be assumed to be the case. I am certain, if Mariana had suggested they move in together immediately, Anne Lister would not only have jumped at the chance, she would have been doing back flips!

Now let us consider Mariana's situation. It appears from her letters to Anne that her relationship with her husband, Charles, had become rather acrimonious. I get the impression that Mariana did not believe that Charles had made any provision for her in his will. If William Lawton had lived, then on Charles' death, Mariana would have become financially dependent on him, and, given that she had been on good terms with him, she would probably have been financially secure. I understand that when Mariana first married, her husband purchased (I suspect with her dowry) an annuity, which would pay out £500 per year after his death. In today's money that equates to £60,000 a year, which would be nowhere near enough to provide Mariana with a house and servants. Believing her future finances to be looking increasingly precarious, Mariana wanted Anne as part of her back-up plan, and, Willoughby Crewe, although most probably a nice man, whose company and attention Mariana clearly enjoyed, was, I suspect, part of the same plan. In fairness to Mariana, she had married a man much older than herself, whom she did not love, in order to secure her own and her family's financial position, but, it would seem, her husband, Charles, had other ideas.

Although the William Lawton and Willoughby Crewe business had created an element of tension between Anne and Mariana, they continued with their plan to travel to London together and set off from Leamington on Tuesday July 2nd, accompanied by their servants, staying overnight at the Angel Inn in Oxford en route. They arrived at the Hawkins Hotel Dover Street apartments in London at 9.35 p.m. on Wednesday, July 3rd. For a week, Mariana and Anne spent their time shopping, and Anne also took the opportunity to call on some of her London friends. On Tuesday, July 9th, Charles Lawton arrived in London and, the following day, Charles and Mariana had a blazing row involving much *'shouting and bawling'*, which Anne found quite shocking. The night of Wednesday, July 10th, was Anne and Mariana's last night together. Anne Lister: *'Mariana and I had our parting kiss'… Mariana has evidently wanted to see if she could get me back. I have not committed myself'*. It appears that Mariana was continuing to press Anne to re-commit to the plan of their living together once Charles had died. That day the two women paid more social calls and did more shopping, with Mariana returning, in the early evening, to stay at the apartment taken by her husband, Charles, whilst Anne spent the evening as a guest of Lady Stuart at Richmond Park and stayed there overnight and most of the next day. Anne returned to her rooms on Dover Street at 8.35 p.m. on the evening of Friday, July 12th, to find a note from Mariana saying that she and Charles planned to leave London on Monday, July 15th, and that she would call on Anne the following morning. Anne and Mariana spent most of the weekend together doing more shopping and paying more calls, but each returning to their own apartments at night, and saying their final goodbyes on Sunday evening.

Anne Lister spent most of Monday and Tuesday with her London friends obtaining travel advice and more letters of introduction to friends of friends living on the continent. On the Tuesday she finished off her letter to her aunt and also hurriedly wrote a three page letter to Mariana, describing the letter in her journal: '.....*affectionate but not compromising myself. Said how much I thought of her. Twenty years a long spell and a strong one'*.

On Wednesday, July 17th, Anne, along with her two servants, Eugenie and Thomas, set off from London to Dover staying overnight at Wright's Hotel, ready to board the steam ship, the Ferret, the next morning, arriving in Calais, France, at one o'clock in the afternoon, to commence her travels on the continent. They travelled leisurely in Anne's carriage to Paris, alighting at the Hotel de la Terrasse, Rue de Rivoli at 2.55 p.m. on Thursday, July 25th.

On Tuesday, July 30th, Anne received two letters and a parcel containing a work case from Mariana, and one letter each from her aunt, and Samuel Washington, who was acting as her estate manager whilst she was on her travels. Anne Lister: *'Poor Mary writes to me very affectionately and I believe is heartily sorry for what has passed'*. Anne loved Paris and remained there for over three weeks, tracking down and visiting old friends, including Maria Barlow.

On Thursday, August 8th, Anne Lister unexpectedly received a letter from Elizabeth Sutherland, Ann Walker's sister. It appears that Elizabeth was concerned about her sister, who was clearly still very depressed. She wrote: *'I am aware from what my sister has repeatedly stated that there is no individual living by whom she would be so much influenced, and my only consolation is that thro' your kind interference and influence she may be directed to do that which will promote her happiness. As at present she is certainly unable to judge for herself, anxiously expecting to hear from you and where I can address you with a certainty of my letter reaching you. I am my dear Miss Lister, very sincerely yours'.*

Interestingly, the next morning, Anne Lister *'incurred a cross just before getting up, thinking of Miss Walker'*. She wrote a kind supportive reply to Elizabeth stating that she believed that Ann required specialised medical advice and suggesting that she be put under the care of Dr. Belcombe in York. Anne also included an address in Copenhagen to which letters could be sent and, at the end of her letter, added *'I cannot close my letter without again begging you to give my love to your sister with a repetition of the assurance that she may count upon my doing all I can for her and that her having too often prevented my doing the <u>best</u> I could, will never deter me from doing whatever may remain in my power. Tell her to consider what I have urged and not reject it too hastily. Removal and skilful medical treatment are, in the 1st instance, absolutely and immediately necessary. Half measures never answer and feeble ones but seldom'.*

Having decided to travel north to Denmark, Anne Lister agreed to allow the niece of a friend of hers, Sophie Ferall, who needed to get to Copenhagen, to travel with her. So, at half past three on the afternoon of Sunday, August 18th, Anne, Sophie, Thomas, and Eugenie departed from Paris, in Anne's carriage. They did not travel directly to Copenhagen as Anne had planned to do a lot of sightseeing on the way. The party arrived in Copenhagen on Wednesday, September 18th. Anne was met by Monsieur de Hageman, a relative of Vere Cameron (Hobart as was), who, with his wife Lady Harriet, would be Anne's hosts in Copenhagen. There were several letters waiting for Anne in Copenhagen, but surprisingly, none from Elizabeth Sutherland.

Anne had a brilliant time in Copenhagen. The de Hagemans introduced her to lots of people, most of whom she found interesting and entertaining, including the Queen of Denmark. So enjoyable was Anne's stay in Copenhagen, she decided to remain there until the spring of 1834, then continue her travels, possibly to Russia. However, on Tuesday, November 19th, a letter arrived for her that would bring her travel plans to an abrupt end. The letter was from her sister, Marian, with two pages from Dr. Kenny, both expressing their concern for Aunt Anne's health. Now, Aunt Anne had been considered frail for at least the previous six years so Anne was not sure how seriously she should take Dr. Kenny's view of her aunt being *'in an exceeding precarious state of health'*. However, fearful that she may never see her dear aunt alive again, Anne decided she had no choice but to make the now treacherous journey (with winter approaching) back to Shibden. In just less than a month later, she arrived at the port of Gravesend, England.

CHAPTER 6: REUNITED

Having arrived at Gravesend, at 2.10 a.m. on Sunday December 15th, 1833, and disembarked from the ship, Anne Lister's plan was to set off as soon as the carriage was released from the custom house at about 11 a.m. that morning, travel all day and arrive at the home of her friend Lady Stuart, in Richmond near London, staying there Sunday night. Set off the next morning, and sleep Monday night in her carriage en route to Leamington, Mariana's home in Warwickshire, arriving late Tuesday night. Off the following morning, sleeping Wednesday night in her carriage, arriving in Halifax on the evening of Thursday, December 19th. To set up this plan Anne had had a message sent to Lady Stuart in Richmond and wrote letters to Mariana and Aunt Anne. In her letter to Mariana, she commented: *'the surprise to my aunt will be very great'*. She ended her letter to Aunt Anne with: *'my dear aunt, believe me very anxiously impatient to see you, and very affectionately yours'*.

There are no further entries in Anne's journal until Saturday, December 21st. She has left pages blank probably with the intention of completing them at some later opportunity but for some reason she did not. Perhaps the journey had not gone quite as planned or maybe Anne decided it was not worth commenting on or maybe something else altogether. Anyway, by Saturday, December 21st, 1833, Anne was already back at Shibden, busy organising further improvements to the Hall. Aunt Anne was in very much better health than she had been led to expect, so much so, that Anne decided to go and stay with her friends, the Norcliffes', at Langton Hall, setting off early in her carriage on the morning of Tuesday 24th December.

On Friday 27th December, whilst at the Norcliffes', Anne received a letter from Ann Walker, who had returned from Scotland on Christmas day and had immediately called at Shibden Hall. Anne and Ann had missed each other by just one day! Ann Walker had assumed that Anne was in Copenhagen and had written a letter for her which she left with Aunt Anne who had forwarded it to Langton Hall. Ann Walker's letter included: *'Whilst you are in England, I hope you will consider my little cottage as your own. I have plenty of accommodation for your servants and 2 rooms entirely at your own disposal to keep your own hours and do exactly as you like'.* Although this was an invitation to Anne Lister to move in with her at Lidgate House, the bit about *'keep your own hours and do exactly as you like'* made it sound like Ann Walker was offering lodgings rather than expressing a desire for the two of them to live together as a couple. In her letter, Ann Walker explained that she had wanted to consult Dr. Belcombe on her passage through York from Scotland but had her Uncle Atkinson with her and so had been unable to do so. Also in her letter, she expressed her desire to meet Anne Lister in York and go to see Dr. Belcombe to get help with her anxiety and melancholy, saying she fully intended to follow his advice. Anne Lister was clearly concerned: *'Poor girl! I fear she is not much better....... How extraordinary, my actions and hers too, so close and unexpected on each other!'* Anne immediately wrote to Ann Walker: *'I am surprised and glad to find you once more at Lidgate. I see from the style of your letter that you are, at any rate, not less well than when I saw you last. This gives me great hope. Cheer up. You are quite sure I will do anything in the world I can for you, and, if you have at last courage to follow my advice, I am sanguine about your being restored to that can alone make life enjoyable, sound health. Again and again all I ask of you is to cheer up. Thank you for your so kind offer of house room. I shall see you as soon as I can. It was the so indifferent state of my aunt's health that caused my return to England. Get over to Shibden again, not earlier than 1 or later than 2 in the day, if you can, and give my love to my aunt, and tell her I have sent you to sit with her ten minutes from today, that I shall write to her again in a few days. It will be better for you not to think of meeting me in York. I will see you first and then plan for you as may seem best. Depend upon it. I can manage for you very willingly. Keep up your spirits as well as you possibly can. I will write to you again as soon as I have fixed the day for leaving here (which will probably be about a week hence) and then if you will have 2 beds for me, I will return by Binstall, see how you are and settle what to do. Write to me again immediately on the receipt of this letter. Give my love to your aunt and my own and believe me affectionately and faithfully yours. A Lister'.* This was a kind letter from Anne Lister, very much like other letters of hers I have read, offering support and advice. Concluding with 'affectionately' in addition to 'faithfully' showing her fondness for Ann Walker. Also, Anne had intelligently organised for Ann Walker to visit her aunt at Shibden every day and to immediately reply to her letter, instinctively knowing that the best thing for someone suffering with anxiety was a daily structure and activities to keep them occupied.

A few days later, on Monday 30th December, Anne Lister received a two-page letter from Ann in which she expressed her gratitude and said she: *'will count each day and hour until Anne arrived'.* Anne Lister immediately wrote her reply to Ann Walker in which she suggested that she keep her cousin, Miss Elizabeth Atkinson, with her until Saturday morning, then take her home saying that Anne Lister was coming that evening but not to mention to anyone about seeing Dr. Belcombe in York until the plan was fixed. In her letter, Anne Lister offered comfort and support, urging Ann to: *'cheer up now she had so much reason to hope all she could desire'.*

On Friday January 3rd, 1834, Anne Lister left Langton Hall at 3.20 p.m. and travelled in her carriage to York. She went to visit Dr. Belcombe to discuss Ann's treatment then spent the night at the Black Swan Inn, setting off to Shibden the following morning. Anne arrived at back at Shibden at 8 p.m., spent some time with her father, Marian, and Aunt Anne, and then at 9.10 p.m. walked, in the dark, to Lidgate House, with her servant, John Booth carrying her night things for her. As usual, the walk took 25 minutes, so at 9.35 p.m., on Saturday 4th January 1834, Anne Lister and Ann Walker were finally reunited. Ann Walker appeared pleased and excited to see Anne. They had dinner, Anne stayed the night and they talked till four o'clock in the morning. Anne Lister: *'She repented having left me. Longed to go after me to Copenhagen. Had had Mr. Ainsworth writing and offering again etc. etc. Once thought she ought to marry, lastly refused him. Her sister told him she was not able to judge for herself, but he did not mind that, so both Captain and Mrs. Sutherland got annoyed at him. I suppose saw through him. Miss Walker talked as if she would be glad to take me. Then, if I say anything decisive, she hesitates. I tell her it is all her money which is in the way. The fact is she is as she was before but was determined to get away from the Sutherlands and feels the want of me...... I touched her a little, but she soon said that exhausted her'*. This journal entry shows just how totally conflicted Anne Lister was about being reunited with Ann. She clearly had very strong feelings for Ann and so wanted for the two of them to live together, but she also knew that Ann's mental health issues could still make this an impossibility. I think the fact that Ann Walker was keen to get the medical help she needed for her anxiety and depression, gave Anne a slight glimmer of hope that they may have a future together. Either way, Anne Lister had promised to help Ann, and she was always as good as her word.

After breakfast on the Sunday morning, the two women talked again for most of the morning, making plans for Ann Walker to be in the care of Dr. Belcombe, probably for several months, and with the intention that she would stay in lodgings to be found for her in York. Anne Lister would continue to live at Shibden but would travel to York periodically to stay with her. Anne Lister then left for Shibden to read prayers to her aunt and the servants. About 4.30 p.m. she walked back to Lidgate to be with Ann. They dined about 6 p.m. then had tea and coffee. Anne

Lister described what happened that night: *'At twelve last night felt her on the amoroso. She thought me asleep, and I pretended to be so till my fondness seemed to awake me. Pressed and partly grubbled and held her near me but had on my drawers. In fact, I had as much a kiss as possible without absolute contact. Said I dared not be nearer, uncertain how she would make up her mind and afraid of attaching myself to her too much. Pressing and feeling her this morning. She let me look at her without seeming to care. In fact, I might do all I could and not do enough. I am older in these matters than I was twenty years ago. She seems bent on taking me, but yet it is uncertain, for she says nothing quite positive. Tis well my care for her will not kill me whether she says eventually yes or no'.* Anne Lister was clearly fearful that her heart may be broken yet again and was trying to prepare herself for the possibility that Ann would ultimately decide not to commit to her. So, what was this business regarding Anne Lister refusing to remove her underwear? For Anne, the ultimate sexual connection with another woman was in achieving simultaneous orgasm through vulva-on-vulva sex. She now believed that this should only happen when she and Ann Walker were in a committed relationship.

After breakfast on the Monday, Anne and Ann walked to Cliff Hill to visit old Miss Walker. Anne Lister then continued on to Shibden to deal with estate matters, returning to Lidgate House at about 5.30 p.m. to have dinner with Ann at 6 o'clock. Ann Walker's estate manager, Samuel Washington, called to discuss several matters, and stayed a long time, in fact *'a pothering long time'* according to Anne Lister. She again spent the night at Lidgate. Anne Lister: *'A little pressing and grubbling… but I am not for more of it than I can help'.* This was quite a turnaround for Anne Lister, who, in the past, had jumped at every opportunity for sex that presented itself.

The next day, Tuesday, January 7th, Anne and Ann walked to Shibden for Ann Walker to make a formal call on Marian and Aunt Anne. They then walked back to Cliff Hill for Ann Walker to visit with her own aunt, old Miss Walker. Wanting to complete her letter to Mariana, and get it in the post, Anne then walked back to Shibden. Her letter to Mariana was full of kindness and comfort. She did mention Ann Walker in the letter but also wrote: *'do not let your conclusions run on too rapidly. Now that I have taken my fate into my own hands, believe nothing till I tell it you myself'*. When Anne had completed the letter, she walked back to Lidgate House to have dinner with Ann and again stayed the night. A good 9 miles of walking for Anne Lister that day!

Anne Lister was still not sure that Ann would ever commit to them having a life together. However, she knew that getting Ann the medical help she needed for her mental health issues had to be their priority. Anne Lister spent the next five nights with Ann at Lidgate. There was grubbling every night except Saturday, when Ann Walker fell asleep and was snoring very loudly. Anne Lister had a couple of wobbles when she again lost confidence that Ann would commit to her but sorted herself out, as usual, with a bit of a rant in her journal. At times Ann Walker was feeling rather low, however, a session of touching, pressing, and grubbling, always seemed to perk them both up and all was ok again, although Anne Lister continued to refuse to remove her drawers.

On Monday 13th January 1834, the two women set off for York at 2.35 p.m. in Anne Lister's carriage arriving at the Black Swan Inn in York just before 9 p.m. Later that evening, Dr. Belcombe, (Steph), called on them for half an hour. Anne Lister: *'Miss Walker makes no complaints of fatigue and seems as well as usual. Saw Steph first and explained a little'*.

The following morning, Tuesday, they had another visit from Dr. Belcombe and then did some shopping in York. They then took a cab to view Heworth Grange, the lodgings where they had planned for Ann Walker to stay whilst under Dr. Becombe's care. Ann Walker was happy with the rooms and the people running the lodgings as well as the arrangements for meals to be provided. She then did some sketching while Anne made a few social calls. They had dinner at 6.15 p.m., then spent most of the evening talking and writing, interrupted for half an hour by a visit from Dr. Belcombe, and went to their bedroom at 11.25 p.m. for a *'long goodish grubbling'*.

The next day, Wednesday 15th January, after paying a social call on Dr. Belcome's wife, they travelled to Selby in their carriage, booked into the Hawdon's hotel and had a meal, which was unfortunately rather poor, and went to their bedroom at 9.25 p.m. for a *'very good grubble. She said better done at last than ever it was before'.*

The following day, Thursday, they continued their travels across Yorkshire, did some sight-seeing and arrived at the Cross Keys Inn in Hull at 6.30 p.m. Using Hull as a base they continued their sight-seeing in the area until Monday 20th January, then made their way back towards York staying overnight at the Tiger Inn, Beverley. The next day they went to Market Weighton for Anne Lister to show Ann Skelfler House where she had spent part of her childhood. They arrived back at the Black Swan Inn, in York, just before six o'clock on the Tuesday evening, having for the most part enjoyed each other's company, although Ann Walker was apt to snore which disturbed Anne's sleep, making her feel grumpy, although she kept this to herself. That evening Anne Lister took Ann's luggage to Heworth Grange, and, on her return, found that Isabella Norcliffe had booked into the Black Swan, so went to her room for a chat for fifteen minutes.

The next morning, Wednesday, 22nd January, Isabella had breakfast at the Black Swan Inn and Anne was able to introduce her to Ann Walker, although she did not write anything about the meeting in her journal. Anne Lister was aware that Ann's relatives, the Sutherlands, had questioned Ann's mental state regarding the making of important decisions, so when Dr. Belcombe called at the Black Swan, at midday, she asked him to assess her and give his medical opinion on the matter, which he did. He expressed the view that Ann was perfectly mentally competent to make decisions. Anne and Ann then went shopping for blankets, which they took to the lodgings at Heworth Grange and then had dinner. That night Anne Lister was due to visit with the Belcombes' at Petergate, so she left Ann at Heworth Grange with the servants that had been engaged to look after her saying she would return the next morning. I suspect that Anne Lister had decided that Ann being introduced to Isabella was enough for the time being and that being introduced to all the Belcombes might be a bit overwhelming. Dr. Belcombe had received a letter for Anne Lister, forwarded from Shibden, from Mariana, saying that she had been ill and assuring her that she was not in love with Willoughby Crewe. Anne Lister: *'Bids me take time and not fetter myself too soon nor too tightly'.*

Next morning, Thursday, January 23rd, Anne Lister returned to Heworth Grange to spend time with Ann. Anne Lister: *'sat talking and eating grapes, then both of us asleep on the sofa'.* Dr. Belcombe came to visit about 2 p.m. Anne described that after his visit: *'we went to her room, and she sat on my knee with her head on the bed and her feet on a chair while I grubbled her pretty well'.* After dinner, Anne Lister said goodbye to Ann, left Heworth Grange and walked back to the Black Swan Inn. The following day, she returned to Shibden leaving Ann in Dr. Belcombe's care.

CHAPTER 7: COMMITMENT

Anne Lister arrived back at Shibden at 10 pm on the night of Friday January 24th, 1834. She ate some roast mutton, had a cup of tea then went upstairs to her study at 11.40 p.m. On Saturday, she walked over to Cliff Hill to visit Ann Walker's aunt, old Miss Walker. Anne was there for 1½ hours endeavouring to explain to old Miss Walker why she had left Ann in York under Dr. Belcombe's care, although old Miss Walker: *'not seeming quite satisfied'*. Back home at Shibden, she wrote a letter to Ann which she described as a *'kind letter bidding her cheer up and think of nothing but the agreeable'*.

Two days later, Monday, January 27th, a letter from Ann Walker arrived at Shibden. I must say the postal service then was very impressive, particularly since the mail was transferred by carriage and horses, which probably could not go much faster than 9 mph. Anne Lister immediately wrote a three-page reply: *'kind enough and cheering and about business of one sort or another'*. On this day, Anne also sent a letter to Mariana which she described as a *'very kind cheering letter'*.

The following afternoon, Tuesday, Anne Lister went to Lidgate to gather together a number of items requested by Ann to be sent to York. She then made another visit to old Miss Walker to try again to convince her that it was right for Ann *'to remain quietly for some time under Dr. Belcombe's care'* although again she was not sure that she had succeeded. I have to say that woman does not give up easily!

The correspondence between the two women continued with Anne Lister writing again to Ann on Wednesday, January 29th, and on this occasion sending the letter with a parcel of things Ann had requested from Lidgate. When Ann Walker's reply arrived a few days later, Tuesday, February 4th, it was clear that she was really missing Anne: *'thinks it longer than all the time in Scotland'*. In fact, Ann Walker was so keen to see Anne that she expressed her desire to leave York to go over to Halifax for two or three days, either on the 8th or 10th February, if Anne would let her. Anne Lister replied to Ann immediately, very keen that she should visit. On the same day, she received a letter from Dr. Belcombe reporting on Ann Walker's progress which said: *'everything goes as well and as smoothly as I could desire'*. Apparently, Ann had twice spent two days with him and his family *'and all parties are mutually pleased'*. He wrote that Ann liked her lodgings, the people, and her servants. Dr. Belcombe also reported that a relative of Ann's, Mr. Charles Priestley, had called on him: *'to say he had received a letter from Mr. Edwards of Pyenest begging him to ask if Miss Walker was under my care and whereabouts, as she had left home without her servants, and he was in some perturbation about her .... I replied that Miss Walker was here in lodgings, highly respectable, chosen by herself and that her wish was to be more completely under my care than she had yet been and for this purpose had resolved to come to York. I am anxious it should be considered and known that she is entirely her own mistress in every way while here. Was Mr Edward's query a fetch (trick) to find out how she came here? If so it answered not. I am in good spirits about her. But however it is not good policy to dream much may be done. A little while and I shall gain more experience about her. Will write again shortly'*.

The next day, Wednesday, February 5th, Anne Lister walked over to Cliff Hill, to see Ann's aunt to put her in the picture regarding Ann's proposed visit. Anne Lister was worried that old Miss Walker would say the wrong thing to Ann and undo the progress she had made under Dr. Belcombe's care in York. She explained that if old Miss Walker showed her disapproval of Ann getting medical help from Dr. Belcombe, it would be unsettling for her and could be detrimental to her mental state. However, uncooperative as ever, old Miss Walker expressed the wish that her niece did not return to York. Anne gently explained that living alone at Lidgate was not good for Ann and cleverly suggested that old Miss Walker should have Ann come to live with her at Cliff Hill, to which old Miss Walker made no response. Anne wrote in her journal: *'Poor girl indeed! They are all against the only plan likely to answer. I shall be much talked of and blamed for all the good I have tried to do'.*

On Saturday, February 8th, Anne received another letter from Ann Walker saying she was impatient to see her and giving her some instructions to be passed on to her manservant at Lidgate. There had been some concern regarding the health of Mrs Atkinson, an aunt of Ann Walker's, who lived in Huddersfield, but who was now reportedly much better. Ann Walker planned to travel to Halifax on Monday 10th February. The following morning, Sunday, Anne Lister was woken at 8.15 a.m. by a knock at the door of Shibden Hall. A message had arrived from Ann Walker saying she was already at Lidgate and could Anne join her there for breakfast. Anne did not delay and set off at 8.50 a.m. arriving at Lidgate, twenty five minutes later. It turned out that on Saturday, Ann Walker had had a message that her Aunt Atkinson had taken a turn for the worse, so she had gone directly to Huddersfield to see her and arrived home at Lidgate at 11.00 p.m. that night. When Anne Lister arrived at Lidgate that morning she found Ann *'not quite dressed, looking and being considerably better than when I saw her last'.* Anne Lister described that they had breakfast and: *'then sat talking as if our being together was all but fixed'.* That morning, a messenger arrived at Lidgate to say that Ann's aunt Atkinson was much improved. The two women took a walk together, then Anne Lister headed back to Shibden to continue supervising the renovation work being done on the Hall, and Ann went to visit her aunt, old Miss Walker.

Well, Anne Lister arrived back at Lidgate at 10.05 p.m. to discover that she had been right to be worried by what old Miss Walker might have to say to Ann. A clearly agitated Ann had been on the receiving end of a lecture from her aunt. Ann

Walker made Anne promise: *'never to name her, to tell anything about her again to old Miss Walker in future'.* The two women spent that night together. Anne Lister: *'She was at first tired and sleepy but by and by roused up and during a long grubbling, said often we had never done it so well before. I was hot to washing tub wetness and tired before it was half over. We talked and never slept till five. Talk of taking her to Paris the end of March. Talked too of taking her to Langton'.*

The following morning, Monday, February 10th, after breakfast, Anne Lister headed back to Shibden whilst Ann set off to Huddersfield to collect her cousin and close friend Catherine Rawson, who had been staying with their aunt Atkinson, and bring her back to Lidgate. That afternoon, Anne Lister noted in her journal that Ann had not suggested going to a church service the previous day nor any reading of prayers. This is significant because previously, one of the symptoms of Ann's mental health problems had been religious despondency and the repeated reciting of prayers. Perhaps this was a sign that Ann's mental health was improving. However, Anne Lister also confided in her journal her continued insecurity about Ann's commitment to their future together. This fear, that their relationship would go pear-shaped again, was totally understandable given what had happened between them previously, however, it unfortunately had the effect of making Anne Lister super-sensitive to anything Ann said that could possibly be misconstrued as indicating a lack of commitment to their relationship. Anne Lister was back at Lidgate that evening joining Ann and Catherine for tea and coffee. She enjoyed Catherine's company and it seems that Catherine was very supportive of the medical help that she had organised for Ann. Catherine expressed her view that Ann Walker appeared much better but also reported that she had heard that there had been talk in Halifax, encouraged by some of her cousins, that she had gone crazy. This was presumably based on their discovering that Ann was under Dr. Belcombe's care. That night Anne and Ann talked. Ann Walker now knew of her relatives' poor attitude to her treatment for her mental health problems and knowing this made it clearer to her just how badly they would be likely to react if she and Anne moved in together. Knowing that Ann was now more aware of what she was going to have to deal with, Anne Lister, always keen to get things settled, asked her to decide if she was committed to their being together for life. Anne Lister: *'She agreed, and it was understood that she was to consider herself as having nobody to please and being under no authority but mine'.* This day, February 10th, 1834, was the day they considered themselves committed to each other and they celebrated their anniversary on the 10th of February on each year that followed. Together that night, Anne Lister: *'She said how very well and quietly I grubbled her'.*

The next morning, Tuesday, February 11th, Ann Walker took Catherine back to Huddersfield. Catherine had become fond of Anne Lister, probably through observing how kind she was to Ann, and told Anne, as she and Ann Walker departed, that she would drive over from Huddersfield to call on her at Shibden. Anne Lister then headed back to Shibden to spend some time with her aunt. She returned to Lidgate in the afternoon to help Ann Walker pack up the many things that she wanted to take back with her to her lodgings in York. Together again that night, Anne Lister wrote: *'Long capital grubbling so that little time for sleep. She is to give me a ring and I her one in token of our union as confirmed on Monday'.*

The following morning, Wednesday 12th February, Ann Walker had a meeting with her steward, Samuel Washington, to discuss Walker estate business, whilst Anne Lister loaded up Ann's carriage with all the things to go to York. They then went to Shibden for Ann Walker to spend some time with Anne's aunt. At 3.15 p.m. they set off for York, with Anne Lister travelling with Ann as far as the King's Head Inn, in Bradford. Anne Lister wrote: *'Affectionate to Miss Walker and told her I should not be long without seeing her'.* They agreed that Anne Lister would visit Ann again in York in about 10 days. Anne then left Ann Walker to continue on to York and she walked back to Shibden. That's a 13 mile walk! OMG that woman had some energy. That evening Anne Lister: *'I certainly feel fond of her now and if I was once really near her (no drawers on) and she was pretty well satisfied, I should be at ease. She has often said she wished to be near myself'*. So Ann Walker had most definitely got over her scruples and wanted to be fully connected with Anne, who, it seemed, was a little anxious as to whether Ann would be sexually satisfied with her efforts.

The next day, Thursday, 13th February, Anne Lister received a short letter from Ann confirming that she had arrived safely at Heworth Grange at 10.30 p.m. the previous night. I know I have already mentioned how impressed I am with the Royal Mail back then, but this is pretty amazing. Anne Lister immediately wrote a three page reply to Ann. Her journal, at this time, was very much taken up with details of the day to day running of the Shibden estate, negotiations regarding Shibden's coal reserves, as well as the Shibden Hall renovations and the extensive work she was having done on the grounds of the estate. Also, the collecting of items from Lidgate that Ann Walker wanted to be sent to her in York along with the communication of Ann's instructions to her servants at Lidgate and to her Walker estate manager, Samuel Washington. Add to that all of her correspondence and the writing up of her journal, it seems to me that Anne Lister was a very busy woman with the ability to pack a lot into each day without appearing to run out of energy. She also, of course, made a point of spending time each day with her, now quite frail, Aunt Anne.

The following Monday, February 17th, Anne Lister received a long letter, three pages close and all crossed, from Ann, which included another list of things for her to collect from Lidgate and take to York on her next visit. Anne Lister commented on the letter: *'says very little alluding to our union but yet enough to shew me she thinks of it as fixed'*. That evening, Anne Lister: *'Talked to my aunt tonight as if the thing was nearly done but I should know better in York, tacitly meaning that I should then make her give me a ring and bind herself by a decided promise'.*

Always very prompt in replying to Ann's letters, Anne Lister sent off a three page letter, small and close, at 8.40 a.m. the next morning, Tuesday, confirming that she would visit Ann in York for two or three days, but could not yet give the precise dates. That evening an affectionate letter arrived at Shibden from Mariana: *'Fred you are more frequently uppermost in my mind than you think. The pleasures of memory still visit me thro' a cloud, as to the future bears close upon its heels. If you had continued always near me, it would have been happier for me. Some of the sorrows of my heart too big to withstand the comfort of sympathy. Would not then have sown the seeds of a regard which I never dreampt of but which I now believe to be as you said of more than yesterday's growth. Mr. Crewe has sent a black profile shade of himself and a remarkably pretty drawing of the two boys, saying that he believed them to be the most welcome present he could send'.*

At about ten o'clock on the night of Friday, February 21st, a long letter arrived at Shibden from Ann Walker: *'do come quickly for I am getting dull, and I want you in a thousand ways'.* Anne Lister wrote *'she seems to have been pleased with my affectionate letter. If she will bind herself to that I can have confidence, I hope and think we shall get on together happily'.* Anne immediately wrote her reply and sent the letter off early the next morning confirming that she would be at Heworth Grange on the following Tuesday evening, February 25th, at about six o'clock, hopefully in time for dinner. In her letter Anne wrote: *'The blackberry sirup has done my cough a great deal of good. I take it the last thing at night. Is it the sweet juice, or the thought of her who gave it that has healing power? God bless you!'.* The warmth of their correspondence seemed to make Anne Lister feel more confident that Ann would fully commit to be her wife. So much so that she had several friendly chats with her sister Marian about the prospect of Ann moving in with them at Shibden. Anne commented in her journal that Marian: *'seems quite prepared for Miss Walker's being here, makes no objection, on the contrary, I could bring no one my father would like better'.*

On Sunday, February 23rd, Anne Lister wrote and sent her reply to Mariana's letter of February 18th. It was long letter full of comforting and supportive statements, including a reference to having taken Ann Walker to stay in York to be cared for by Dr. Belcombe, Mariana's brother.

A further exchange of letters took place between Anne Lister and Ann on Monday 24th February, then on the following morning at 10.40 a.m., Anne Lister set off in her carriage for York arriving at Heworth Grange at 4.45 p.m. Anne Lister: *'Miss Walker very pleased to see me but she looked not quite brilliant about the eye'.* It turned out that Ann Walker was having her period, the first one in twelve months, so I can imagine that she must have been feeling pretty rough, hence looking *'not quite brilliant about the eye'.* That night had meant to be their first time ever that they had sex *'without drawers on',* however, as Anne Lister wrote: *'tho not a thorough grubble, she having a napkin on, yet she had a thorough pressing and squeezing outside of it and we were both considerably excited'.*

The following evening, Wednesday, the two women took a Fly (a small carriage pulled by a single horse) to Dr Belcombe's house for dinner. Anne Lister took the opportunity to check with Dr. Belcombe if it would be ok for her to take Ann to call on the Norcliffes at Langton. He agreed. That night, Anne Lister: *'no drawers on, first time and first attempt to get really near her. Did not succeed very well but she seemed tolerably satisfied'.* Scissoring can take a bit of practice to perfect with a new partner. Also, I do feel I should clarify Anne's use of the word 'tolerable'. She uses this word to mean 'okay', 'quite good' or, as we might say, 'not bad'.

After breakfast the next morning, Thursday, February 27th, Anne Lister helped Ann with her French studies. At 12.50 p.m. they set off in Ann Walker's carriage to make a social call on the Norcliffes at Langton, arriving at 3.05 p.m. and were met by

Mrs. Norcliffe and Charlotte Norcliffe, they being the only ones at home. Just before they arrived, Ann Walker put a gold wedding ring on the third finger of Anne's left hand as a *'token of our union'*. Ann Walker had felt unwell before arriving at Langton which Anne thought was due to her being nervous of meeting the Norcliffes. However, Mrs. Norcliffe and Charlotte were very civil to Ann, and she relaxed, felt better and *'she seemed much pleased with her visit'*. That night, Anne Lister wrote: *'Tolerably near her last night. She said not quite as well as last night, but I think we shall do in time. She seems very fond of me. Is very proper during the day but very sufficiently on the amoroso at night that I am really or soon shall be satisfied with her and I really hope we shall get on very well together'.*

The next two days, Friday and Saturday were taken up with long leisurely walks, visits to Dr. Becombe, and on Saturday night they *'sat up eating oranges'*. On Sunday morning a message arrived informing them that Ann Walker's aunt, Mrs. Atkinson had died. They cancelled their plan to make social calls, read prayers aloud and wrote a number of letters as the situation required. About Sunday night, Anne Lister wrote: *'Two goodish ones last night. (She) said I had never felt her so well before'.*

The following day, Monday, March 3rd, Anne Lister travelled back to Shibden in her carriage with her two servants. Just as she was leaving, Dr. Belcombe called: *'fearing his patient might be dull due to my leaving her'.* In actual fact, Ann Walker had expressed a wish that nobody call that day. Anne arrived back at Shibden at 7.40 p.m.

Next morning, Tuesday, March 4th, before breakfast, Anne Lister wrote a long letter to Ann taking care not to be overly affectionate on account of Mrs. Bagnold, the post mistress in Halifax, having developed the habit of opening and reading the mail. Anne wrote: *'Said that as I wrote for the eye of Mrs. Bagnold more than ordinary caution was required. Miss Walker had begged me not to write anything particular, not to get ourselves laughed at. I be-*

lieve she is fond of me, and, however unreserved and on the amoroso at night in bed, no allusion to these matters ever escapes her in the day. In fact, she is then really modest and nicely particular enough'. Anne Lister then walked to Lidgate to collect some more things that Ann wanted sending to her at Heworth Grange. She then called on Ann Walker's aunt, old Miss Walker, at Cliff Hill who appeared to still be annoyed that Ann was remaining in York and declared that she would write and tell her to come home. Anne Lister: *'oh! oh! thought I, but said nothing'.* Anne showed a huge amount of patience with old Miss Walker, as she did with most people. Personally, I think I would have kept my distance from the grumpy so and so.

The following day, Wednesday, March 5th, Anne Lister wrote a four page letter to Ann and sent it with a box containing a crape bonnet, worsteds, velvet brush and some biscuits. The next day, Thursday, a letter arrived from Ann Walker. Pleased with the letter, Anne Lister wrote: *'I think all will go well'.* Anne replied to Ann Walker's letter and sent it off to the post at 8.30 p.m. that evening.

On the evening of Friday, March 7th, a servant brought a parcel and a letter to Shibden from Samuel Washington, Ann Walker's estate manager, for Anne Lister to send on to Ann. The following day, Saturday, Anne Lister wrote a letter to Ann and sent her servant, Thomas, off to the post with the letter and the parcel from Samuel Washington. Later that same day a three page letter arrived at Shibden from Ann Walker. Be aware that their letters were crossing in the post, so this letter of Ann's was a reply to Anne Lister's letter sent on Thursday evening, with the box containing the bonnet, biscuits etc. Ann Walker had been well pleased with the bonnet that Anne had sent her and wrote: *'You quite astonish me with your expedience in the execution of all my wants and wishes'.* However, she then went on to write: *'I am thinking about Lidgate and will say more when I write next. Will it be wise to irritate or brave public opinion further just now? For the same reason, ought or can I accept your kind proposition about Shib-*

den?' Oh dear, just when Anne Lister was starting to believe that their future together was confirmed, her hopes are once again dashed by Ann's fear of what people might say about them. Anne Lister wrote in her journal: *'Does she mean to make a fool of me after all... now declines taking the straight course of shewing our union or, at least, compact, to the world. Public opinion has been too much or too little braved and whatever force there is against her coming here (Shibden) is the same against my going there (Lidgate House). I don't like all this. I distrust her and feel as if the thing would again, and this time forever, go off between us. I shall not be played with'.* Ann Walker's letter continued: *'I long for the sketch of the Chimney piece, but don't pay the carriage. Why did you do it for the box? I suspect the affront was Thomas's not yours'.* The key word in the statement was *'affront'.* So, Anne Lister had paid the postage on the parcel rather than leave it for Ann to pay when the parcel was delivered, and this appeared to have caused offence. Anne Lister: *'Affront! Does this seem as if she really thought us united in heart and purse'.* It does seem that, from time to time, Ann Walker could say exactly the wrong thing. In her letter, she also expressed the view that they should not go on a long journey whilst Anne Lister's aunt was still alive: *'there are plenty of places nearer home, unseen and which would be disgraceful not to visit'.* Anne Lister thought: *'this would be well enough if I did not shrewdly suspect she wishes to avoid going abroad or doing anything that would too decidedly be speak our compact'.* It was very much Anne Lister's dream to live at Shibden Hall with her wife *'at her elbow'.* She wanted Ann to move into Shibden with her and let out Lidgate. Although Ann Walker was clearly concerned with what Halifax society might think of her moving into Shibden Hall, I also think she was, understandably, very attached to her home, and it would have been a wrench for her to give it up. Although very sensitive to Ann Walker's needs, I suspect that Anne did not quite realise just what a wrench it would be for her to leave the Walker estate.

The following evening, Sunday, March 9th, Anne Lister confided in her aunt: *'told her Miss Walker's hesitation about letting Lidgate and coming here and my feeling about it, saying it was touch and go with me. "Yes" answered my aunt, "I should not be surprised if it is all off". "No, no" said I. "I don't quite know that".*

Anne Lister started to compose her reply to Ann Walker on Tuesday March 11th: *'writing little paragraph in answer to Miss Walker's indecision about Lidgate'.* That day, Anne also received a long letter from Mariana, who had sent the letter care of her brother, Dr. Belcombe, thinking Anne was still in York with Ann Walker. It was beginning to dawn on Mariana that Anne's re-established relationship with Ann Walker had become serious and she was starting to worry. In her letter, Mariana asked after Ann Walker, hoping she was better. She was also asking about the nature of Ann Walker's health problem and whether Anne and Ann had made any commitment to each other. Mariana: *'Has anything passed in reference to the occurrences of last spring, and have you any reason to believe an answer on the same subject, if again requested, would be different from that which you received last year? Freddy, since you have been in York, my thoughts have perpetually full of you. I do love you dearly and fondly come what may. My heart is not unfaithful and still as formerly and forever my joys by yours are known'.*

The following day, Wednesday, March 12th, Anne Lister continued writing her letter to Ann although it still was not finished. It was not unusual for Anne's writing of a letter to be spread over several days, sometimes even longer, but whilst Ann Walker had been staying at Heworth Grange in York, Anne had been in the habit of writing and sending her reply the same day she received a letter. However, after receiving the letter which had upset her on Saturday, Anne had not sent her reply. The next morning, Thursday, a long letter arrived from Ann Walker including the line: *'I am still in the mire about Lidgate'.* Anne Lister: *'poor girl! I am getting over my annoyance. She wants guiding and I must begin as I mean to go on or give her up at once'.* Anne Lister had wisely delayed writing back to Ann Walker until her 'annoyance' had subsided. When she did reply, she sought to ease the pressure that she recognised Ann was experiencing. Anne Lister's letter included the following: *'I impatiently waited your answer about Lidgate. It is couched in less than one line "I am still in the mire about Lidgate". Indecision must press on you no more. Had I been at your elbow, you would have been wiser – it cannot be just yet, therefore leave the matter in status quo for the present and advertise house and land together next year'.*

On Saturday 15th March, a letter arrived at Shibden from Ann Walker. It contained details of money she had either given or loaned to certain relatives and she wanted Anne to advise her who she should write to and what she should say in the letters. In her letter, Ann also said that she was quite satisfied to let Lidgate and land together next spring, and, in reference to the onyx ring that Anne had given her as a wedding ring, she reassuringly said that it was *'only off her finger at night and to wash hands'*. Ann Walker asked Anne to visit her at the end of the month. Anne Lister: *'The tone of her letter, manner of writing affectionate and proper enough as if she really did mean to submit, so said I was quite satisfied'*. Just a note about Anne's use of the word *'submit'*. I have read in another part of the diaries where Anne refers to herself as *'submitting'* to Isabella and also to Mrs Norcliffe, the context suggesting that she was letting them have their own way or she was doing whatever they wanted. Therefore, I am sure Anne thought that a committed relationship with Ann Walker would involve them both *'submitting'* to each other. In fact, in Anne Lister's reply to Ann she wrote: *'I would do anything in the world to give you pleasure'*.

For the next two weeks the two women continued their correspondence with Anne Lister sending parcels to Ann with items from Lidgate she had requested as well as biscuits baked by one of Ann's servants at Lidgate. On Saturday, March 29th, Anne Lister left Shibden at 12.25 p.m. and travelled in her carriage to Heworth Grange arriving at 5.18 p.m. Anne Lister: *'Miss Walker very glad to see me'*. They had dinner, then tea and coffee, and as usual, talked a great deal. That night, Anne Lister: *'Three kisses, better to her than to me'.* So multiple orgasms for Ann Walker, good for her! It's great to see her scruples have disappeared.

Anne and Ann had previously promised themselves to each other, exchanged rings as a token of their union, and now the final stage of their commitment was to take the sacrament together in church. The next day, Sunday, March 30th, at 10.35 a.m., they arrived at Holy Trinity Church, on Goodramgate, in York. Anne Lister: *'Miss Walker and I and Thomas* (Anne's servant) *staid the sacrament, almost all the congregation staid and, tho' the church too small to hold many, the service took 40 minutes. The first time I ever joined Miss Walker in my prayers. I had prayed that our union might be happy'.* Holy Trinity Church in York, where Anne and Ann took the sacrament together, is a very special place. Just before Christmas 2019, my wife and I decided to take a short break in York specifically to visit this little church. I booked, what turned out to be, a very plush apartment, for a two-night stay, about a 25 minute walk from York city centre. It was going dark as we arrived, so we quickly unpacked, had a cup of tea, then set off to walk to the Christmas market near the Shambles. If you are not familiar with the Shambles in York, Google it, it's amazing. The road we walked along into the city centre was lined with large Victorian houses each with Christmas trees lit up in their bay windows. It was a beautiful clear night, very cold. It was a lovely walk. From the Christmas market we made our way to York Minster, our aim being to find the narrow road, lined on one side by a high wall, shown in the final scene in the final episode of season 1 of the Gentleman Jack tv show. In this scene, Anne and Ann are walking towards the Minster discussing what to do next having just taken the sacrament together. I had committed to memory the particular view of the Minster shown in that final scene to help us with our search. We walked around the outside of the Minster, and, after a few minutes, we found that view and there, opposite, was the road we were looking for. We very excitedly walked the length of this little narrow road and then turned back in the direction of the Minster re-enacting, word-for-word, that final scene from 'Gentleman Jack' (fortunately there was no one else around). The following morning, we set off to find Holy Trinity Church. The scene in episode 8 of the first season of 'Gentleman Jack' showing Anne and Ann taking the sacrament was filmed in this very church, (very clever of HBO and the BBC). Holy Trinity is not at the end of the narrow road, that we had found the evening before, as suggested in the tv show. Holy Trinity is on Goodramgate and is accessed through a gate between two shops. Excitedly we crossed the road to get to the gate. Gutted! The gate was locked. A notice on the gate said the church was shut all day and there was no indication when it would next be open. Visiting this church was the main reason for our York trip so not surprisingly it took me a few moments to get over the disappointment. Pulling myself together, I decided that we would try again in the morning before having to set off home. I got out my little map of York and we set off down Petergate to try to find the houses where the Belcombes lived and also where the Norcliffes had a property. We found number 9 Petergate which I think belonged to one of these two families. We then set off to find the Manor School that Anne Lister attended. We discovered a collection of beautiful old buildings in Exhibition Square. One of these buildings had housed the school and I could picture a 14 year old Anne Lister (looking remarkably like a young Suranne Jones) chatting up some of the other girls in the courtyard. Next morning with some apprehension we walked back to Goodramgate. Thankfully, the gate to the church was open. The blue plaque commemorating Anne and Ann's marriage was just inside the gate. How wonderful to see a gay marriage being so visibly recognised. We followed in Anne and Ann's footsteps into the little church. This church is over 500 years old. It is stunning with its cute boxed pews and delightful altar, behind which is a beautiful stained glass window that was fitted in 1470 A.D. This church would be a joy to visit even without the Anne Lister-Ann Walker connection, but sensing the presence of these two inspiring women, I have to admit, I felt very emotional. For those of you who have watched 'Gentleman Jack', my wife and I sat in the very pew where Suranne Jones and Sophie Rundle sat for the sacrament scene, how cool is that!

Taking the sacrament together at Holy Trinity was Anne and Ann's way of confirming their union in the eyes of God. After the ceremony they took a walk finishing at the Monk-bar church at 2.30 p.m. to listen to the sermon there. Although the taking of the sacrament was an incredibly important part of confirming their commitment to each other, it was not this date, March 30th, that Ann and Anne considered to be the anniversary of their union. For them, their anniversary was February 10th, when they made their promise to each other.

CHAPTER 8: A TASTE OF MARRIED LIFE

Having made a promise to each other, exchanged rings and taken the sacrament together on Sunday March 30th, 1834, Anne Lister and Ann Walker considered themselves to be a married couple. However, they could only actually be together for relatively short periods, whilst Ann remained under Dr. Belcombe's care in York, which they expected would continue for a few more months.

Anne Lister, having arrived at Heworth Grange on Saturday, March 29th, had planned to return to Shibden on Sunday April 6th, so for this visit, at least, they would have had eight days together. Monday and Tuesday, April 1st and 2nd, were quiet days, with Ann Walker seeing Dr. Belcombe and also having a drawing lesson from her drawing master, Mr. Brown. However, on the Wednesday, the two women set off in their carriage, heading north to visit Duncombe Park and Crayke Castle, at Ann Walker's suggestion. They stayed overnight at an inn, then visited Rievaulx Abbey the following day. There are so many beautiful places to visit in Yorkshire. They then continued on their travels to Langton Hall to stay overnight with the Norcliffes before returning to Heworth Grange on the evening of Friday April 4th.

Ann Walker's estate manager, Samuel Washington, had come to York to meet with her to discuss Walker estate business. He arrived at Heworth Grange for their meeting at 7.00 a.m. on Saturday morning. The meeting lasted two hours. I had mistakenly got the impression, from various sources, that Ann Walker had a lot of time on her hands because she did not work. From my own transcribing of Anne Lister's diaries, I have found that not only did Ann Walker have a major role in the running of the

Walker estate, it seems she did the job very effectively. Ann and Anne attended St. Saviours Gate Church at 10.40 a.m. the next day for the Sunday service. They had an early dinner at 3.00 p.m. and then at 4.25 p.m. Anne Lister set off back to Shibden in her carriage, arriving at 9.45 p.m. in time to spend half an hour with Aunt Anne.

Although apart, Anne and Ann were very much in each other's thoughts. Before breakfast the next morning, Monday April 7th, Anne Lister wrote a three page letter, with the first page crossed, to Ann, who similarly must have written to Anne Lister that same morning as a letter arrived at Shibden from her the very next day. That evening, a letter arrived at Shibden from Mariana who was clearly distraught. From what was a long letter, Mariana: '*I have never loved any but you, this you know. A wife for eighteen years, with nothing but the name, your image alone awakened feelings for which otherwise I had no use. I love you dearly and fondly and can neither understand nor account for the influence which circumstances, in spite of inclination, have had over me....... I am sick, I am sorry my Fred, I could be miserable, love me, think of me, in pity do both. Yes, you have indeed been my friend, a tried a steady one and you are still the kindly prop which supports me under sorrows which even time has not taught me to bear...... I can say no more than that I am still yours, affectionately and entirely, Mariana*'. Anne Lister: '*What a letter!*' Poor Mariana had become very distressed on realising that Anne was committed to her relationship with Ann Walker.

The next day, Wednesday, Anne Lister was incredibly busy with Shibden estate business. After dinner in the evening she wrote to Ann, sending the letter to the post office at 9 p.m. The two women had already decided that Anne Lister's next visit to York was to be on Tuesday April 15th. The plan was that Anne should set off very early from Shibden on the Tuesday morning, travel to York, collect Ann and then travel back to Shibden, the same day, for Ann's first sleepover there, assuming of course that Dr. Belcombe gave his permission. Ann Walker's next letter arrived at Shibden on Friday, April 11th, to which Anne immediately replied with encouraging words designed to allay her anxiety about her visit to Shibden: *'you will see from the moment you enter the house that not one soul in it considers you a stranger. The feel of home will soon cling closely round you and I have no doubt of your interests and happiness growing up quickly together... I know not what I said to make you answer "Don't talk about being grateful" .... but I am always grateful to everyone who does me kindness or service and to you who will do me the greatest of both in making me happy'.*

Ann Walker's next letter arrived at Shibden on Sunday 13th April. She wanted Anne to go to her at Heworth Grange the next day rather than wait till Tuesday as they had planned. Thinking about this request, Anne Lister: *'My first impulse was to go tomorrow .... but after thinking about all the afternoon, saw it would be best to keep to Tuesday now it had been fixed. She would understand all this on coming here or seeing me. Very impatient to see her, the time will seem an age'.* Clearly Ann and Anne had now become so close that they were both finding it difficult to be apart from one another.

Having given herself a few days to think about that letter from Mariana, on April 13th, Anne Lister needed to put pen to paper and construct her reply before heading back to York. Previously whenever Mariana had become upset, regardless of the reason, Anne always sought to make her feel better, so not surprisingly her letter to Mariana was full of concern and comfort: *'I shall still watch over your happiness with more affectionate solicitude than you think. The heart that has truly loved never forgets and you will always find me a friend whose sincerity you may trust. Regret not the past. Be thankful and be assured that heaven has ordered all things well. I hope you will find me a great and safe and lasting comfort'.* However, in response to Mariana's hope that they would see each other that summer, Anne knew her reply had to be non-committal because, having married Ann Walker, she was no longer a free agent: *'I will see you in the summer if I can, but I dare not count upon it for I can't be quite so much under my own control as formally. My days of solitude are surely drawing to a close'.* Also, in her letter to Mariana, Anne commented on how supportive her sister had been regarding her relationship with Ann Walker: *'Marian has really taken me by surprise. I had certainly no right to calculate upon her being half so kindly accommodating'.*

On Tuesday April 15th Anne Lister set off in her carriage at 6.17 a.m. and arrived in York at 10.53 a.m. Anne and Ann left Heworth Grange together at 2.20 p.m. and travelled to Shibden in Ann Walker's carriage, arriving at Shibden at 7.55 p.m. Anne Lister: *'Miss Walker a little nervous in coming along but soon got over it on arriving. 10 minutes with my father and Marian. Coffee in the drawing room, cozy and comfortable. Congratulated her on our arrival at Shibden, the only home I hope we should both have by and by. Marian came and sat with us. ¼ hour with my aunt, who was really glad to welcome us but seemed very suffering and poorly. Came upstairs at 10.15 p.m. Siding and settling ourselves'.*

Ann Walker was to stay at Shibden with Anne and her family for very nearly two weeks before returning to her lodgings in York. This was a big step for them both, but particularly for Ann Walker. Staying at Shibden when her own home was only two miles away would make it clear to her relatives that she was now with Anne Lister.

Whilst probably not knowing the intimate details, Anne Lister's family were totally accepting of her relationships with women. In fact, Anne's aunt, father, and sister all seemed quite delighted to welcome Ann Walker into the family. The following morning, Wednesday April 16th, Ann and Anne walked to Cliff Hill to visit old Miss Walker, who Anne Lister now sometimes refers to as 'Miss Walker Senior'. *'Miss Walker senior received us very graciously, <u>for her</u>'.* It was incredibly courageous of Ann Walker to commit her future to Anne Lister given the opposition of her relatives and the likely hostility of Halifax society. She was so brave, bless her. That evening after dinner, the two women played four games of backgammon, sat with Aunt Anne for a little while, then together with Marian, looked over Watson's History of Halifax.

Thursday morning, April 17th, Anne Lister: *'One good one last night and both asleep directly. Twenty minutes dalliance in the midst of dressing'.* That evening a letter arrived for Ann Walker from her sister, Elizabeth, in Scotland. Anne Lister: *'She had foolish letter from Mrs. Sutherland enclosing one from Sir Alexander Makenzie, to be returned unopened with short decided tho' coolly civil copy of answer I wrote for Miss Walker'.* Alexander Makenzie, a relative of Captain Sutherland had, some years previously, asked Ann Walker to marry him, but she had sensibly refused, him being of dodgy character. Also, that day, Anne Lister received a short letter from Mariana*: 'dated the 15th, written probably immediately on the receipt of my last of the 13th inst. as follows: "dearest Fred, I have received your letter. The die is cast, and Mary must abide by the throw. You at least will be happy, and this will teach her to be so, who has nothing to hope for herself, ever yours Mariana".* Anne Lister: *'Miss Walker, being at my elbow, put the letter into her hands, but she has no idea of the real state of our former connection, wondered, but I talked all off as well as I could and she thinks it is merely about as Catherine Rawson will feel about her, Miss Walker, but luckily our talk turned chiefly of Mrs. Sutherland's folly'.* Clearly Anne Lister had decided that it was better that Ann did not know the intimate nature of her past relationship with Mariana. Whilst asleep together that night, Anne Lister: *'She awoke me by a scream in the night for I was biting her lip through. She got up and put spirits of wine. Great laughter'.*

Next morning, Friday April 18th, Anne Lister walked down the old bank into Halifax to attend to some estate business whilst Ann wrote a reply to her sister. Anne Lister had had the table in the library passage moved into her study for Ann so that when they were both writing they could sit with each other. At 3.00 p.m. they walked to Lidgate. It took them 45 minutes, much longer than Anne Lister's usual 25 minutes so I suppose it was more of a stroll. I have noticed that when Anne Lister was with Ann, she made sure they took plenty of walks, I suspect she thought this would be good for Ann's well-being. The two women spent an hour and quarter at Lidgate then called at Cliff Hill to visit with old Miss Walker, who received them *'most graciously'*. I wonder if she was beginning to come round. That evening, back at Shibden, they had dinner at 6.30 p.m. then played backgammon. Ann Walker was an excellent player of backgammon and Anne Lister's wins came infrequently.

Anne Lister had made comments in her journal regarding her aunt's frail health since the mid-eighteen twenties. In the previous couple of years, she wrote of the pain her aunt suffered with ulcers on one of her legs. More recently however, she had also been expressing concern about the health of her father, who had been experiencing bouts of biliousness. At this time, April 1834, brother and sister were aged 82 and 69 respectively. On the afternoon of Saturday, April 19th, Dr. Kenny called to see Aunt Anne, and suggested she may live only another 48 hours. Anne Lister was very close to her aunt so obviously this prognosis would have been very distressing for her.

Although Dr. Kenny was Aunt Anne's usual doctor, the next day, Sunday, Anne Lister arranged for a different doctor, Mr. Sunderland, to see her aunt. Mr. Sunderland's assessment of Aunt Anne was very different. Anne Lister: *'the sore on my aunt's leg enlarged but not looking at all alarming and no symptoms to make one uncomfortable. There was certainly no gangrenous appearance at present and my aunt's pulse was very fair and he saw no symptoms of alarm greater than ordinary, in fact, my aunt had kept up her strength very well'*. That afternoon, Anne and Ann went to St. Matthew's church in Lightcliffe for the Sunday service. This was the first time that they had attended this church, together. Ann Walker was involved with the Sunday School at St. Matthews, and, after the service, she was required to test the thirty Sunday School boys on their catechism. That evening Ann Walker was poorly having started her period. Anne Lister: *'Miss Walker not quite well. Her cousin came before prayers this morning the first time, except the little bit two months ago, this twelve month or more'.*

Ann Walker experienced irregular periods, and, when she was having her period, she suffered particularly badly for the first couple of days. She did not venture out on Monday and Tuesday, spending most of the time sat on the sofa. Anne Lister was in the middle of organising significant structural changes to Shibden Hall, referred to as the *'castle plan'* and on the Monday had a meeting with her architect. In the evening, she completed her letter to Mariana that she had started on Saturday. Anne Lister: *'Told Miss Walker she might read it. She did and approved exceedingly'*. A section of Anne Lister's letter to Mariana: *'Your few hurried lines, my dearest Mary, of the 15th, and which I received on Thursday evening, must surely have been written at the moment of your receiving my last letter. I need not say how much I have thought of you. You are quite aware that my own happiness must be imperfect, till I am better assured of yours. But I still hope, and still persuade myself, that you will, by and by, see things thro' a brighter medium, and that you will live to acknowledge I have been a juster steward than you think, both for your comfort and my own. I am quite sure you have no reason to disapprove what I have done. It is what you yourself have repeatedly advised and what you must have seen I was determined to do from the moment you had taken the only possible means of convincing me that your advice was sincere. God grant my dearest Mary, that we have both been right'.*

By the evening of Tuesday April 22nd, Ann Walker was feeling much better. Anne Lister: *'All the evening till nine and a half, playing with and handling her on the sofa and lastly on the bed where she came and lay down. She so well inclined for it all as to lead me on…. one good kiss and both fell asleep. One good kiss also this morning'.*

Now that she was back in action, Ann Walker wanted to make calls on some of her friends and relatives. At 11 o'clock, Wednesday, April 23rd, the two women set off in their carriage so that Ann Walker could call on Mrs. Ingrams, Mrs. Winfield and then Mr. Atkinson. As I have already mentioned, the protocol at the time was to only call on a person at their home if you had previously been formally introduced to them at some event for example at a ball or concert. Since Anne Lister had not previously been introduced to these individuals, she remained in the carriage reading and napping, whilst Ann Walker made the visits. They then both called together on Mrs. Stansfield Rawson and her daughters, then Mr. Wilkinson and his daughters.

On the morning of Thursday April 24th, Anne Lister walked with Ann to Lidgate and left her there to get on with Walker estate business. Anne Lister returned to Shibden via the hut where she had an hour's sleep in the rustic chair. That afternoon she was very busy sorting accounts and paying bills. In the meantime, Ann Walker walked from Lidgate to Cliff Hill to visit with her aunt. At 4.20 p.m Anne Lister walked to Cliff Hill to collect Ann, stayed for a little while to see old Miss Walker, then they walked back to Shibden arriving at 6.20 p.m. and had dinner at 6.50 p.m. I have noticed that Ann Walker liked to have a nap at some point during the day, and, if she did not get her nap, could be a bit grumpy. The ever patient Anne Lister: *'She would have been crossish tonight with any but me, but I left her and let her lie down and she soon followed me to my study and began writing. Steph was right, I shall have a good deal of trouble with her, but I shall perhaps get her right in time.'*

The routine of making social calls, sorting estate business, sitting with Aunt Anne, and playing backgammon continued on Friday and Saturday, with prayers and church on Sunday. At 2.05 p.m. on Monday 28th April, the two women set off in their carriage for York, arriving at Heworth Grange at 7.30 p.m. having had nearly two weeks of happy married life at each other's elbow at Shibden.

CHAPTER 9: BACK TO HEWORTH GRANGE

On Tuesday, April 29th, 1834, Anne Lister returned to Shibden leaving Ann in Dr. Belcombe's care at Heworth Grange. Anne Lister: *'Miss Walker evidently nervous at my going tho' she said little about it. She certainly cares for me more and seemed much pleased at finding I had ordered a seal to be ready by her birthday and when I said "you see I thought of you", she answered "yes, when do you not think of me." I think we shall get on very well together'.* Anne Lister set off from Heworth Grange at 4.35 p.m. and arrived back at Shibden at 10.55 p.m. to find everybody had gone to bed. The journey had taken longer than usual because Anne had decided to take a different route and go on a new road, which turned out to have a poor surface so the carriage could only travel at walking pace.

Before breakfast the next morning, Wednesday, April 30th, Anne Lister wrote to Ann: *'Beginning how are you my love and ending ever dearest, faithfully and affectionately yours'.* I am aware, from a diary of Ann Walker's discovered in Oct/Nov 2020, that her pet name for Anne Lister was *'dearest'*.

The following day, Thursday, May 1st, a 2½ page letter arrived at Shibden from Ann Walker. Anne Lister wrote that Ann *'had thought of me all Tuesday night and all Wednesday morning'.* For most of this day, Anne Lister was working with the men on the estate planting laurel, yews, lavender etc. That evening, as usual, she went to sit with Aunt Anne and suggested that her aunt might like to go and see the planting that had been taking place. Sadly, this suggestion distressed her aunt. Anne Lister: *'She said she should never go out again till she was carried out another way (meaning to her funeral) and burst into tears. I never saw her, my aunt, so low on this subject before'.* Although Aunt Anne's poor health had been a cause of concern for many years, she always seemed to carry on regardless, so seeing her in tears would have been very upsetting for Anne.

The following morning, Friday, May 2nd, another letter arrived at Shibden from Ann Walker. The first two pages were for Anne Lister, but the third page was a set of instructions for her steward, Samuel Washington, one of which was to send Sarah, one of her servants at Lidgate, to Heworth Grange, as her servant there was ill in bed. After dinner that evening, Anne Lister wrote a kind letter in reply to Ann's letter.

And so things continued, with the two women writing to each other every day or every other day. In their correspondence they were planning a tour of a few places in the north of Yorkshire and in County Durham to give Ann Walker the opportunity to practice her sketching. Anne Lister was also very keen to be at Heworth Grange in time for Ann's birthday on May 20th but was concerned that the poor state of her aunt's health may prevent this. In one of her letters to Ann, Anne Lister wrote: *'but surely I shall be at your elbow to wish you your health and many happy returns of that day. I shall be glad for that day to be the last of my solitude. Nothing can be more good and kind than your conduct about my aunt. When two parties are each so anxious to do all they can to oblige the other, how can they fail to go on well?'*

In addition to her worries about Aunt Anne's health, Anne Lister was becoming increasingly concerned about her father, Jeremy. On May 12th, he experienced numbness in his left arm which Anne described as a *'slight paralytic affection'*, a diagnosis which was confirmed by Mr. Sunderland when he attended Jeremy.

Mr. Sunderland continued to attend Aunt Anne and Jeremy, and on Sunday, May 18th, told Anne that she could *'safely go from home for a week, on Tuesday'*. So, on the night of Monday, May 19th, Anne said goodbye to her aunt, her father and her sister, and at 6.20 a.m. the following morning, she set off in her carriage, with Eugenie and Thomas, to Heworth Grange to be with Ann on her birthday. She arrived at Heworth Grange just before midday and, soon after Dr. Belcombe called. Several others called about one thing or another so it was gone two o'clock before Anne and Ann could set off in their carriage for their sketching holiday. They passed through the village of Leeming at about five o'clock, then as they travelled, ate a dinner of boned shoulder of veal, ham, and oranges they had brought with them. Anne Lister: *'grubbling as we came along in the carriage just before and after Boroughbridge'*. They arrived at the King's Head hotel in Richmond and had tea. Anne Lister described their accommodation as *'very comfortable, large excellent sitting room and bedroom adjoining'*. The King's Head still stands and has been providing hospitality for 300 years. In 1834 it was the hotel of choice for the nobility and the gentry. I have not visited the King's Head, but it is certainly on my list.

After breakfast the next day, Wednesday, May 21st, Anne and Ann sauntered around Richmond looking particularly at the 11th century castle, the Friary and the marketplace, hoping to find suitable views for Ann Walker to sketch. They decided on the Friary and returned to the Kings Head and were both asleep on the sofa when Mr. Brown, Ann's drawing master, arrived at about half past two, having travelled by coach from York. At about half past three, after Mr. Brown had had lunch, Anne and Ann set out with him, Eugenie, and Thomas to the Friary for Ann's sketching lesson. Unfortunately, Ann Walker's period had started in the early afternoon and the poor woman felt unwell but soldiered on regardless. That night she was in bed by 10 p.m., but by the time Anne Lister retired, she was feeling much better. Anne Lister wrote: *'playing and squeezing and pressing for an hour and a half last night and almost as long this morning. She says she gets fonder of me and certainly seems to care enough for me now, I think we shall get on very well. Nobody would care for me more or do more for me'*.

Thursday, Friday, and Saturday were taken up with Ann Walker sketching and Anne Lister going off exploring the location, then in the evening, enjoying each other. Thursday evening: *'Miss Walker having me near her on the sofa and being on the amoroso, grubbled her well'.* Friday night/Saturday morning: *'goodish kiss last night and an hour playing this morning. I am really getting fond of her for the play was all my own bringing on'.*

On Saturday evening at about half past seven, Mr. Brown headed off from the King's Head in a gig to Darlington to catch the coach back to York the next morning, and Anne, Ann, Eugenie, and Thomas set off in their carriage to the village of Greta Bridge. Anne Lister described the route: *'fine, rich, wooded, beautiful hill-and-dale country'*. They arrived at Mr. Chamber's Inn in Greta Bridge at 9.05 p.m. and had tea.

The following morning, Sunday, they attended the local church. Anne Lister fell asleep during the sermon so presumably it was not particularly scintillating. They explored the local area, walked alongside the river Tees and Ann did some sketching. After dinner they set off at 5.37 p.m. and travelled to the town of Barnard Castle arriving at 6.05 p.m. They were given a tour of the 12th century castle, then had a dinner of roast fillet of veal, cabbage, potatoes, salad followed by cheesecake and tarts, and Anne Lister had a pint of *'very good ale'.* I visited both Barnard Castle and Richmond Castle as a seven-year-old child, although I do remember being very cross on the trip to Richmond Castle on account of being required to wear a dress. I mean, who wears a dress to a castle when there are battles to be fought and dungeons to escape from. After dinner, the party set off to the village of Staindrop, alighting at the Queens Head Inn at 7. 20 p.m., and then had tea.

The following morning, Monday, May 26th, Anne and Ann visited Raby Castle, about two miles from Staindrop. This castle was built in the 14th century and is pretty much intact. They were then off to Bishop Auckland to see the 12th century Auckland Castle, which, in 1834, was the home of the last prince-bishop of Durham. The two women were certainly keen to see as many castles as possible on this trip, and at Auckland Castle, Anne Lister was getting ideas for her potential additions to Shibden. From Bishop Auckland they travelled to the King's Head Inn at Marsham arriving at 6.55 p.m., and during the last half hour of the journey, Anne Lister: *'had grubbled her well just once before driving into the town'*.

The party was off from King's Head Inn, Marsham, at 9.30 a.m next morning, Tuesday, and visited Hackfall, an extensive woodland garden and now a Site of Special Scientific Interest (SSSI) near the village of Grewelthorpe. They then drove about 10 miles to the Brimham Rocks, a rocky moorland area and now also an SSSI, arriving at 2.15 p.m. Ann Walker was getting tired by this time so at the Brimham Rocks House they had a late lunch/early dinner of bacon and fried eggs, bread, some of their own roll of veal and ginger beer. Refreshed, they were taken on a guided walk by the woman of the house. Sometimes, I think Ann Walker appeared to be tired when, in fact, she was actually hungry. Although having said that, Anne Lister did have her getting up pretty early every day, so they could pack in as much sight-seeing as possible, so it is likely she was in need of a lie in. They spent the night at an inn in Boroughbridge, having tea, bread, butter, and honey on arrival.

Wednesday morning was spent at Newby Hall, near Ripon, built by Sir Christopher Wren in the 1690's, so it was over 140 years old when Anne and Ann visited. Sixty-seven years before their visit, Richard Adams was commissioned to remodel the interior of the house to make it beautiful and elegant, and so now Newby Hall is described as an Adams house. The afternoon was spent at Fountains Abbey, and while Ann sketched the interior of a nearby church, Anne Lister took a nap. They returned to the inn at Boroughbridge for the night, and were up early, at 6.30 a.m. on Thursday morning, travelled to explore Knaresborough, and then back to Heworth Grange arriving at 4.25 p.m.

Dr. Belcombe called the following morning, Friday, May 30th. Anne Lister: *'I think Dr. Belcombe seems now aware of the business between Miss Walker and myself. Asked me if I thought her being so well would last? Yes! I had no fear'.* Even before their holiday, Anne and Ann had been discussing the possibility of Ann Walker now leaving Dr. Belcombe's care, letting out Heworth Grange until their lease ran out, and setting up home together at Shibden. Now the decision was made, and they began packing up Ann Walker's belongings. Anne Lister would return to Shibden the following day loaded up with Ann's things, then return the following Tuesday to Heworth Grange. Their plan from then depended on the condition of Aunt Anne's health. I am not sure of the precise nature of Aunt Anne's health problem, although Anne Lister had mentioned dropsy, which is related to a heart condition. I am aware though that her state of wellness fluctuated and if Anne Lister found Aunt Anne improved, Anne and Ann would go to France and Switzerland on honeymoon, but, if not, they would return straight to Shibden.

Anne and Mariana's correspondence had continued, and, showed that Mariana was becoming more despairing. A letter arrived from Mariana, having been forwarded from Shibden. Anne described the letter as *'composed, proper enough letter, tho' owning she repented her conduct and its consequences, tho' if I was really happy, she could not at least be indifferent to the person who made so'.* Mariana: *'tho' probably a little time may elapse before I could meet any individual under such circumstances with composure. But strange thoughts and feelings pass upon me. At least there is yet one in which you have never had a rival, most probably never will, for in some particulars Mary is not like every other woman, for tho' her heart may be moved, there is still a string which never vibrated to any touch but yours. Who knows, but it is now silenced for ever.... Your pages crowd so many thoughts upon my mind that I almost seem deprived of the power of arranging my ideas. I could think I could look back upon the past and know and feel perhaps all you tell me to be true, but the mind that can gain nothing by regret ought to find no leisure to look back. All is now decided, and if I cannot make you happy, I ought to rejoice that any other can. That I have and do love you dearly and fondly you cannot doubt. Heaven forbid that our friendship should ever cease for without it, Fred, I should indeed be wretched. I am grateful for the kind assurances you give me of your continued regard. If my love has sometimes perplexed you, it has been more from the waywardness of circumstances than from inconstancy of my nature'.*

Anne Lister set off from Heworth Grange at 4.10 p.m. on Saturday, May 31st, and arrived back at Shibden at 9.35 p.m to find Aunt Anne so much better that she had even spent some time out in the garden. Anne stayed up till midnight talking about her plans to Marian, who was very supportive of her sister's relationship with Ann Walker, and had already realised the possibility of them travelling abroad for a few months now that Aunt Anne's health had improved. Anne and Ann were both very much aware that their going abroad would leave Marian caring for both Jeremy, and Aunt Anne, and had decided, in that event, they would give Marian £100 (about £11,000 in today's money). Anne Lister wrote that Marian said: *'that she thought it was too much. I said it certainly was not'.*

The following morning, Sunday, June 1st, Anne Lister wrote and sent a letter to Ann and later that day a letter arrived from Ann, to which she wrote a reply and sent it off to Heworth Grange within a parcel containing biscuits and buns. Another letter arrived at Shibden the next morning, Monday, from Ann Walker to which Anne immediately wrote and sent a reply which arrived at Heworth Grange the following morning. The mail service then was so efficient it was almost as good as email!

Being incredibly busy catching up with estate business, Anne Lister did not set off to York till 5.00 pm, on Tuesday, June 3rd, so only arrived at Heworth Grange at 9.28 p.m. and found Ann alarmed that she was later than expected. The following morning Anne Lister wrote: *'a tolerable kiss last night but my bowels having being heated and wrong these ten days took two teaspoonfuls of salts at eight this morning, getting up, and they had worked off by twelve'.*

CHAPTER 10: THE HONEYMOON

Anne and Ann's honeymoon, began on Wednesday, June 4th, 1834. It lasted 12½ weeks and involved a journey of about 2000 miles, mostly in their own carriage but also by boat, by char-à-banc, on foot, and by mule. The trip they had planned would take them first to London, then to Paris, then Switzerland. It was to be Ann Walker's first experience of travelling abroad, and, also, the longest time that she and Anne had spent together thus far in their relationship. In reading opinions expressed about Anne Lister and Ann Walker from a variety of sources, I have come across some negativity regarding their travels abroad. For example, the suggestions that Ann Walker did not want to travel abroad but Anne Lister insisted, and that Ann Walker had to pay for these trips, and also, that she was far from being the perfect travelling companion for Anne Lister. Well, I will now tell you what happened on their first holiday abroad and throw in a few opinions of my own.

The trip was to be a learning experience for both women, but more so for Anne Lister, who would discover that Ann was, actually, a very good traveller. It transpired that Ann Walker, unlike Anne Lister, did not suffer from sea sickness. Also, it turned out that Ann Walker could cope perfectly well with long carriage journeys, including getting up very early, travelling all day, and all through the night on occasion as well. There were, however, two rules that Anne Lister was required to learn in this regard. Firstly, that Ann Walker needed lunch. Now Anne Lister was very much in the habit of having just two meals a day, breakfast, and dinner in the evening. Not so for Ann Walker, she needed three decent meals a day. Secondly if she was up and about early, she required a nap after lunch. This rarely presented a problem when they were travelling in their carriage, since she just slept as they went along. She was, in fact, a very good sleeper, and could take a nap at almost any time she chose, quite handy when you're travelling.

The couple set off from Heworth Grange, at 3.10 p.m. on that Wednesday, with servants, Eugenie and Joseph, and headed for London. However, Anne Lister was starting to feel unwell. At 9.45 p.m. they stopped at an inn in the village of Barnby Moor in Nottinghamshire. Anne was feeling so ill that Ann Walker had to put her to bed. The following day, Anne was feeling even worse. She was feverish, her limbs were painful, and she had a sick headache. There was no alternative but for her to remain in bed all day. Ann Walker remained by her bedside. Anne stayed in bed until late in the afternoon of the next day, Friday, June 6th, when she was able to drink a little boiled milk and eat a few pieces of bread. However, she wanted to get on with their travels, so at 4.18 p.m. they set off in their carriage from Barnby Moor, arriving at The George Inn at Grantham at 9.05 p.m. where she was able to eat some bread and drink a little more boiled milk. The following day, she felt a little better, although still very weak, so they continued their journey and arrived at Stevenage at 8.35 p.m. having had, at 5 p.m., a little cold ham in the carriage which she relished. The next morning, Sunday, whilst reading prayers aloud, she was overcome with fatigue and had to lie down on the sofa till 1 p.m. The party then set off in their carriage and arrived at the Hawkins Hotel, 26, Dover Street, in London, about four hours later. Unfortunately, the apartment on Dover Street, that Anne Lister had booked, had, in error, been let to someone else, and an alternative apartment, on Albemarle Street, had been reserved for them instead. This apartment was on the third floor accessed by *'bad stairs'* and had *'dirty bedding'*. Alas, not the best of starts to the honeymoon.

Anne and Ann stayed in London, for four nights, from Sunday, June 8th, to Thursday, June 12th. This provided the opportunity for Anne Lister to pay social calls on two of her London friends and for Ann Walker to visit her dentist and also to shop for a new riding habit. Ann actually had a tooth removed at the dentist but seemed none the worse for the extraction. On the Monday night, Ann Walker wrote a long letter to Aunt Anne at Shibden, to which Anne Lister added a few more lines. It was becoming clear that Ann Walker had really warmed to Aunt Anne during her two week stay at Shibden. By the way, at half past twelve on the Monday night, Anne Lister recorded the temperature as 66°F, yes, she had taken her thermometer on holiday (well it's not illegal!)

At 1.40 p.m. on Thursday, June 12th, Anne and Ann set off from London for Canterbury arriving at the Fountain Inn at 10.15 p.m. having eaten sandwiches in the carriage, en route. Next morning, after breakfast, they visited the stunning Canterbury Cathedral, built in the Gothic style in the 11th century, and, in the early 19th century, Anne Lister: *'all new-done-up, white and clean'*. Throughout her travels, whichever inn or hotel, she was staying at, Anne Lister referred to as *'home'* in her journal. After their visit to the cathedral, Anne Lister: *'home at 1.10 p.m. Tired, somehow I do not get up my strength. Lay on the sofa till off from Canterbury at 2.05 p.m. and alighted at the Ship Inn, Dover, at 4.15 p.m'*.

After dinner at the Ship Inn, Anne Lister wrote a three page letter to her aunt Anne containing some instructions regarding which letters arriving at Shibden for her and Ann should be forwarded on to them. Samuel Washington was Ann Walker's estate manager and also acting manager at Shibden when Anne Lister was on her travels. Any letters from Washington were to be sent on to them in Paris as well as letters from Anne Lister's solicitor, Mr. Parker, and Ann Walker's sister, Mrs. Sutherland, but no others. Anne Lister still rented a little apartment in Paris, number 27, Rue Saint-Victor, and their mail was to be forwarded to her at that address. I expect Anne was trying to ensure that Ann Walker did not receive any potentially distressing letters from her tribe of relatives in Halifax whilst on holiday.

The next morning, Saturday, June 14th, Anne Lister: *'Breakfast at 7.30 a.m. On board the Ferret packet, Captain Hamilton. Having been put off from shore in a small boat, at 8.30 a.m., under weigh at 8.45 a.m. Miss Walker and I sat in the carriage, she not sick at all, I very soon got rid of my breakfast'.* The Ferret was a steam powered packet boat, which carried the mail for the Post Office and crossed the English Channel in just three hours. The captain's priority would have been to get the mail off the boat and on its way. Passengers, however, had to wait about an hour to be ferried by a small boat to the pier in Calais. It would take another two hours before Anne and Ann's carriage was taken ashore, and then a further hour before it was released from the custom house. So, leaving Joseph in charge of the carriage, Anne, Ann, and Eugenie walked to the local hotel, eating and napping in the lounge there, before setting off in the carriage from Calais at 5.12 p.m. After travelling for about four hours, en route to Paris, they arrived at the Hotel de Londres, in Boulogne, where they spent the night. Although Anne Lister was still not fully recovered from her illness, it had not prevented them continuing their sex life. Anne Lister: *'a little kiss last night'.*

The next stage of their travels involved a nine hour journey in their carriage from Boulogne to Abbeville where they alighted at the Hotel de l'Europe at 7.05 p.m. Ann Walker had pain in her neck and head so rather than take a walk they just went to the nearest church to listen to the Sunday service. Apart from being poorly when she had her period, and also when she had a bowel complaint towards the end of the trip, this is the only diary reference to Ann Walker being in pain, during their twelve week holiday. This was very much in contrast with the frequency with which she experienced pain, related to her weak spine, when she was at home. After the church service and back at the hotel they had a particularly good dinner, so much so that Anne Lister noted the details: *'soup, fish (pike?), fricandeau, roast chicken, pigeon smothered in peas, potatoes, cauliflower, compote des pommes and desert'.* After dinner Anne Lister: *'Adney lay down while I wrote out yesterday and today'.* This is the first occasion, that I am aware of, that Anne Lister refers to Ann Walker as 'Adney' in her journal.

The following day, Monday, June 16th, they set off from Abbeville at 9.40 a.m. and, after another nine hour drive, they arrived at the Hotel de l'Ecu de France in Beauvais, in time for a short wander around the cathedral, then dinner at 8.05 p.m. The food was poor, but the beds were comfortable. The following morning, rather than having breakfast in the hotel, Anne and Ann walked to the market and bought strawberries for theirs and the servants' breakfasts. Whilst they were out and about, Anne Lister called in at the coaching inn, Hotel d'Angleterre, to order the horses for the next stage of their journey to Paris. Just as in the UK, an extensive network of coaching routes and inns existed across western Europe at this time and enabled a traveller, who owned their own carriage, to change horses and coach driver at frequent intervals. This enabled journey times to be significantly reduced compared with travelling using the carriage owner's own horses. Presumably, the hotel where Anne and Ann were staying, the Hotel de l'Ecu de France, was not a coaching inn. They set off to Paris from Beauvais at 10.05 a.m., a journey of about 70 miles. Just outside Paris, they stopped for half an hour to look around the beautiful, Gothic abbey church of Saint-Denis, then entered Paris by the barrière de Clichy at 5.20 p.m.

One of the best hotels in Paris was Le Meurice and this was where Anne and Ann had hoped to get rooms. Isabella Norcliffe, her sister Charlotte, and their friend Miss Beckett were already staying at Le Meurice. However, the only rooms available were on the fifth floor, so Anne Lister decided to drive to the Hotel de la Terrace where they took rooms on the second floor overlooking the garden. Isabella appeared at the Hotel de la Terrace just as Anne and Ann were sitting down to dinner at 8.40 p.m. After dinner, Ann Walker excused herself and went to bed and left Anne and Isabella *'tête-à-tête'*. Anne Lister: *'Isabella Norcliffe wounded at my choice but did not say much when she found the thing so settled. I said she (Miss Walker) had more in her [than] people thought and was a nice girl, as would appear more by and by'.*

After breakfast, on their first full day in Paris, Wednesday, June 18th, Anne and Ann went to the hotel Le Meurice to call on Isabella, Charlotte and Miss Beckett. Whilst there Anne Lister inquired about hiring a valet de Place, which was a man who acted as a guide to travellers. Oh, by the way, Anne Lister spoke fluent French. They then went to Fèrrere Laffitte and Co., a Parisian bank, to cash in three of their circular notes for a total of £75. Circular notes were fixed denomination promissory notes which were purchased at a bank in England prior to departure to mainland Europe. These circular notes, usually referred to as '*circulars*', could be cashed at specific banks across Europe provided they were supported by a letter of introduction. Anne Lister also collected her mail from her little apartment on Rue Saint-Victor. A letter there from Aunt Anne to both of them confirmed that all was going on pretty well back at Shibden. In the evening, after dinner at their hotel, Anne and Ann went to the opera to see 'La muette de Portici', the earliest French grand opera and believed to have been the trigger for the Belgian revolution of 1830. Anne Lister: *'very good dancing and the whole thing beautifully got up'*. They left the opera a little while before it had finished on account of Ann Walker feeling tired and having just started her period. On the Friday night, they went to see the Comédie Francaise at the Theatre Francais, having received tickets for a box, from a friend of Anne Lister, a Miss Berry. Anne Lister: *'Miss Walker tired. Asleep between pieces lying along the bottom of the box'*. OMG the woman could sleep anywhere! It was however not surprising that Ann Walker got tired as she was rarely able to have a lie in, and also a day spent with Anne Lister tended to be a busy one.

On the morning of Thursday, June 19th, Anne and Ann visited the Louvre Museum on the Rue de Rivoli. The Louvre had been established about forty years earlier, in 1793. The paintings they were particularly keen to see were 'La Belle Jardinière' by

Raphael and 'The Young Beggar' by Murillo. They then walked all around the Palais Royal, which was opposite the Louvre. As its name suggested, the Palais Royal had once been a royal palace, owned by Louis XIV, but, in the early nineteenth century, it was famous for its shopping arcades. In one shop they ordered a hundred calling cards for Ann Walker and then called at Chez Maurisset, Anne Lister: *'and found he had still kept for me the nacre snuff box for Isabella Norcliffe, with her initials, he had since I forgot it in 1831!'*. They then went for a snack of gateau and lemonade at the patisserie opposite Rue Vivienne followed by more shopping. I am beginning to get the impression that Ann Walker was rather keen on shopping. Later in the afternoon, they visited the Exposition des produits de l'industrie Francais and in the evening they went to a concert at the Champs-Élysées. Back at their hotel, they had strawberries and lemonade for supper.

On the morning of Friday 20th June, Anne Lister left Ann at the hotel and went off with Francoise, the valet de Place she had hired at Le Meurice, to try to complete the task of getting the passports sorted for herself, Ann, and their two servants, Joseph and Eugenie, for the next stage of their journey. This task had been proving difficult as it involved several agencies including the British Embassy. I am, however, slightly puzzled regarding the passport for Joseph. In her journal, Anne wrote that she was sent a passport for George Joseph Booth, and from then on, she referred to Joseph as George. Back at the hotel at 11.00 a.m., Anne and Ann were visited by Isabella. Anne Lister: *'Isabella Norcliffe came and sat with us above an hour and drank a tumbler and half of sheer vin de penas, strong Spanish wine'*. That afternoon, the saga of the passports continued. Anne Lister: *'Out again at 2 to go back to the prefecture to identify Eugenie and George and get all the passports done. Sent mine and George's to the Swiss Charge d'affaires and Eugenie's to the French foreign office'*.

Anne Lister was busy again the following day, Saturday, June 21st, still trying to get their passports authorised for their planned journey through France to Switzerland. She was even required to get a passport for the carriage! The whole business seemed rather hit and miss and depended on a variety of documents being sent to a variety of people. It was a hot day and when she got back to the hotel at 4.00 p.m., feeling the heat, she took off her clothes and sat in her dressing gown. While she had been out, Ann Walker had written a 2½ page letter to Aunt Anne at Shibden, so Anne added to it to complete the third page. Ann Walker had also written to her own aunt at Cliff Hill, and to her sister, Elizabeth in Scotland. The two women had dinner in the hotel at 6.15 p.m. then lay dozing together on the sofa in their room till 9.30 p.m. when Anne Lister went out to visit her old friend Madame de Bourke. She returned to the hotel at midnight to find that Ann had waited up for her and together they ate strawberries and drank wine till after 1 o'clock.

At last, on Sunday afternoon, June 22nd, the authorised passports and visas arrived at the hotel so Anne, Ann, and their servants, would now be able to continue their journey through France to Switzerland. First things first though, they arranged for the hairdresser to come to their room. It had been a rainy day in Paris but was fine in the evening, so they drove to the Bois de Boulogne, where they walked in the woods for about forty minutes, then back to the hotel for a *'double kiss'* (two orgasms without losing contact).

Monday, June 23rd, was devoted to getting things ready for leaving Paris on Tuesday morning. Also, a few notes were sent here and there, and a bottle of champagne was bought to take on the journey. In the evening, when all was sorted, they went to the Café de la Rotonde for a café au lait for Ann Walker and a strawberry ice for Anne Lister.

Ann and Anne had, by this time, spent about a week in Paris and were certainly having a thoroughly good time. In her letter to her aunt, Anne Lister had written that she was *'glad to have come'*. Apart from Anne Lister having to get the passports sorted and make a few social calls on her friends, the couple were together most of the time and appeared to be very happy and relaxed in each other's company. During the week of their stay in Paris, the weather had been hot and mostly dry. I mention this not just because I'm British, and yes, we do like to talk about the weather, but because the weather did subsequently change, and this did affect their holiday plans. Anne and Ann had decided that they would travel the 350 miles from Paris to Geneva and then go on to explore the alpine mountains, in particular Mont Blanc. This seems to me to be a long way when you are only travelling between 5 and 10 miles per hour, but it did not seem to faze either of them at all, they just enjoyed the journey. In fact, with their explorations en route, it took them about a week to reach Geneva.

Anne, Ann and their servants, Eugenie and George, set off in their carriage from Paris on the morning of Tuesday 24th June. After 6½ hours on the road they arrived at the Hotel de la Ville de Lyons in Fontainebleau, the latter stage of the journey having been through the beautiful forest surrounding the Palace of Fontainebleau. Anne and Ann immediately went off to visit the palace. This palace was originally built for the French royal family but subsequently became the residence of Napoleon Bonaparte, and, on their visit, the interior was *'put as it was in Napoleon's time'*. Before dinner at the hotel, they walked in the gardens surrounding the palace, which were then, as now, *'very pretty'*. The rooms that Anne and Ann had in the hotels in which they stayed in France tended to be either two single beds in one room or a single bed in each of two adjoining rooms, usually with a small sitting room (or salon). In either case, the beds were rarely large enough for two people to sleep together comfortably all night. Anne Lister: *'crept into my own separate bed without kissing or awaking her'*.

On Wednesday, June 25th, they set off from Fontainebleau at 10.13 a.m., a bit later than planned because one of the springs on the carriage had to be repaired. They arrived at Joigny at 7.10

p.m. having stopped at a café in the town of Sens for Ann Walker to have a mug or two of café au lait. They booked into the Hotel des Cinq Mineurs then went off for a much needed walk, having been sat in the carriage for over eight hours. After dinner in the hotel, they drank the champagne they had brought with them from Paris and then, Anne Lister: *'An hour with Miss Walker, two kisses'*.

Next morning, Thursday, they set off from Joigny at 7.18 a.m. heading for Rouvray, via Avallon, another whole day of travelling. Now Anne Lister could usually demonstrate a lot of patience but occasionally something pretty insignificant could irritate her. As I have explained previously, she was good at not showing her irritation but would subsequently have a bit of a rant in her journal and that would ease her annoyance. On the drive to Rouvray, two things irritated her. Firstly, Anne Lister: *'At Auxerre, delayed 22 minutes, Miss Walker on the pot all the time. Had I known I would have gone to see the cathedral (not far off)'.* I assume Ann Walker was having a bit of difficulty, and Anne Lister wasn't good at just waiting with nothing to do. Although, timing how long someone takes to have a poo? Well, I suppose we all have our quirks. The second irritation was Anne Lister's own fault. As they drove through Vermenton, Ann Walker requested that they stop at what looked like a *'good looking café'* for her to have her café au lait. Anne Lister: *'but I persuaded her to wait and dine at Avallon, at the hotel de la Poste'*. Uh-oh, big mistake! Anne Lister was still trying to get Ann to go for as long as her without stopping for sustenance. When they did eat, at 5.40 p.m., having also had to wait an hour for the meal to be prepared, Ann Walker was absolutely ravenous and ate and drank far too much. Anne Lister: *'She ate a large dinner and drank altogether about two tumblers of vin du pays, a good common red burgundy, some without water and the rest with very little. I could not have drank at that rate.... Then on getting to the carriage again, she was heated and had the fidgets. Was in all positions and saying how ill and tired she was. Steph was right enough, I shall have plague enough, but I must manage as well as I can'.* Ann Walker had been an excellent traveller thus far, but Anne Lister had not quite yet learned that she needed lunch, even if it was just a mug or two of milky coffee. They left Avallon at 6.56 p.m. and arrived at the hotel de la Poste in Rouvray at 9.05 p.m. Anne Lister: *'Miss Walker lay down immediately'.*

Next morning, Friday, June 27th, Anne and Ann had breakfast at 6.30 a.m. and were off from Rouvray at 7.33 a.m. heading for Dijon. The weather was still hot and dry. It was a beautiful drive to Dijon but they could see black clouds and hear thunder in the distance. They arrived at the Hotel de la Cloche at 4.28 p.m. and had dinner at 5.40 p.m. At 7.10 p.m. they went to explore the Palace of the Dukes of Burgundy, referred to by Anne Lister as the *'old ducal palace'*, taking George with them. Although originally built in the 14th century, most of what they saw was built in the 17th and 18th centuries. They were back at the hotel by 8.55 p.m. Anne Lister: *'With her from ten to eleven and a quarter and a long very good kiss to her and tolerable to me'.*

On Saturday morning the couple explored the gothic Cathedral of Saint Benignus of Dijon and the Arquebus botanical garden, before setting off from Dijon at 10.47 a.m. On reaching the top of the first hill, after leaving Dijon, they saw their first view of the mountains of the Jura range. About twenty miles from Dijon, they entered the fortified town of Auxonne where they had to show their passports and also where they found a café where Ann Walker could have her café au lait. They arrived at the town of Dole at 4.11 p.m. but although they were able to change the horses, there was no driver available, so they decided to have an early dinner at the Hotel de Paris. They had a very good dinner and set off again at 6.22 p.m. and, arrived at the town of Mont sous Vaudrey just over two hours later, where they spent the night at the auberge at the post office.

The next morning, Sunday, June 29th, they set off from Mont sous Vaudrey at the incredibly early time of 5.38 a.m. Anne

Lister had had the idea that they should set off before breakfast rather than having an early breakfast and then setting off. They stopped at Poligny for breakfast at 7.35 a.m. Anne Lister: *'Miss Walker lay down [in the carriage] for ½ hour and as long after breakfast and having eaten biscuits in the carriage going a stage before breakfast seems to have suited her very well. I have not enjoyed my breakfast so much since leaving home, for on breakfasting immediately after getting up, I never eat with relish'.* Sunday night was spent at the Hotel de la Poste at Morey after a journey of 70 miles from Mont sous Vaudrey. The following morning, they set off at 6.18 a.m. and had breakfast at Roussess, where they were also required to show their passports. Ann Walker had pickled trout for her lunch in the town of Gex and then a little further on they had their first view of Mont Blanc. Anne Lister: *'Miss Walker thought I wanted to go to the top of Mont Blanc and she certainly would go with me'.* Ann Walker seemed up for pretty much anything. As they entered Geneva, they handed in the passports to the police and at 5.40 p.m. alighted at the Hotel de Bergues. Letters were waiting for them at the Post Office, three for Ann Walker and one for Anne Lister. The letter to Anne Lister was from Aunt Anne. Anne Lister: *'from my aunt, Shibden. Better account of herself and begs us not to hurry home. All going on well in and out of doors. My father pretty well, ditto Marian. [Old] Miss Walker of Cliff Hill takes it ill [we] never told her of going abroad tho' it had been publicly talked of so long – what nonsense!'* Two of Ann Walker's letters were from her sister and one from Samuel Washington regarding Walker estate business.

That night a problem arose between the two women. What had happened was that Ann Walker had developed thrush like symptoms which she described as *'the whites'*. She felt too embarrassed to tell Anne, so she came up with a lie to put off them having sex. Unfortunately, her choice of lie was to prove very hurtful. Anne Lister: *'Ten minutes with her tonight. She was tired. Said I was long about it. That I gave her no dinky, that is, seminal fluid, and I excused myself and came away to my own bed'.*

The following morning, Tuesday, July 1st, after breakfast, Ann Walker went back to bed, in need of more sleep. Most of the day was spent writing letters including a letter containing instructions from them both to Samuel Washington regarding the Walker and Shibden estates. Clearly both of them were still very much involved in the day to day running of their properties, despite being on holiday. That evening they sauntered around the town, taking George with them. Anne Lister bought a little guide to Chamonix, which she read the whole of when they returned to the hotel. Anne Lister: *'Lay quietly by her twenty five minutes and then to my own bed'.*

Out and about in Geneva the next morning, Wednesday, Anne and Ann went to see a scale model of Switzerland, took their letters to the Post Office, and purchased a shawl for Ann Walker. In the afternoon Anne Lister paid a call on a Miss Pickford, a woman she had been friends with in Halifax, many years ago, and who was on holiday with a Miss Maitland. Miss Pickford was a lesbian and had been open about this to Anne. Her partner had been a Miss Threlfall, but she had died two years previously. It had been Miss Pickford who had ended the friendship, annoyed that Anne would not admit to having sexual relationships with women, having been sworn to secrecy by Mariana. Reading between the lines Miss Pickford was not altogether pleased to see Anne. That evening the weather changed. Anne Lister: *'heavy rain and a thunderstorm, lightning very vivid and one peal so near, the house seemed coming down'*. Also that evening, having realised that she had upset Anne Lister, Ann explained the real reason why she had been reluctant to have sex. Anne Lister: *'Miss Walker owns she has had whites again, had them years ago and since these last two or three days. Said she had rather affected me on Monday night'.*

At 12.40 p.m. on the following day, Thursday, July 3rd, they set off on their drive to Chamonix, about sixty miles from Geneva. During the first hour of the drive, they enjoyed the magnificent scenery but then the weather deteriorated, Anne Lister: *'The thunder was so near and the lightning so frequent and vivid, Ann's lips turned pale and she was a good deal frightened'.* The thunderstorm continued, so when they arrived in Bonneville at 4.15 p.m., they decided to have dinner there, at La Poste, and stay the night. They had an excellent meal, the beds were comfortable, and they had sex, having cleared up the misunderstanding between them. Anne Lister: *'Goodish kiss last night'.* Nice to see normal service had been resumed.

The next morning, Friday July 4th, Anne and Ann were up early and set off from Bonneville at 6.12 a.m. After travelling for about 3½ hours they arrived at the Hotel de Bellevue in Sallanches, where they had breakfast and enjoyed the *'fine view of Mont Blanc from the balcony'.* It was here, at Sallanches, where they would begin their *'mountain wanderings'*. They left Eugenie, most of their belongings, and their carriage at Sallanches, and with only their travel bags, travelled by char-à-banc, with George, to Chamonix, arriving at the Hotel de Londres at 7.05 p.m. A nineteenth century char-à-banc was essentially a wagon with benches. It may be covered but the sides were open to the elements, and, since it had rained for the whole of the journey, by the time they reached Chamonix, they were wet through, Anne Lister: *'Adney, wet, put her to bed immediately before dinner at 8 p.m. and had the table placed at her bedside'.*

The next morning, Saturday, July 5th, Anne, Ann, and George were taken by two guides David and Michel, on a two hour journey, by mule, to see the Montanvert glacier, known as the Mer de Glace. They had boiled milk at the Pavillion, then completed the descent back to the Chamonix on foot in an hour and a quarter. Back at the hotel. Anne Lister: *'Adney not tired tho' much heated as well as myself. Adney took off her habit and went to bed for an hour and we all had boiled milk again. Adney up and out with me at 3 p.m. Went into the church, neatly kept and good, in the Italian style of gilded finery about the alters'.* They had dinner at 6.30 p.m. and, since it was raining heavily, remained at the hotel for the rest of the evening, Anne Lister: *'Half hour with her and good long kiss'*.

On Sunday, July 6th, Anne, Ann, and their servant, George, were to begin a tour of the Alps in the region of Mont Blanc, returning to Chamonix on Sunday July 20th. Since they were to travel sometimes on foot but also by mule, they were required to travel light, so Anne Lister had to leave her journal at the hotel in Chamonix. She subsequently left twenty journal pages blank with the intention of writing the entries after the tour had been completed. However, she only made entries for eight of the twenty pages with the other fourteen pages remaining blank. The journal entries she did complete corresponded to Sunday July 6th to Wednesday July 9th, 1834. During the previous night, Ann Walker had suffered from sickness, but, despite this, she and Anne Lister got up early on the Sunday morning, and were dressed and packed in time for breakfast at 8 a.m. They set off from Chamonix at 10.30 a.m. with their two guides, David and Michel, and three mules, one for the baggage, one for George, and one for Anne and Ann to ride. Anne Lister: *'rode ¼ hour, then walked to les Ouches, there at 12.30 p.m.'* I am pretty sure she meant 'Les Houches'. There is a town called Ouches in France, but it is not in this region. Anne Lister then wrote that they reached the top of the mountain de Vauzaz at 3 p.m. Googling this mountain produces no results. Looking at the map, I have found a Col de Voza on the walking route from Les Houches to Les Contamines, which was where they spent the night. Col de Voza is a mountain pass not a mountain which makes sense since they reached it in a few hours. They then made the descent, mostly on foot, arriving at the village auberge at Les Contamines at 5.10 p.m. Given that Anne Lister wrote the details of this part of their journey over two weeks later, it would not be surprising if she made some mistakes on the exact names of some of the locations. This journey from Chamonix to Les Contamines is about 13 miles and involved a steep ascent of over 2000 ft during which there were frequent rain showers. Given that Ann Walker was not used to this level of exertion, and had been sick the previous night, I have to say I admire her fortitude. At 6.30 p.m. they had a good roast veal and chicken dinner at the auberge and drank two bottles of vin d'asti blanc. Ann Walker went to bed at 7.45 p.m., Anne Lister: *'found her fast asleep <u>on</u> the bed. Helped her to get her things off and put her to bed. She was literally tipsy'.*

Next morning, Monday, July 7th, the party set off from Les Contamines at 6.40 a.m. continuing their ascent into the Alps. They travelled past the series of waterfalls on the Saint Gervais river and arrived at an auberge at 8.15 a.m. for a breakfast of milk, bread, and honey. By midday they were walking through snow, and George slipped and fell 20 or 30 yards. At 3.35 p.m. they arrived at an auberge in a small settlement that Anne Lister referred to as la ville de Motets, where they had a *'splendid chalet'* with *'a small double bedded room'* and George, seemingly none the worse for his tumble, had the room next door. I have found that there is a place, known as the Refuge des Mottets, which is described as a former alpine chalet, and am confident it is in the correct location for it to have been the place Anne referred to. The dinner of mutton and potatoes that they were given was quite poor, so Ann Walker had the cold fowl and some of the vin d'asti they had brought with them from Les Contamines, and Anne Lister had some brandy and water. After dinner, they both then lay down and slept for an hour and a half. Anne Lister: *'Adney has borne today very well, a little frightened at the last snow, thought her legs would have failed her, but got on, followed me and George, and hanging on David's arm'.*

The following morning, Tuesday, July 8th, they set off from the chalet at 6.20 a.m. and began a steep ascent on a track alongside a sheer drop down to a fast flowing river, Anne Lister: *'Adney frightened, nervous and sickish'.* The level of physicality expected of Ann Walker was far in excess of anything she had previously experienced, but, it does seem that she rose to the occasion. However, one night's sleep was clearly not sufficient to enable her to recover from the exhaustion caused by the previous day's activity. At 9.a.m. they stopped at a chalet for an hour to eat breakfast and to let Ann have a rest. The terrain they were covering was not suited to riding the mules, so they had to walk most of the time. They rested again after another hour then pressed on and arrived at the hotel de L'Ange at Courmayeur at 2.08 p.m. No more travelling that day so Ann would have the opportunity to recover from her exertions.

The following morning, Wednesday July 9th, George informed Anne Lister that there had been a lot of rain in the night so Anne Lister made a change to their plans and instead of taking the Col de Ferret mountain pass, they would head off in the direction of Aoste. The party set off from Courmayeur at 7.30 a.m. and arrived an hour later at the town of Prés-Saint-Didier, *'beautifully situated at the bottom of [a] deep green valley'.* They had breakfast there and Anne Lister went to see the thermal baths whilst Ann rested before setting off again at 10.05 a.m. I get the impression that they were riding the mules for most of the travelling they did this day. I have read, in Anne Lister's diaries, that Ann Walker was a very accomplished horsewoman, so riding a mule, when the terrain was suitable, would have been relatively easy for her. As they continued on their way, they had a fine view of Mont Blanc and, at 4.45 p.m., had their first view of Aoste in the distance. The later start time of 7.30 a.m., the change of route, the longer the breaks to eat, and increasing number of rest stops suggested that Anne Lister did realise that her original itinerary was too demanding for Ann and changes had to be made to accommodate her.

Although there are no more entries in Anne Lister's journey related to their tour of the mountains, it is reasonable to assume that it continued until Sunday 20th July, given that they spent that night at the hotel de Londres in Chamonix, and Anne Lister returned to her journal the following day, writing: *'an end of ascending Mont Blanc'.* She subsequently wrote in a letter to her Aunt Anne that their mountain wanderings had been brought to an end by the bad weather. It appears that if the weather had been better, they would have attempted to get closer to the summit of Mont Blanc than they had actually been able to achieve.

The following day, Monday, July 21st, at 12.30 p.m., Anne, Ann, and George were driven in a small one-horse carriage from Chamonix to Sallanches, arriving at 5.15 p.m. to be reunited with Eugenie, who *'appeared to be very well'*. Since she had just enjoyed two weeks of peace and quiet without Anne Lister telling her what to do, I am not surprised she appeared to be very well. Anne and Ann had dinner at 6.15 p.m. then immediately set off in their carriage heading for Bonneville despite the heavy rain which subsequently developed into a thunderstorm. It would appear that Ann Walker had too much to eat and drink at dinner, probably knowing that it was going to take over five hours to get to Bonneville, and not being sure when she would next eat (a concern I frequently have when travelling). During the journey, Anne Lister: *'never in my life saw such fidgeting in a carriage. She was in all postures and places till at last she luckily fell asleep about an hour. She had too much Roussillon wine which made her feverish, without being tipsy'*. They arrived at the hotel La Couronne, Bonneville at 11.45 p.m. and had to wake up the hotel staff to attend to them.

The following morning, Tuesday July 22nd, Anne and Ann must have had a lie in because they only went down to breakfast in the hotel at 11.30 a.m. Anne Lister: *'she came for an hour and half to me this morning quietly talking'*. They set off from Bonneville at 12.20 p.m. heading for Geneva, Anne Lister: *'from there the mountains wear out into rounded beautiful, green, wooded hills and extensive valleys. At 2.50 p.m. stopt at Amenas to shew passports. At 3.50 p.m. stopt at Heutsch's bank. Sent up to them and they brought me down the money for two £25 circulars'*. There were two letters waiting for them at the Heutsch Bank, one being from Mariana marked *'Leamington, June'*. The 2nd letter dated June 27th was from Aunt Anne, the first two pages for Ann Walker and the third page and ends for Anne Lister: *'all going well. My father has ordered a little carriage to go about in'*. They alighted at the hotel des Bergues, Geneva at 4.00 p.m. then went out to the Poste restaurante office, where there were three letters waiting for them. One for Ann Walker from her sister, one for Anne Lister from Lady Gordon, dated Saltzburg July 10th, and another from Aunt Anne dated July 9th, in which she wrote that Anne's father was: *'tolerable but very feeble, he does not appear to gain strength at all. He walks out a little every day, generally to the top of the bank and in the course of the day, 2 or 3 times, a little in the garden'*. Aunt Anne added: *'As to myself, sometimes I have a very poorly day, and then better. Mr. Sunderland is very attentive, and upon the whole, I think I am much the same as when you went'*. In her letter, Aunt Anne reassured them that there was no need for them to return home on her account. She did however express concern about a letter she had received from Mariana who wrote that she had been very ill and had not heard from Anne Lister in several weeks. Anne Lister: *'my aunt begs me to write to Mariana immediately'*. In her letter to Anne Lister, Mariana wrote: *'For the 1st time in my life, my dearest Fred, 3 weeks have passed without my hearing from you, and for the 1st time in my life you are in England and Mary knows not where to find you. What can all this mean?'*

Mariana included a reference to Mr. Willoughby Crewe and his two sons in her letter. It transpired that Anne had written to Mariana before leaving England and had sent the letter to Warrens as that was where Mariana was meant to be going. However, Mariana was too poorly to go there and Anne's letter for some reason had not been forwarded on to her. As a consequence, Mariana did not know where Anne was, and this had caused her great distress. Clearly Mariana had sent her letter to Shibden and Aunt Anne had forwarded it to the Poste restaurante office in Geneva. Besides describing how ill she had been, Mariana, in reference to Anne's relationship with Ann Walker, who she referred to as *'your friend'*, also wrote: *'Your happiness and comfort is very dear to me, and I am not the last of your friends to rejoice that you are satisfied of having secured both. May it be so! But for all our sakes perhaps it is best that at present I should tell you this on paper. An unsophisticated mind I think is more likely to secure your permanent happiness than any such worldly one as that which falls to the lot of those who of late years had been your associates. You have lived long enough on hope, dearest, now the desire has come I trust it brings with it all you have so often longed for. Your friend will always be a source of interest to me and I will never rob her of her due. But you can tell me about her and I will believe all you say which at least will be much for her advantage because I am by no means sure that I could be an impartial judge'.* I do feel sad for Mariana. Anne Lister had been the person who Mariana could trust to always put her feelings and needs first. The situation however had changed, and Mariana had realised that it was Ann Walker who was Anne's first thought, not her. That night, Anne and Ann stayed up till 2.00 a.m. writing letters. Ann Walker replied to her sister's letter, Anne Lister wrote to Mariana, and they wrote jointly to Aunt Anne. In the letter to Aunt Anne, Anne Lister mentioned that, since bad weather had ended their mountain tour, they might consider returning to the mountains for a few days, weather permitting. Anne Lister wrote a very affectionate and kind letter to Mariana. Anne Lister: *'should be ill at ease till I heard she was better'.* Then, after all the letter writing, Anne Lister: *'long kiss at twice last night and with her for an hour and a half'.*

The following morning, Wednesday July 23rd, Anne Lister finished off her letter to Mariana. In the letter she begged Mariana to write to her, addressing the letter to her little Paris apartment on Rue Saint-Victor. Anne was already in the habit of showing her correspondence with Mariana to Ann Walker, who then helped Anne to write a copy of the letter before they went down to breakfast in the hotel at 10.40 a.m. It was a warm dry day so after breakfast Anne and Ann went shopping. They purchased some earrings for Mariana, some prints, and Anne Lister placed her order for the model of Switzerland she had previously enquired about, and which was to cost 1500 francs and measured 7 by 5 French feet (about 2.3 by 1.6 metres). After dinner, Anne Lister studied her maps and planned where they would go next.

Anne Lister: '*Went to her bed for thirty five minutes... long good kiss*'.

Thursday 24th and Friday 25 of July were leisurely days spent in Geneva. On Thursday afternoon Anne and Ann attended a concert at the cathedral, taking Eugenie and George with them, and then on Friday afternoon they went to another afternoon concert at the theatre, after which Ann Walker was hungry and thirsty, Anne Lister:
'*obliged to take her to a café for [a] bun and lemonade*'. That night, Anne Lister: '*Her bed stocks creaked so that the people in the adjoining room being up, I put Miss Walker's bedding on the floor, and we had a good long kiss. About three quarter hour with her*'.

The following morning, Saturday July 26th, Anne and Ann were out at 11.40 a.m. shopping for books and bought Bardon's Antique Costumes of the Greeks, Baily's history de l'Astronomie, the Dusseldorf Gallery of engravings, maps illustrating the travels of Anacharsis, all for Anne Lister, and Michelet's Abridgement of Modern History for Ann Walker. I am not sure that Ann Walker enjoyed looking round bookshops quite as much as Anne Lister. At 12.20 p.m. they set off in their carriage from the Hotel de Bergues, called at the Heutsch Bank to cash in two £25 circular notes, called at the bookshop to collect their parcel of books, then headed to the medieval city of Annecy, about thirty miles south of Geneva. The journey was very pleasant, the roads were good, and the scenery they viewed from the windows of the carriage included Mont Salève and Mont de Sion. They arrived at the Hotel de Genève at 7.00 p.m., took a quarter of an hour's walk to view Lake Annecy, then ate dinner in the public dining room in the hotel at 7.50 p.m. during which they were serenaded by a man playing the harp and a girl singing. Back in her room, Ann Walker got into bed and Anne sat with her, writing her journal.

The next morning, Sunday, July 27th, after breakfast at 7.45 a.m. they read prayers for forty minutes before being taken for a drive alongside Lake Annecy in a char, a little two wheeled, one horse carriage. Lake Annecy is a beautiful lake surrounded by alpine mountains. They stopped at a little auberge for Ann Walker to have some cold chicken for lunch then returned to their hotel in Annecy. At 3.33 p.m. the party set off in their carriage heading for the town of Aix-les-Bains, about 25 miles southwest of Annecy. They arrived at Aix-les-Bains at 7.25 p.m. and were taken to view the Roman baths. They had intended to spend the night at Aix-les-Bains but the hotels were full so at 8.08 p.m. they set off to Chambéry, a town about twelve miles further south, arriving at the hotel La Parfait Union at 10 p.m., and then dined at 11 p.m. Anne and Ann stayed four nights at the hotel La Parfait Union in Chambéry.

The next morning, Monday, Anne Lister had ordered a calêche (a small carriage with a folding roof) to come to the hotel to take her and Ann for a drive. However, the calêche was dirty so she refused to accept it. Instead, they went out on foot. They had a quick look round the cathedral, then stumbled upon a bookshop where Anne Lister ordered a set of Courtois and Aubert Lithographs. The two women then called at the Post Office to order a little carriage to collect them from the hotel later in the afternoon, then walked to Les Charmettes, which had been the home of the Genevan philosopher, Jean-Jacques Rousseau, and his mistress, Madame de Warens, in the 1730's. Ann Walker was, however, starting to feel hungry, so they walked back to the hotel so she could get something to eat. At 4.30 p.m. the carriage they had ordered arrived at the hotel to take the two of them for a drive to view a waterfall. Back at the hotel, they dined at 8.15 p.m. and this time it was Anne Lister's turn to overeat: *'too much dinner. Very hot. Asleep in my chair, after Eugenie left me, till near 11 p.m.'*

The next morning, Tuesday, July 29th, Anne and Ann, along with Eugenie and George, were taken for a drive in a calêche along the valley of Chambéry. They took a boat ride on Lake Bourget, near the town of Aix-les-Bains, however, the wind was starting to pick up, Anne Lister: *'Adney rather frightened but be-*

haved very well'.

On Wednesday, the weather was particularly bad, with heavy rain and thunderstorms. Anne, Ann, and George ventured out at 5.20 p.m. but the rain and thunderstorms returned and continued all evening and all night. The plan for Thursday morning was to visit the Monastery of the Grande Chartreuse in the mountains north of Grenoble but the heavy rain made this impossible. At 6.00 a.m. Anne Lister sent George to the Post Office to cancel the carriage she had booked for the trip. Feeling cold, she then got back into bed: *'Miss Walker came to me at eight and ten minutes. Had shewed me her bosom and, on my asking her, took off her night things and stood naked, so then got into bed and we had a kiss'.*

On the afternoon of Thursday, July 31st, they set off in their own carriage, heading south to Les Échelles, where they would stay for two nights before returning to the hotel La Parfait Union in Chambéry on Saturday August 2nd. They arrived at the Auberge de la Poste in Les Échelles at 6.23 p.m. and had dinner at 7.45 p.m. Now Anne Lister only occasionally recorded in her diary the details of the food she ate, and, on the occasions when she did, the food was either very good or very bad. On this occasion, the food was very good, Anne Lister: *'good potage, one trout, chicken, roast mutton, rice pudding, and plenty of strawberries'.*

Although there was heavy rain, thunder and lightning during the night, Anne Lister was up early the next morning, Friday, and went out with George to arrange for mules and a guide to take them up the mountain to visit the Monastery of the Grande Chartreuse. They set off at 10.30 a.m. and arrived at the Monastery at 1.00 p.m. only to discover that women were not permitted to enter. By this time Ann Walker was hungry. They entered a building a short distance from the monastery where Ann Walker sat down on a bench and ate some cold fowl, which they must have brought with them from the auberge. She then lay down on the bench and had a nap, using a cloak for a pillow.

When she awoke, she found that the not only had the heavy rain returned but it was accompanied by thunder and lightning. She also found that Anne Lister had made the decision that they would return to the Auberge de la Poste in Les Échelles, the weather having finally got the better of them. Their journey back to Les Échelles was not easy on account of one of the mules having stumbled and gone lame, so they were very glad when they arrived back at the auberge. They sat down to a good dinner at 6.33 p.m. and spent the remainder of the evening writing. Anne Lister wrote a letter to her friend, Lady Gordon and updated her journal and Ann Walker wrote 2½ pages to Aunt Anne then went to bed at 10 o'clock.

The following morning, Saturday, August 2nd, they set off in their carriage from Les Échelles heading back to Chambéry. En route they stopped at les Grottes de St Christophe which is an extensive natural cave system. Anne and Ann were able to view a large cavern, but the effects of the recent heavy rain prevented any further exploration. They arrived back at the hotel La Parfait Union in Chambéry at 2.25 p.m. On this occasion it was Anne Lister that was feeling tired, so she took a ½ hour nap, then she and Ann went out to the post office to post the letters they had written the previous evening. Back at the hotel, at 5.40 p.m. they had very good dinner which, along with veal cutlets, included a type of fish they had never eaten before, lavaret, which Anne Lister had seen being caught by the fishermen on Lake Bourget. And, that night: *'long, very good kiss to her'*.

On Sunday morning, they set off in their carriage from Chambéry at 9.00 a.m. heading south to Grenoble travelling along the valley of Grésivaudan, which Anne Lister described as a *'wooded rich beautiful valley …perhaps the most beautiful valley I ever saw'*. They arrived at the Hotel des Ambassadors in Grenoble at 3.50 p.m., which Anne Lister described as *'not a handsome looking hotel but had two double bedded rooms. Have just had (from 5.50 to 7 p.m.) a good dinner and are very comfortable'*.

Next morning, Monday, August 4th, Ann Walker had started with a particularly bad bowel complaint from which she did not fully recover until the following Friday. She stayed in bed on Monday morning and lay on the sofa in the early afternoon having had biscuits and brandy with water. Feeling a little better, she went out for a walk in the town with Anne Lister, but they had to return to the hotel after an hour, as she was too unwell to continue. On Tuesday morning they went out for a drive in a calêche taking George with them. They drove across a suspension bridge, over the Drac river, then after driving through the village of Sassenage, they drove as far up a very steep hill as was possible, got out of the carriage to walk to the top of the hill to view a quarry and the junction of the Drac and Isère rivers. No doubt it would have been Anne Lister's interest in geology that prompted this particular exploration. However, Ann Walker at this point was trying her best to soldier on despite being unwell with her bowel complaint. After walking for about twenty minutes, she could go no further. She sat down and rested while Anne continued up the hill to the viewing point. After about 50 minutes, Anne returned to find her eating the cold fowl they had brought with them for lunch, using one stone as a seat and another stone as a table. Back at their hotel, in Grenoble, after dinner, Anne Lister: *'Dawdling with Miss Walker. Her bowels grumbling and she wanted petting'*. Well, we all need a bit of mollycoddling when we are poorly.

Still feeling unwell the next day, Wednesday, Ann Walker decided to remain at the hotel to rest while Anne explored a chateau fort north of the town. Anne returned to the hotel 3.30 p.m. and about an hour later they set off in their carriage heading north-west along the valley, *'a fine beautiful drive'* to the town of Voreppe. They had intended to spend the night in Voreppe but the auberge was very shabby and Ann Walker feared there was a risk of them getting fleas, so they continued their drive to Voiron, alighting at the Hotel du Cours at 9.40 p.m. where they had a nice supper.

The following morning, Thursday, August 7, Anne Lister: *'She came to me about eight to warm her stomach. Still bowel complaint, and I tended in a long good kiss to her and our lying till tolerably cool'.* I do love Anne Lister's belief in the medicinal benefits of sex. They had a late breakfast then Anne made tea for Ann Walker using the Jones' boiler that she had brought with them. I have not been able to find an image of this device but since Anne described it as having a spirit burner, I imagine it was probably similar to the little meths burning Trangia stove I used when camping in my youth. Ann Walker, feeling much improved after having sex, followed by breakfast, and a nice cup of tea, proceeded to eat large bowl of strawberries. The weather now being much improved, the two women went out for a long drive in a light, one horse calêche.

The following morning, Friday August 8th, they set off in their carriage from the Hotel du Cours, in Voiron, at 10 a.m. heading north-west to the city of Lyon. This was a long drive, about sixty miles. They travelled all day, arriving at the hotel de l'Europe, Lyon, at 8.15 p.m. They took a *'very good, handsome apartment'* on the 1st floor comprising a salon, with two master bedrooms and an ante room, and were very comfortable. They spent three nights at this hotel. Over the next few days, Anne and Ann enjoyed themselves out and about in Lyon. They went shopping for shawls for Marian and old Miss Walker, visited the Roman temple of Diana, and the Roman baths. On the Sunday night, Anne Lister: *'Long good kiss last night, twenty minutes with her...... she came to me for about an hour this morning, lay talking'.*

On Monday morning, however, there was a misunderstanding between the two women. It transpired that Anne Lister had said something inadvertently that had upset Ann, although Anne Lister had no idea what it was that she had said to cause the upset and Ann would not tell her, which, in turn, upset Anne Lister. As a result, during the rest of the day, things were a bit strained between them. They set off in their carriage from the hotel de l'Europe, Lyon, at 4.45 p.m. and at 9 p.m. arrived at the hotel Saint Jacques at Rive-de-Gier about 25 miles south-west of Lyon. Anne Lister: *'Not inclined to talk. Miss Walker fancied I said something this morning that I did not. Could not get her to tell me what and this disappointed me. She observed my silence but thought me not well'.*

Before breakfast on Tuesday morning, August 12th, Anne and Ann spent an hour visiting a local foundry and coal pit. During breakfast back at the hotel, they sorted the misunderstanding between them. Anne Lister: *'Made all right with Adney. She told me she thought I had said all we had (meaning all we were now spending) was hers and I ought to think it as much mine as hers. I said I could not bear her to refuse me anything or keep anything secret from me and we were both attendries [softened] and better friends than ever'.* Clearly Ann Walker was keen that she and Anne treated their individual incomes as belonging to them both. Visiting a foundry and a coal pit whilst on holiday may not seem the most enjoyable of activities, however, this was the first of a series of such visits, they made between the 12th and 16th August, that formed a fact-finding tour aimed at developing their knowledge of coal mining given their plans to further develop the coal reserves at Shibden. They set off from hotel Saint Jacques, Rive-de-Gier, at 11.33 a.m. heading south-west to the town of Saint-Étienne, alighting at the hotel de l'Europe at 2.20 p.m. Anne Lister ordered a small one-horse carriage, and they went to the école des mines to speak to the mining engineer there. They then visited the Côte Thiollière coal pit and went underground to view the mine workings. The descent was very steep, so Anne Lister sent Ann back to the surface while she continued deeper into the mine but only for a short while as she was *'afraid of leaving Adney so long'.* Over the next few days Anne and Ann continued their mining research staying overnight at Montbrison, Pont du Chateau, and Clermont. On Sunday, August 17th, at 1.30 p.m. they left Clermont, essentially heading back to Paris. They stayed in Vichy on the Sunday night, in Saint-Gérard-le-Puy on Monday night, in La Charité-sur-Loire on Tuesday night, and slept overnight in their carriage on Wednesday night, arriving in Paris at 10.29 a.m. on the morning of Thursday, August 21st, Anne Lister: *'neither of us the worse for being up all night'.* I imagine that Ann Walker would have been able get some sleep in the carriage as they travelled, what with her being able to sleep anywhere, anytime. Anne Lister, however, would have to be involved each time they stopped at a coaching inn to change the horses, so any sleep she did get would have been disturbed.

On arriving in Paris, they went straight to Anne's little apartment on the Rue Saint-Victor to collect their mail. However, their mail had just been forwarded to Geneva, Anne Lister: *'How terribly unlucky!'* Next, they were off to Meurice's. Unfortunately, all that was available was a tiny apartment on the third floor consisting of a single bedded room with a small sitting room, so a type of camp bed had to be brought in for Ann Walker. Anne Lister wrote a letter to the director of the post office in Geneva requesting their letters be sent back to them, they then washed and dressed and went out for a walk. Saturday was devoted to shopping, mostly for presents, and the daytime on Sunday was spent letter writing and getting everything sorted for the journey back home. That evening, they set off from Paris in their carriage at 5.35 p.m. heading for Calais.

Their journey from Paris to Calais was impressive, to say the least. Approximately two hundred miles with no overnight stops. On the road for about 36 hours. Anne Lister: *'Adney has borne the 2 nights up uncommonly well, seems not at all tired, slept very well and quietly all last night'.* Their arrival at Calais at 5.25 a.m. on the morning of Tuesday, August 26th, luckily coincided with the scheduled 6.00 a.m. passage of the steam packet, the Ferret, so by 9.15 a.m. they were in Dover.

I so admire their stamina. I suppose in those days, if you chose to travel long distances, and wanted to make good time, it was accepted that you might have to travel during the night. Already aware that Anne Lister was a seasoned traveller, I must now conclude that Ann Walker, on her first trip abroad, took to travelling like a duck to water. Good on you, girl! They were off from Dover at 2.45 p.m. having had to wait for their carriage to be landed and then released by customs. Then drove the fifty miles to Rochester arriving at the Wright's hotel at 9.35p.m. They had a supper of tea and shrimps then slept together in a comfortable double bed, Anne Lister: *'Long good kiss. Slept together, first time since Paris'.*

The following day, Wednesday, August 27th, they had a leisurely morning then set off in their carriage heading for London at 11.25 a.m. arriving at the Hawkins Hotel, Dover Street, at 4.18 p.m. where they took a very comfortable first floor apartment. Anne Lister immediately wrote a letter to her Aunt Anne saying that they expected to be at Shibden on Saturday night, or possibly Sunday morning, then she arranged for a hairdresser to come from Truefitts of Bond Street, to cut hers and Ann's hair. Before breakfast the following morning, Thursday, a kind letter arrived from Mariana, Anne Lister: *'still thinks of me too often and loves me too well but time ceases all things'.* In her letter, Mariana requested that Anne go to Wilks on Regent Street to get her 10 shillings worth of coronation braiding. After breakfast, Anne and Ann were very busy out and about shopping in London. In the afternoon Anne Lister called on Lady Stuart in Whitehall while Ann did more shopping on Oxford Street. That night, at 10 p.m. Anne Lister made a second visit to Lady Stuart in Whitehall. As was the custom, she could not take Ann with her not having, as yet, been formally introduced.

After breakfast at 10.15 a.m. on Friday morning, and having spent half an hour settling a dispute between Eugenie and George, Anne and Ann set off in their carriage heading back to Shibden. They planned to travel all of Friday night and took the route to Halifax via St. Albans, Newport Pagnell, Leicester,

Sheffield, and Huddersfield. As they passed through Newport Pagnell, Anne Lister bought Eugenie a pair of thick large lambswool stockings to put on over her shoes during the night, the temperature being significantly lower than when they were in France. Anne Lister: *'Both Adney and I slept a good deal. She, very comfy, not having to awake at each stage as I did'*. Anne and Ann did some shopping as they passed through Sheffield mid-afternoon purchasing a portable teapot containing a coffee pot, cream and sugar basins for £6. They arrived back home at Shibden at 8.55 p.m. on Saturday night and went straight to see Aunt Anne.

Well, their honeymoon had begun as they left York on Wednesday, June 4th, and finished when they returned to Shibden on Saturday, August 30th. During those three months, there were a couple of minor misunderstandings but certainly not a single cross word. In fact, not only were they very much at ease with each other, they appeared to be well entertained by each other's company. Travelling huge distances in their carriage was not a problem for Ann Walker, in fact she clearly was a happy traveller, particularly since she could always take a nap as they went along. There were just two occasions in those three months when Ann Walker was fidgeting in the carriage, having eaten too much, causing some irritation to Anne Lister. Fortunately, Anne Lister did learn from this that Ann, unlike her, needed lunch. Although Ann did not have Anne Lister's level of physicality, well, not many people did, she was up for everything that Anne had planned and showed drive, determination, and increasing levels of stamina as their travels continued. Anne Lister was able to decide pretty much everything that they did, and she got to have sex most nights, both of which would have pleased her, and also, certainly for this trip, they shared the expenses. So, was Ann Walker the perfect travelling companion for Anne Lister? Absolutely she was!

CHAPTER 11: SETTING UP HOME AT SHIBDEN

Sunday, August 31st, 1834, was the first full day for Anne Lister and Ann Walker living together at Shibden as a married couple. The next month or so would be exciting and, at times, exhausting for them both as they brought Ann Walker's possessions from Lidgate to Shibden, made extensive changes to some of the rooms at the hall and bought new furniture and furnishings to create their own space where they could be comfortable and cozy. For Ann Walker, however, the relaxed carefree time she had enjoyed whilst her and Anne were travelling abroad was over. The reality of the consequences of her decision to move into Shibden would hit her that first day when she and Anne went to Cliff Hill to visit her aunt, old Miss Walker, after they had attended the Sunday service at St. Matthews. Old Miss Walker shook Anne Lister's hand on their arrival but did so reluctantly. Anne Lister described old Miss Walker's actions: *'scolded Adney all the time. No shew of pleasure to see us'*. Ostensibly, old Miss Walker was annoyed because her niece had gone abroad without informing her, although I think, in reality, it is more likely that she was simply angry that Ann had decided to live at Shibden Hall.

The following day, Monday, September 1st, Anne and Ann's letters, that had mistakenly been forwarded from Paris to Geneva, arrived at Shibden. There was one letter for Ann Walker from her sister, Elizabeth, two letters for Eugenie, and two letters for Anne Lister from Mariana. In her letters, Mariana suggested that Anne's infrequent letters to her whilst abroad showed that she was neglecting her. Mariana also suggested that Anne would not have neglected Sibbella McLean or Vere Hobart in this way. Anne had written only a few letters whilst she had been on her honeymoon, which I suppose was to be expected, but Anne and Mariana had always corresponded quite frequently, probably every two to three weeks, so it was not surprising that Mariana was upset. Anne was certainly quite shocked that Mariana had charged her with neglect and in her reply she wrote: *'I never suspected the possibility of reproach from that quarter whence I least deserved it. But those who might be supposed to know us best are not always those who do us most rigorous justice. Mary, I leave your own heart to judge'.*

Since their arrival back at Shibden, Anne and Ann slept together in what had been Anne Lister's bedroom, known as the blue room. However, Anne Lister, being very keen to ensure Ann's comfort now that she had moved in with her, decided to make the upper kitchen chamber into a bedroom for the two of them. I understand that the upper kitchen chamber was the room above the upper kitchen, which would surely mean that it would be relatively warm, which would be nice for them given how cold Shibden Hall was in winter. Work began on their new bedroom on Monday September 1st, with the start of the construction of a *'tent wise top'* which would cover a large part of the ceiling. Having a tented room in your property was considered very fashionable in the 19th century, the idea being to use large swathes of fabric to make the room look like the interior of a luxurious tent. Anne and Ann's new bedroom was therefore to be called the *'tent room'*. Apart from a walk in the Shibden estate and measuring up the north parlour for a new carpet, this day had not been particularly busy for the two women, but that night Anne Lister described Ann as being *'much tired'*. I do wonder if Ann Walker's tiredness was a symptom of her increasing level of anxiety on her return to Halifax.

Ann Walker had been very upset by her aunt's hostility towards her on her first visit to Cliff Hill after their return from the continent. A few days later, Thursday, September 4th, her cousins, William and Eliza Priestley, called at Shibden Hall. However, both Ann and Anne were at Lidgate packing up china so the

Priestleys sat with Marian for a little while. Later, when Anne and Ann returned, Marian described the visit. George had answered the door to the Priestleys who gave him their card on which they had made it clear that they wanted to see Ann Walker, not Anne Lister. Marian described William Priestley as being in a bad temper. He had made reference to Ann Walker being at Shibden and *'said how long she would remain was another thing'*. He also complained that *'Ann had not consulted any of her friends. Had not named her intention even to her aunt of Cliff Hill'*. Marian's description of the visit clearly indicated bitterness on the part of the Priestleys. Whilst Anne and Ann were at Lidgate House, some of Ann Walker's other relatives called there, but the servants turned them away as Ann Walker had given orders that no one was to be admitted. Ann Walker was clearly trying to avoid her relatives knowing they may be hostile to her moving into Shibden. It is no wonder that she was becoming increasingly stressed.

Anne and Ann were continuing the huge task of organising the transfer of Ann Walker's favourite possessions from Lidgate to Shibden and packing up the remainder to go into storage. In addition, Ann Walker, with the help of Samuel Washington, was trying to find a suitable tenant to rent her former home. On Saturday, September 6th, Anne Lister recorded in her journal that a Mr. Hird: *'took Lidgate and all the land and the house furnished for 10 years at £100 per annum'*. At the same time, Anne Lister was trying to find a new tenant for Northgate House, part of the Shibden estate but so far without success. Both Ann and Anne had frequent meetings with Samuel Washington regarding estate business. He appears to have been a massive help to them both, being reliable and thrustworthy and even collecting their rents for them. Anne Lister, also with Samuel Washington's help, was still having discussions and gathering information regarding the sinking of a coal pit in Cunnery wood, although at this point, September 1834, little significant progress had been made. I will apologise now for including only minimal references to coal related issues, just not my cup of tea, sorry.

The following Monday, September 8th, Ann Walker again went to visit her aunt at Cliff Hill. This time she went alone, although Anne Lister did subsequently go to Cliff Hill to collect her. Anne Lister: *'no shake-hands with her aunt, who had been crosser than ever. How tiresome. Gets upon Adney's nerves and undoes all good. Surely she will cease to care for such senseless scolding by and by. All sorts of bitterness against me. I am said to have said in York, I would have nothing to do with her "troublesome friends" and indeed her friends, said Mrs Ann Walker [Adney's aunt], would not trouble her (Adney) much at Shibden. The poor old woman's head is crammed full of potheration and untruths'.* After her sister Elizabeth, Ann's aunt at Cliff Hill was her closest living relative, so experiencing this level of hostility from her, particularly as Ann had always been her most attentive niece, must have caused her great distress.

The transfer of Ann Walker's belongings from Lidgate to Shibden was done by cart and took about three weeks to complete. Packing things up at Lidgate then unpacking and siding when they arrived on the cart at Shibden was an exhausting task for the two women. Some of the items transferred were a mahogany wardrobe, two mahogany bureaus, a mahogany chest of drawers, a table, a large collection of glassware, china, crockery, and linen. The wine cellar at Lidgate House contained a huge collection of both alcoholic and non-alcoholic beverages and preserves. In fact, Anne Lister had a new wine cellar created at Shibden simply to house the collection. Whilst they were away on their honeymoon, a coach house had been created in the barn with the area outside the coach house then being repaved. During Anne and Ann's first month or so at Shibden together, further changes were made to the barn including a new laundry with a fire range and chimney, a shoe black workshop, a new coal place, as well as a new window created at one end of the barn for a workshop for wood seasoning. At the front of the hall, flower beds were designed and created, mostly under Ann Walker's supervision.

Inside Shibden Hall the refurbishments continued at a pace. Dressmakers came to make the tent for Anne and Ann's new bedroom ceiling. A new mantlepiece was also designed for the north parlour along with new curtains and a window blind. The new carpet for the north parlour was fitted by a Mrs. Lee. I mention this just because I had not expected a carpet fitter in 1834 to be female. New fire grates were fitted in the north parlour, north chamber and the tent room. The bed curtains on the couple's bed were taken down by Ann Walker and Eugenie and sent to Leeds to be cleaned, and Anne Lister did a clear out of the Hall Chamber closet and organised for a window to be created. This closet would then be used to store all the linens they had brought from Lidgate.

On Thursday, September 11th, a letter arrived at Shibden from Mariana. She was staying in Scarborough with her sisters, Anne Belcombe and Harriet Milne. Mariana was feeling very poorly so I wonder if the trip to Scarborough had been taken primarily for the benefit of her health. Apparently, Anne Lister's friend, Lady Stuart had also not received a letter from her for some time and had written to Mariana to inquire about her. Realising that Anne had not written to her other friends whilst abroad, had been a comfort to Mariana. In her letter she wrote: *'what you say on the subject of not writing, while you were abroad, gives me all the consolation that you intended… may our friendship, which while we could see each other never suffered one moments interruption and which I firmly believe no length of absence will lessen burn bright until our last here and be renewed in a better world to last for ever and ever. I have loved you long and fondly, I love you no less at present tho' our position with regard to each other is so changed, that I cannot now, as hitherto I have ever done when in Yorkshire, anticipate the happiness of our meeting.… now the material for hope seems worn out and I begin to think this blessing is beyond my reach'*.

About five days later, Anne wrote a long letter to Mariana which included words of comfort, an attempt to cheer her, and a lot of *'chit-chat'* about one thing or another.

Those first few months back at Shibden were certainly hectic and this did appear to take its toll on the couple. Anne Lister taking daytime naps whenever she got the chance, and Ann Walker going off to bed early, was a clear indication that they were feeling more tired than usual. However, for Ann Walker there was more to her fatigue than just being very busy. Besides going early to bed, with increasing frequency, she had Anne rub her back with brandy as the back pain that had plagued her in the past had returned. Given that the strenuous physical demands of their travels round France and Switzerland had not upset Ann Walker's supposedly weak spine, I think it is likely that its reoccurrence was due to the stress caused by her fear of what people thought of her moving in to Shibden Hall with Anne Lister. Unfortunately, this fear was made much worse by the behaviour of her aunt at Cliff Hill and other members of her tribe of relations.

On Thursday, September 25th, a letter arrived at Shibden from Mariana, sent from Scarborough, thanking Anne for the parcel she had sent containing stays, laces and the earrings that Anne had bought her whilst travelling on the continent. Unfortunately, Anne's last letter to Mariana had failed to provide her with any comfort and she was again complaining about the lack of correspondence from Anne whilst she was abroad with Ann Walker. Mariana was also now denying all remembrance of having told Anne that she would not leave her husband. Anne Lister: *'How strange! How inconceivable a lapse of memory! vide Journal of May 1832'.* The knowledge that Anne was in a committed relationship with Ann Walker was clearly too much for Mariana to bear.

At Shibden, work on the tent room was progressing well, and although not quite finished, on Saturday, September 27th, Anne and Ann's bed was moved from the blue room into the tent room and that night they slept there for the first time. Despite the bed curtains having not yet returned from the cleaners, they slept *'very comfortably, very warm'*. The tent room and the blue room opened on to the opposite ends of the library passage. The blue room was to have a new sofa, similar to one they had admired in Paris, new curtains, and also a new ornate mantlepiece. It would serve at times as a dressing room, a breakfast room, a sitting room, and occasionally a dining room. Greenwoods, in Halifax, were commissioned to make a large bookcase for the blue room. The bookcase was to be about 7 ft by 6½ ft and would take six weeks to make. The tent room and the blue room were also linked by interconnecting doors, so these two rooms along with the study at the end of the library passage effectively formed a private suite for the two women.

On the afternoon of Monday, September 29th, Ann Walker had a few visitors call at Shibden Hall to see her. Her cousins Miss Atkinson and Charles Atkinson, called at 2.30 p.m. followed by Mr. Plowes and Mrs. Dyson at 3.00 p.m. Anne Lister wrote: *'I kept out of the way, not, of course, being asked for by either party'.*

A few days later, Thursday October 2nd, Anne Lister called on elderly Mrs Rawson at Stoney Royde, Halifax. Mrs. Rawson told Anne that Ann Walker was the subject of gossip in Halifax. Anne Lister: *'all the town talking of Adney's coming here [Shibden]. So cruel to leave her aunt and how did my father like so many femmes [women] in the house. With her fortune, so strange to give up her house and come and live so out of the world'.* Anne, deciding to set the record straight, explained to Mrs Rawson that Ann's aunt had not wanted Ann to move in with her at Cliff Hill, and in moving to Shibden, Ann was actually only 2 miles from her aunt. She pointed out that both her and Ann were alone and how much better and comfortable to be living at Shibden together, and that her aunt, father and sister were pleased with the new living arrangements. Anne said to Mrs. Rawson: *'people should know all sides before they judge'.* Mrs. Rawson agreed and seemed satisfied but did have some news for her. Ann's aunt at Cliff Hill had invited one of her other nieces, Mary Rawson, to live with her. On returning to Shibden, Anne told Ann all she had heard from Mrs. Rawson which, not surprisingly, caused her considerable upset.

Not only was she the subject of gossip, which was one of her greatest fears, but that her aunt had deceived her by implying that Mary Rawson, who Ann had seen at Cliff Hill, was just visiting not actually moving in with her.

The following Tuesday morning, October 7th, no doubt at Anne Lister's request, her father and sister paid a formal call on Ann's aunt at Cliff Hill. Although Anne, herself, was persona non grata with Ann Walker's relatives, the Lister family was high up the pecking order in Halifax society, certainly much higher than the Walkers, so Jeremy and Marian calling at Cliff Hill would be seen as an honour to old Miss Walker. I am sure this was what Anne Lister was counting on. Her plan worked, and when she and Ann called at Cliff Hill that afternoon they were very well received. The following Saturday, October 11th, when again they called on Ann Walker's aunt, they were graciously received. Looks like Anne Lister had got the measure of old Miss Walker.

Besides her relatives' disapproval, there was another issue that was bothering Ann Walker. This was a financial matter that appeared to have been ongoing for many years. In 1830, when Ann's brother died, she and her sister, Elizabeth, had jointly inherited the Walker estate in accordance with their father's will. It seems that the caveats in the will prevented Elizabeth's husband, Captain Sutherland, from automatically getting his hands on his wife's property, as would have been expected in the 19th century. So, Elizabeth, herself, had settled her property on her husband, much to Ann's annoyance. Ann, it appears, thought that Elizabeth should have settled the property on her children not her husband. As a consequence, Ann wanted it recognised in law which parts of the estate were hers and which now belonged to Captain Sutherland. Well, the Walker estate was extensive, and the required legal process very complex, so the whole business was taking a long time, and Ann was getting fed up with it all. In fact, on the evening of Saturday, September 27th, she was somewhat more than fed up: *'She had four glasses of madeira at dinner.... would have a division of the property, what she would say to Captain Sutherland about it. She enraged against them'.*

Just a word or two here about Anne and Ann's plans for their own finances. Although they believed, in the eyes of God, they were married, legally they were not and never would be. So, any suggestion that Anne Lister wanted to marry Ann Walker to get control of her fortune, as a potential husband might, is clearly incorrect. The two women agreed to consider their incomes to belong to them jointly. This was something that Ann Walker was very keen on, despite the fact, at this time, her income exceeded Anne's. Anne Lister did borrow capital from Ann to make improvements to Shibden Hall and to develop the profitability of the Shibden estate. These loans, of course, were approved by Ann Walker, and were secured and arranged at 4% interest. Yes, there would be occasions during their marriage, when the two women disagreed over a financial matter, but Ann Walker was no mug, and for the most part, in this regard, they were as harmonious as most couples.

I daresay you may be wondering just how active Anne and Ann's sex life was during their first month at Shibden. Well, you can decide for yourself. Their first week at Shibden saw Ann Walker stressed and tired and therefore retiring to bed early. On September 7th, clearly disappointed, Anne Lister described the previous night: *'she always tired'*. However, she described the night of September 8th: *'good kiss last night'*. Another week passed quietly, followed by a flurry of activity with Anne writing on both the 16th and 18th September: *'very good kiss last night'*. Then on September 19th: *'Long grubbling last night. Really tolerable kiss to me, the best I have ever had of Adney, but very bad one to her'.* She wrote: *'good one last night'* for the nights of Monday and Tuesday, the 22nd and 23r September, and then a week later: *'pretty good one last night'.*

Regarding matters of business, both Anne and Ann were intent on purchasing additional land for the Shibden and Walker estates, and Anne Lister's plan, to mine Shibden coal, was getting ever closer to realisation. On the evening of Friday, October 3rd, at the Stags Head Inn, an event, organised by Samuel Washington and James Holt, acting for Anne, was held for interested parties to bid for the contract to sink a pit in Cunnery wood on the Shibden estate. The event was very well attended and the contract, to sink what was to be called the Walker pit, was won by the Mann brothers. By the way, the folly-like tower that was the ventilation shaft, built for the Walker pit, still stands on the edge of Cunnery wood.

One thing I have noticed about Anne and Ann's first month or so at Shibden was the increasing amount of time that they were spending in the company of Marian, Jeremy, and Aunt Anne. I think Ann Walker was becoming much more comfortable with the other members of her new family and they appeared to be genuinely pleased to have her living with them. Indeed, when Anne Lister was out on the Shibden estate organising the workmen, Ann would often be sat in the parlour with Marian and Jeremy. After dinner, in the evenings, Anne and Ann often played backgammon in the parlour in the company of Marian and Jeremy, and occasionally Aunt Anne, who, because of her failing health, did spend quite a lot of time in her bedroom, being visited periodically, during the day, by Marian and Ann Walker and always, every evening, by Anne Lister. Jeremy was also becoming increasingly frail, and to help himself to get out and about, he splashed out on a new carriage, a Briska phaeton, that he would drive himself.

On October 8th, Anne Lister wrote a reply to Mariana's letter received on September 25th. In her letter Anne was as usual, affectionate, reassuring and comforting to Mariana, but also commented on Mariana's claim that she had no recollection of having said to Anne, during her visit to Lawton Hall in May 1832, that she intended to live and die at there.

On the morning of Thursday, October 16th, Anne and Ann were sat with Marian and Jeremy, in the little breakfast room at Shibden, whilst Marian explained about a possible change in her circumstances. In previous conversations with Anne Lister, Marian had expressed her concern regarding the likely size of her income after the death of their father, Jeremy. It is my understanding that the bulk of Jeremy's income came from two sources. Firstly, he received an income, for his lifetime, from the Shibden estate as specified in his brother James' will and secondly, from his small Skelfler estate in Market Weighton. At this time Jeremy was financially supporting Marian, but after his death, Marian was to inherit Skelfler. She said that her income after her father's death would be about £300 per year (equivalent to £36000 in today's money) most of which can be assumed to be generated by Skelfler. Now, suppose Marian wanted her own home, say with one or two servants, the income generated by her inheritance from Jeremy, would obviously not be enough. Anne had told Marian that she would always have a home at Shibden and that she would give her money should she require it. However, as I have said before, life was particularly precarious in those days, so it was understandable that Marian had been considering other options regarding her future financial security. The two options she was looking into were either sharing a house with a female friend, a Miss Posey, who had her own independent income, or marriage to a man who had lately been showing an interest in her, a Mr. Abbott, who lived in Halifax. Well actually it was more than showing an interest, it would seem that he had proposed marriage to Marian. So back to the conversation in the little breakfast room that morning. Anne Lister: *'It seems she had made up her mind to marry Mr Abbot. I promised not to name it to anyone. Said I would not advise against it, but I did not think it would answer so well as she might think. She did not know the mortification of giving up her own family .... agreed she could not live happily alone but to mind not to leap out of the frying pan into the fire'.* Although Marian did say she liked Mr.

Abbott, her discussion of her finances plus her plan to only marry after her father had died, does suggest that the marriage was motivated primarily by the need to secure her financial future. Mr. Abbott was not a landowner. He was involved in the wool trade and Marian could only guess at the size of his income, hence Anne's comment regarding the frying pan and the fire. The following day, Friday, October 17th, Marian told Anne that: *'she had not determined on taking Mr. Abbott. Did not know that she should do it'.* Clearly, Marian was confused and uncertain of the best course of action to take.

Although Anne and Ann had settled happily into their daily life together, Ann Walker continued to get tired, so took herself off to bed usually by ten o'clock, whilst Anne Lister read or wrote in her study. I think it can be assumed that Anne Lister would have been up for having sex every night given the opportunity, so I suspect that she would have been disappointed that, during the month of October, she and Ann Walker had sex on just four occasions, and even then, according to Anne Lister, not overly successfully. Anne Lister described the night of October 13th: *'A tolerable kiss last night. Weight of two blankets and quilt rather much. She a little exhausted and said "it is killing work".* Anne's journal entry describing the night of October 16th, showed her increasing confusion: *'A kiss last night but no better than the last. She said I did not give her dinky as at first. How was it that she did not feel moisture from me as before?'* I think that Ann Walker was a woman who needed a lot of sleep. You may recall from the honeymoon chapter, that she was in the habit of taking a nap at some point during daytime. This did not seem to be happening once they were back at Shibden so by bedtime she was too knackered to have any interest in sex. My theory is supported by the events of Sunday, November 2nd, and Tuesday November 11th. On the Sunday, Anne and Ann had dinner at 6.05 p.m. and afterwards sat chatting with Marian and Jeremy. They then had coffee upstairs in the blue room and Anne Lister read aloud to Ann Walker from her Chinese history book till 9.15 p.m. Anne

Lister described what followed: '*She on the amoroso. I happening to say I wished we were in bed. She said "well let us go and take off drawers" which we did and in quarter of an hour had a pretty good kiss. Then put on my pelisse etc. again, at 9.40 p.m.*' On the Tuesday evening, Ann Walker hid the key to Anne's study so as to get her into bed early and make love, which they did. So, a bit earlier in the evening, before she was too tired, Ann Walker was not just up for having sex, she initiated it.

On Friday, October 31st, a letter arrived at Shibden from Mariana who was now back at Lawton Hall, having spent six weeks in Scarborough. However, it transpired that her route home from Scarborough had been via York and Halifax. Apparently, Mariana's carriage had passed within a hundred yards of Shibden Hall but she had decided not to visit, presumably she was not yet ready to meet Ann Walker. Anne Lister was shocked. Mariana wrote: '*Be my friend, be all that a new engagement will admit of, and for this, Mary will not be ungrateful. She has loved you dearly, fondly and faithfully. She loves you no less at present, but she loves you too well to be a source of discomfort to you. Tho' we should never meet again my wishes and prayers for you will not cease and to know you are happy will be always a source from which I myself can draw comfort and pleasure*'. Again, Anne Lister was shocked. Realising just how bad a state Mariana had got herself into, Anne immediately wrote a reply. Her letter was supportive and comforting but also firm, insisting that Mariana should never again leave her in ignorance of her whereabouts. Anne Lister: '*why should we never meet again? Of what comparative use or pleasure, the affection of one whom we never can see? Why put off meeting? There is no moral courage in this delay. But it is not I who may determine. You must judge for yourself, and heaven grant that your judgement is right*'.

In early November, Anne and Ann decided that it was time for them to pay social calls on some of Ann Walker's many relatives. At 9.30 a.m. on Monday, November 3rd, they set off in their carriage, and three quarters of an hour later, arrived at Mill House, where they sat with Mary Rawson and her daughter Caroline for fifteen minutes. Then off to Thorpe to visit Mr. John Priestley. Followed by a call at Haugh End to visit Mary Priestley, then on to Willow Field to call on Mrs. Dyson and Lucy Atkinson. After this they continued on to Darcy Hey to visit with Mr. and Mrs. John Edwards who Anne Lister described as *'very properly civil'*, with Mrs. Edwards declaring that she had never seen Ann Walker looking so well. As they continued on their travels Ann Walker ate the sandwiches they had taken with them for her lunch. Some of her relatives were not at home and a few others chose not to receive them, but they did go on to call on Mrs. Catherine Rawson then old Mrs. Rawson at Stoney Royde, who Anne Lister described as *'very glad to see us and very kind and civil'*. Half an hour at Heath with Mrs. and Miss Wilkinson and home at 5.45 p.m., dinner at 6.45 p.m. followed by coffee at 7.30 p.m. A little while afterwards, Marian called for Anne and Ann to go out onto the flags in front of the house to look at an amazing circle of light covering about two thirds of the sky. I am guessing this was the optical phenomenon known as a halo with the moon at its centre. The phenomenon was clearly very extensive as it was reported in the Liverpool Courier, the Birmingham Advertiser, and the Herald.

As I have already mentioned, Ann Walker had, for a long time, been trying to separate the Walker estate property she had jointly inherited with her sister, Elizabeth. Ann intended that the Sutherland children would be her eventual heirs but, in the meantime, she was not happy that Captain Sutherland still had a say in her business. At this point in time, the two big estates, Cliff Hill and Crow Nest, making up the bulk of the Walker property, belonged to Ann and Captain Sutherland respectively. However, Captain Sutherland treated his Crow Nest tenants ruthlessly, and Ann, being the kind, caring person that she was, disapproved, and did not want people to associate her with his cruel behaviour. Up to this point, the partition of the Walker estate had been in the hands of an administrator, a Mrs. Clarke, although little progress had been made, seemingly because Captain Sutherland was dragging his feet. Anyway, annoyed at this, Ann wanted to go to York to see her solicitor, Mr. Gray, to try get things moving.

On Tuesday, November 25th, at 9.39 a.m. Anne and Ann set off in their carriage to York, accompanied by their servants, Eugenie and George, and also Charles Haworth, a carpenter who had been doing a lot of work on the refurbishments at Shibden Hall and on the estate. The party travelled via Leeds and Tadcaster, did some shopping here and there en route, and arrived at the Black Swan in York at 4.25 p.m. Anne and Ann had a hairdresser come to their room to cut their hair, then, at 5.30 p.m. had dinner. In the evening, they visited old Mrs. Belcombe, Mariana's mother. Charlotte Norcliffe, Harriet Milne and two other ladies were also there, and they all had tea together. Both Anne and Ann observed that Charlotte and Harriet were rather cool with them. Anne Lister explained: *'It seemed Mrs. Milne and Charlotte fancied I must have known Mrs. Norcliffe arrived in London on the 8th of June, the very day Ann and I arrived!!! And that I did not choose to call upon her in London!!! How absurdly untrue! I saw, however, that all I could say was in vain. Adney as much surprised at Charlotte Norcliffe's huffiness as I was'.* I wonder if, in reality, Charlotte and Harriet were jealous that Anne Lister was no longer as attentive to them as she had been previously.

The following morning, Wednesday, at ten o'clock, Ann Walker's solicitor, Mr. Gray arrived at the Black Swan to advise her about the partition of hers and Captain Sutherland's joint property. He explained that Ann may have to file a bill in the Chancery to compel the partition at a cost about £150, equivalent to about £18000 in today's money. That was a lot of money, but those of you familiar with Charles Dickens' Bleak House, will know all about the goings on at the Chancery. Ann also asked Mr. Gray about the two large pews in St. Matthew's church that the Sutherlands claimed should belong to them. Although I can imagine there may have been many minor issues such as this that Captain Sutherland and Ann were unable to agree on, I do wonder if Captain Sutherland was hoping to get his hands on the whole of the Walker estate. Then, after paying a call on Dr. and Mrs. Belcombe, Ann and Anne returned to the Black Swan for Ann Walker's lesson with her drawing master, Mr. Brown. After an early dinner, the two women set off in their carriage at 4.30 p.m. with their servants, Eugenie and George, to travel to Hull. Charles Haworth had set off a few hours earlier, travelling by public coach to Hull, with a note for management of the Cross Keys Hotel to make ready for the arrival of *'Miss Lister and Miss Walker'*. The party alighted at the Cross Keys Hotel, the Market Place, Hull, at 9.48 p.m. and had tea. Hull is a port on England's east coast and their journey from York to Hull had taken over five hours, so why did they choose to travel there? Well, Hull was the best place for the purchase of wood, and the continuing refurbishments at Shibden needed wood in large quantities.

The next day, Thursday, November 27th, Charles Haworth checked out Hull's timber merchants looking for the best deals, whilst Anne and Anne went out shopping. After breakfast, the following morning, Friday, Charles reported back to Anne Lister which timber merchants had the best deals for the wood they required, then Anne and Ann went out to look round a few bookshops in the town centre. Besides books, these shops also sold a variety of pamphlets, maps and other publications and Anne Lister was specifically looking for any information related to the new form of transport that was just starting to appear across England, the railway. She had shares in companies running parts of the country's canal system and these shares had been contributing significant amounts to her income. So, it was important that she found out if the railways were likely to impact on the transportation of goods by canal and thereby affect her dividends. Anne and Ann had an early dinner at their hotel and the party set off in their carriage at 3.57 p.m. arriving at the George Inn, Selby, at 9.30 p.m. and had tea. They were a bit peckish and ate the score of cooked smelts they had purchased in

Hull. The landlord of the George Inn told Anne Lister all about the Leeds and Selby Railway, the first mainline railway in Yorkshire, which had opened just one month earlier. Well, I suppose a good way to learn about trains was to travel on one, so that was what they did. The next morning, Eugenie and George set off in the carriage to travel to Leeds, and Anne, Ann and Charles walked to the railway station and boarded the train for Leeds. It rained for the whole of the journey causing the train wheels to slip making the journey slower than it should have been. Anne Lister: *'the 800 yards tunnel into Leeds being quite dark, took Adney and me by surprise and she did not like it at all'*. Anne, Ann and Charles met up with Eugenie and George in Leeds and, after having lunch, set off in the carriage at two o'clock and arrived back home at Shibden a little before six o'clock on Friday, November 28th.

The following Monday, December 1st, Anne Lister and Marian had another conversation about Mr. Abbott. Marian had now made up her mind to marry him and told Anne that she had informed her father of her plan and that Anne was now free to tell Aunt Anne and Ann Walker, who she described as *'now one of the family'*. Anne had already expressed her concern to Marian about Mr. Abbott's finances and although Marian thought he might have two thousand pounds a year, she still had not actually inquired. Anne told Marian that she sincerely wished her to be happy, it was clear that she was concerned about her sister's choice of potential husband. My understanding is that Anne believed it was beneath a member of the landed gentry to marry a man who generated his income in the wool trade. Yes, this was snobbery, although I expect it was a commonly held point of view in early nineteenth century England, where the strict hierarchy regarding social class governed who one might or might not receive into one's home. The consequence of this was that if Marian and Mr. Abbott made their home in Halifax, Anne and Marian would not be able to pay social calls on each other. Anne Lister: *'Marian was almost in tears. I could have been but would not.*

Spoke calmly and kindly, said I should probably not tell my aunt as she would be much hurt'. Sat ½ hour with Adney, she wondered what was the matter, and was as much astonished as I was. She consoled and calmed me'.

Over the next week or so, Marian kept her sister up to date about her marriage plans including her discussions with Mr. Abbott about financial settlements. However, Marian had not, as yet, put Mr. Abbott in the picture about the situation regarding who was to inherit Shibden, although Anne had asked her to do so. Anne wanted to be sure that Mr. Abbott knew that neither he nor Marian, nor any children they might have, would ever inherit Shibden. Shibden had been left to Anne by her Uncle James to whom she had given a promise to make her distant Welsh Lister cousins her heirs, to ensure that Listers continued to live at Shibden. It was also Anne's intention to give Ann Walker a life interest in Shibden, so that it would continue to be her home if Anne predeceased her. However, this could not be arranged until after Anne's father and aunt had passed away, as they had a legal entitlement to a share of the income from the Shibden estate. At last, on December 19th, Marian passed on this information to Mr. Abbott, who appeared not to be concerned.

On December 5th, Anne wrote to Mariana. She wrote a particularly kind conclusion to the letter, knowing that this would be a comfort to Mariana, who was still in low spirits. Anne Lister: *'Thank you again my dearest Mary, fall all your good wishes and kindness about me and mine. The heart that has truly loved never forgets. Ever very affectionately and especially yours. AL.'* However, Anne was now in the habit of either giving her letters to Ann Walker to read or actually reading them to her. Anne Lister: *'read Adney my letter to Mariana. I saw she did not like the conclusion. I said I knew what she was thinking. It struck myself too that the poetical quotation was equivoque, and I would write the letter over again. I see Adney would soon be jealous without care on my part'*. Mariana's next letter arrived at Shibden on Thursday, December 18th. Anne Lister: *'She now wishes to see me and so earnestly asks me to go over to Lawton before the end of this month that I cannot refuse'.* Anne immediately wrote her reply to Mariana: *'My dearest Mary, I had your letter this morning. It rejoices me exceedingly that you are able to give so good an account of your improved health. I was certainly not prepared for so entire a change in your feelings respecting our meeting, but I think your present decision the better. I must entreat you to excuse my entering further upon the subject just now. In fact, it is unnecessary as I shall hope to see you early in next week'.* So, the plan was for Anne to travel to Lawton Hall in Cheshire to see Mariana either on Monday or Tuesday, December 22nd or 23rd respectively.

The following day, Friday, December 19th, Anne and Ann were out looking over the Walker estate. Recently the local hunt had trespassed on to Ann Walker's property and she was not pleased so she and Anne had gone to make their objections known to the huntsmen. That evening, when they had coffee together in the blue room, the two women talked about Mariana. Anne Lister did not write about their conversation in her journal except to say: *'Adney lowish at the thought of my leaving her on Monday'.*

When Monday, December 22nd, arrived, Anne Lister set off in her carriage, just after midday, heading for Lawton Hall in Cheshire, with Ann travelling with her as far as the post office in Halifax. And yes, they would be apart over Christmas, but as I have previously explained, Christmas, for the landed gentry, was no more than an additional church service, to be attended if you could be bothered and it wasn't raining.

CHAPTER 12: CHRISTMAS 1834

Anne Lister arrived at Lawton Hall at nine o'clock on the evening of Monday, December 22nd. For the best part of twenty years, Anne would have been excited and agitated as she travelled to a rendezvous with Mariana. However, on this occasion, she described herself as calm and having given little thought to Mariana during the journey. She was shown into Mariana's room and Mariana soon came to her. In her journal, Anne described Mariana as being *'nervous, sobbing but she got over it pretty soon'*. They had dinner and sat talking till 11.35 p.m. Anne: *'Mariana came upstairs with me to my room and staid ten minutes. A little nervous again and hung on me..... talks of giddiness in her head and not living long'*. Once Anne was alone, she wrote a two page letter to Ann Walker to let her know she had arrived safely at Lawton Hall and included an account of her journey.

The next morning, Tuesday, December 23rd, after having breakfast at 10.20 a.m., Anne and Mariana sat talking till noon then walked, about two miles to make a call on a Lawton Hall tenant who had been badly injured in an accident. Anne sat with Mariana and her husband Charles while they had luncheon, then at 4 p.m. Anne and Mariana took another walk to call on other tenants. I assume these calls were Christmas related. I get the impression that whilst the landed gentry did not celebrate Christmas, the working classes did, to some extent at least. During all this walking the two women talked a great deal. Mariana told Anne of some of the comments made by Harriet Milne and Charlotte Norcliffe about Ann Walker: *'Charlotte said Ann was not ladylike and she and Mrs Milne thought she [Mariana] would not be flattered if she saw her successor'*. They also implied that Anne Lister was only interested in Ann Walker's money, which Anne strongly denied. I suspect Harriet and Charlotte's nasty comments were motivated by jealousy. Mariana also talked about Mr. Crewe and told Anne that whilst she had been in Scarborough with her sisters, Mr. Crewe had been there with her. Anne was glad that she had not been aware of this at the time and that she heard it first from Mariana. Mariana claimed that she had never been in love with Mr. Crewe and wondered if she ever would be. It appears that he was aware of this but was *'very calm on that subject'.* She also talked of taking a trip to Geneva, with her uncle and sister Louisa, next summer, with the plan that Mr. Crewe, and his two sons, would join them there. Anne did endeavour to speak pleasantly regarding Mr. Crewe, but she told Mariana that, but for him, she might have acted differently. Anne and Mariana had dinner at 6.10 p.m. then coffee, followed later by tea, all of which I expect was in the company of Charles, Mariana's husband. In fact, Anne was surprised at how friendly and attentive Charles behaved towards her. Anne went upstairs to her room at 10.30 p.m. and Mariana sat with her for half an hour. Anne Lister: *'She has kissed me as warmly as she dared venture and given me licence enough if I chose to take it. But in answer [to] "do you love me", my "yes indeed I do" bespoke nothing beyond friendship. The fact is I am really indifferent to her, but she would lead me astray if she could'.* By *'indifferent to her',* I understand that Anne meant sexually, because Anne's kindness and attention to Mariana clearly showed that she still loved her as a very dear friend. Anyway, not surprisingly, Anne was puzzled by all Mariana's talk of Mr. Crewe alongside her persistence that all her love was for Anne and led her to write: *'I cannot quite understand Mariana'.*

The following day, Wednesday, December 24th, a letter arrived at Lawton Hall from Ann Walker for Anne: *'3 pages and the 1st page crossed, nice kind chit-chat letter from Adney. Her aunt all kindness.. my aunt not so well as when I left. If worse would write by the next post'.* After lunch, Anne and Mariana sat talking in Anne's dressing room. Anne Lister: *'She asked to look at the hand-*

writing and I read her the letter, she looking over me. She said it was a nice simple minded letter. She was better satisfied to have seen it'. At two o'clock, Anne and Mariana went out to call on a woman, presumably a tenant, who lived at Lawton Hall lodge. After this they continued their walk till 4.45 p.m. Anne Lister: *'Much talk about Mr. Crewe'.* Anne Lister described Mariana as *'Glad to have seen me, for till she saw me, could scarce believe things really as they are. She wondered if she could ever love him [Mr. Crewe], perhaps it would come, but thought she should feel as if she was breaking the seventh commandment'.* This sounds to me as if Mariana had not had sex with Mr. Crewe, despite having some sort of dalliance with him for the previous seven years. Having also talked about Ann Walker, Anne described Mariana as: *'very well satisfied with Adney. Should like her all the daytime but could not bear her at night. Could not bear to see her go off to bed with me'.* They also talked of when they first got together: Mariana said *'she had often thought she had known me too soon or too late. Had she been another year, her mind would have been above minding all she heard against me, but before my first visit there, her father had said I should not enter the house. Till she cried and made herself ill. A separate bed was then made up for me... Mariana felt that I should have made her happier than anyone else could'.* Anne Lister: *'spoke highly of Adney's high principle and honorable feeling, and that even in any case if it cost me life itself, I would not willingly give her uneasiness. She trusted me and she was right'.* To give some comfort to Mariana, Anne explained that when Charles died, and if Mariana needed a place to go to, she would be welcome at Shibden, even if Anne and Ann were abroad, since servants would always be left there. They had dinner at 6.20 p.m. and afterwards returned to Anne's dressing room. Anne Lister: *'She being so low she could not stand it. Drank cold water, sobbed and was almost in hysterics. Then asked if I loved her, "yes" said I, "you know I do". We then kissed, our lips seeming glewed together and somehow tongues meeting. She sobbed and said it is hard, very hard, to be a friend for one who has been a wife. We both cried'.* They were then informed that tea was being served downstairs.

The next morning, Thursday, December 25th, Mariana went to Anne's bedroom and got into bed with her and stayed talking for an hour. Anne Lister: *'she cannot get over her love for me, but I behaved with perfect propriety. She said, well, if anything happened to Adney and Mr. Crewe, would I take her back again? I made no answer till she said "would I not" when I replied "I would not shut the door against you" on which she thanked me and said I was very good'.* After breakfast Anne and Mariana went to church, and took the sacrament, it being Christmas Day. After lunch they went to the Red Bull Inn to wish a Merry Christmas to the fifty boys and girls of Mariana's school who had dined there. When they got back to Lawton Hall, a letter had arrived from Ann Walker, *'properly affectionate'*, but wanting Anne back home. Anne immediately walked to the Lawton Arms coaching inn to order horses for 9.00 a.m. the following morning. The Lawton's had three additional guests for dinner that evening, and they all sat down to eat at 6.15 p.m. After dinner, they discussed a range of topics but later on, Anne and Mariana sat talking in Anne's dressing room till 1.00 a.m., after which they went down to the housekeeper's room to wish Merry Christmas to the servants, who were still enjoying their Christmas party. On going upstairs to bed, Anne Lister: *'[Mariana] seemed low and nervous. I tried to cheer her. Advised her going to London to her uncle, and Louisa, for a week to see little Mariana, till she told me the history, at length, of Charles and Eliza Lawton, then told her not to be away. Said I saw her mind wavered about leaving Charles but that she must not do it unless he compelled her for refusing to have the girl to live with them or unless something between him and the girl came out. She had taxed with it, with what the girl said, and he declared it was a lie. The girl did not like to be alone with him, he put his tongue into her mouth, which, said Mariana, is you know the last thing but one to which I agreed'.* I am not quite sure what to make of this. It certainly appears that Charles may have taken advantage of a girl or young woman. Interesting that her surname was also 'Lawton', could be a coincidence I suppose. Anyway, it was obviously getting very late and Anne was heading home the next day, so this would be Mariana's last opportunity to make her move, and that was exactly what she did. Anne Lister: *'Mariana began kissing me and we got on to such tongueing, warm work that she got excited. I kept my hands over her clothes and my arms decently round her, till the right wandered to queer outside, till she took up her petticoats and put it to her. I gave her a thorough grubbling…. I certainly felt oddish, but no wish to be near to herself, tho' she said, in the midst, "can you not come near to me for a minute or two". I made no reply but went on never opening my eyes. She asked if I loved her. I merely said "yes". When I did look at her, it was in silence, neither as if ashamed nor as if attendri, nor caring much. I was grave and silent. She said she was better and hoped I should have a good night'.* So there you have it. Some grubbling, but Anne made sure there was not a full connection with Mariana. And what did Anne herself make of it? Anne Lister: *'I despise it. She has tried always to upset me. I have done what I have done, but she shall never gain more nor ever I hope a repetition even of this. I could have done without it, but somehow, I thought, gratify her passion by one parting grubble'.* So it was a bit of comfort sex for Mariana, but just to be on the safe side, that night, Anne slept in her clothes.

The next morning, Friday, December 26th, Mariana went to Anne's bedroom before eight o'clock. Anne Lister: *'she seemed in good spirits. Said she had had a very good night and hoped I had had one too. I said not much on this part of the subject. She saw that I did not think of last night's business quite as she did… She seemed rejoiced at the sort of liberty she thought she had gained and argued against my fancying there was any wrong in it. Said it had done her good and she was now much happier. Begged me not to abuse her in my heart…. She was satisfied to have found, as she thought, that all her influence over me was not gone….. she said she still could believe herself belonging to anyone but me'.* Anne did make it clear to Mariana that she would be showing Ann Walker all the correspondence between them, and Mariana did not object. After breakfast, Anne set off from Lawton Hall in her carriage at 11.50

a.m. accompanied by Mariana, who wanted Anne to take her to Middlewich for a consultation with a medical woman. Mariana would then be collected in Middlewich by one of the Lawton Hall servants in her own carriage. It was 2.21 p.m. when Anne was able to set off from Middlewich heading back to Shibden. She experienced a long delay at Altrincham awaiting a change of horses and required a second change of horses at Rochdale. Anne arrived at Shibden at 10.55 p.m. to find everyone had gone to bed except Cordingley, although John Booth quickly arrived on the scene, Anne Lister: *'Adney jumped up and came to me in her dressing gown and cloak, delighted to see me back again. Had given me up in despair. Had tea. The first thing we did was to laugh aloud at her droll figure and the bustle I had made... sat talking, told her I, myself, was astounded how little I had thought of Mariana, either going or returning. Very glad to be back again. Mentioned how I had offered her [Mariana] the use of Shibden in the event of Charles' death'.* They then went to their bedroom and made love. Anne Lister: *'One very good kiss soon after getting into bed and not long after this another not quite so good but very fair'.*

The next day, Saturday, December 27th, Anne and Ann had a lot of catching up to do and were both quite busy. During and after breakfast, they had Samuel Washington updating them on estate business. They were then able to spend some time with Jeremy, Marian, and Aunt Anne, before Anne was visited by the Mann brothers to discuss the pit sinking. Mr. Sunderland, the doctor called to see Aunt Anne and Jeremy, and was generally pleased with them both but did say that the sore on Aunt Anne's leg was getting larger. After Ann Walker had had lunch, she and Anne walked to Cliff Hill to look over the plantations and call on old Miss Walker. They returned home at 5 p.m. and Ann Walker went to sit with Aunt Anne. They had dinner at 6.10 p.m. then spent some time chatting with Jeremy and Marian. That evening, Samuel Washington called again, this time with money, from navigation shares, for Ann Walker and Aunt Anne, sent from their solicitor, Mr. Parker. Samuel Washington stayed for coffee, and Anne then went and sat with her aunt. Anne and Ann retired about half past ten and despite a busy day, made love, having *'one pretty good kiss'*.

Sunday, December 28th, was a quiet day. Anne read prayers for her aunt and some of the servants. In the afternoon, Anne and Ann went in the carriage to St. Matthew's for the Sunday service. On retuning to Shibden, Anne wrote to Mariana, and Ann Walker had two of John Booth's children, little John and Ann, I assume for some Sunday school type of activity. Ann Walker had not felt well this day on account of having her period, so once she was in bed that night, Anne gave her a warming drink of hot wine with water.

After breakfast on Monday, December 29th, Mr. Parker, their solicitor, called at Shibden, with documents for Ann Walker to sign regarding the separation of the joint Walker inheritance. Anne Lister was out on the Shibden estate for most of the morning and part of the afternoon discussing and planning pit sinking related matters with various workmen. She arrived home at 2.50 p.m., and then she and Ann went out and spent an hour walking along Shibden's ornamental walk. On their return they spent some time talking and writing upstairs in the blue room before coming down to dinner at 6.25 p.m. followed by coffee. That night, Anne Lister: *'a little while with my father and Marian… half hour with my aunt. Saw Adney into bed and gave her warm wine and water'*. Anne then meticulously recorded all the conversations and quotes she had had that day regarding coal mining at Shibden. This took up two pages in her journal, and if you have ever seen a page in one of Anne's diaries, you will know that amounted to a lot of information. She wrote till midnight, sat in the blue room adjacent to their bedroom, as it was too cold in her study, there having been no fire in the stove all day.

Tuesday, December 30th, saw Anne and Ann sorting bills, Anne Lister writing a long letter in reply to Mrs. Norcliffe's long letter and, it being a much milder day, the two women went out for a fifty minute walk, late in the afternoon, it being almost dark when they got home. Anne Lister was very keen that she and Ann took a walk each day, weather permitting, believing it to be good for their physical and mental wellbeing.

The following day, New Year's Eve, a letter arrived at Shibden from Mr. Gray, one of their solicitor's, regarding Anne and Ann's efforts to prevent the local hunt from trespassing on the Walker estate. It appeared that not much could be done. Caroline Rawson, one of Ann Walker's many cousins, paid a call on her, although Anne Lister noted that Miss Rawson asked after Aunt Anne and Jeremy, but not after her and Marian. Very easy to cause offence in those days. Anne and Ann sat talking over lunch. Anne Lister did not eat between breakfast and dinner, but was in the habit, whenever possible, of sitting with Ann while she ate lunch. That night, Anne wrote in her journal: *'Another year is gone! How altered my position since last year at this time! Deus nobis haec otia fecit! God be thanked!'* Whilst not the literal translation, the Latin phrase is generally taken to mean: 'God has granted us this ease'.

So here we are, at the end of 1834, and these two amazing, courageous women are choosing to live together, in a committed loving relationship. So brave and so inspiring. Anne Lister finally had what she had spent most of her adult life wishing for: a woman to live with that she loved and who loved her. Ann Walker now had a lover and a caring companion and was no longer alone, and, having lost all her immediate family, except for her sister who lived about four hundred miles away, had acquired a new family, that had welcomed her with open loving arms.

ABOUT THE AUTHOR

Lynn Pharaoh

Lynn Pharaoh is a published author, having written several science books based on her 35 years experience as a physics teacher. 'Anne Lister, Ann Walker, and me' is her first historical biography, having gained a passionate interest in the life of Anne Lister through her transcribing of Anne's diaries for the West Yorkshire Archive Service. Lynn's other great passion is gardening, growing most of her own fruit and veg. She lives with her partner, Julie, in Liverpool, in the UK.

Printed in Great Britain
by Amazon